DANCING FULL TILT
IN THE LIGHT

DANCING FULL TILT
IN THE LIGHT

Naomi Pevsner

Green
Fire
Press

Housatonic
Massachusetts

Cover photo by Alex Sava
Cover and page design by Anna Myers Sabatini
Library of Congress Control Number: 2020904939
Print ISBN: 978-1-7347571-0-1
E-Book ISBN: 978-1-7347571-1-8

Green Fire Press
PO Box 377 Housatonic MA 01236
Some of the names in this memoir have been
changed to protect the privacy of individuals.

Pevsner, Naomi.
Dancing full tilt in the light / Naomi Pevsner.
Housatonic, Massachusetts : Green Fire Press, [2020], ©2020.
287 pages ; 14 cm
9781734757101
1. Pevsner, Naomi. 2. Pevsner, Naomi — Family. 3. Depression,
Mental — Treatment — United States. 4. Grief in women —
United States. 5. Women jewelers — United States — Biography
6. Women fashion designers — United States — Biography.
7. Depressed persons — United States — Biography.

For Karen

"I know now that we never get over great losses; we absorb them, and they carve us into different, often kinder, creatures. We tell the story to get them back, to capture traces of their footfalls in the snow."

~Gail Caldwell

"Where there is ruin,
  there is hope for a treasure."

~Rumi

PROLOGUE

Any fear I had of public speaking vanished entirely as soon as the show started. I was the featured diamond designer for the prime time evening hour, on home-shopping giant QVC, where an enormous digital clock near our feet blinked away the minutes of my very first show.

Bobbing robotic cameras moved in for close-ups as flashing red numbers glowed: 8:25...8:26 and 8:27... one minute morphing into the next; and just like that, at 8:28, I was as relaxed as if in my own living room. Calm and cool as any cucumber, I quipped with the show's hostess, smiling widely at whichever mechanized camera blinked with a red light, as instructed.

By all accounts, my first live appearance on QVC was going splendidly. Several affordable adaptations of my high-end diamond jewelry designs sold out within minutes, the red "SOLD OUT" banner crossing through the 'no-longer-available' item on the screen, meaning that viewer had missed the boat and had better hop to it next time. By 8:56, the show host, Antonella Nester, and I were left with four minutes at the end of the show, a veritable eternity in television time, during which we ad-libbed and chatted casually about the miracle of online ordering, the joy of owning beautiful jewelry, and even each other's manicures (she needed to get a fresh one, she told viewers). Dutifully, I said I thought her nails looked lovely anyway; she appreciated this and called me a doll.

A producer, speaking through a tiny earbud-microphone, gave Antonella and me updates in real-time on what was selling and what we should do next. From where he sat, a voice identifying himself as Alan could see sales rise (or not) minute by minute on a screen, and he'd relay this pertinent information to both of us through our earphones. "We're about to sell out on this one, in three...two...one..." Alan would say, and based on customer comments and sales per second, he'd add, "The customer *loved* what you just said. Please keep talking about it."

This wasn't hard to do because there were stories and inspirations behind each conception and only I knew them. The most personal comments I made—ones that included a personal note or the inspiration behind a piece—directly affected orders. For example, a "statement ring" available with three different colored stones promptly sold out, just after I'd referred to the jewel-toned center stones which I said reminded me of the *Ju-ju-bees* I ate at the movies, as a kid. "They're candy-colored," I'd ad-libbed. The stories behind the jewelry—or my thoughts about even the smallest, most intimate details of the design itself—interested the viewers and prompted them to buy, so that eventually, even without Alan's prodding, I kept it up, confiding to the viewers, for example, that "My mother loves this ring and wears hers every day!" This not only spiked sales, but sent my mother over the moon with joy. Indeed, one of the first things she said to me on the phone after the show was "And I *loved* that you mentioned me!"

Antonella's big voice and boisterous laugh could have traveled a good distance without amplification, but even with Alan in one ear, I knew that the delighted screams of my parents would have drowned both of them out. I knew—without sound or a picture—that they were sitting at the end of their bed in front of the larger of their two TVs, where they'd planted themselves a full hour before my scheduled appearance that evening. Without audio, I knew that my mother's high-pitched shouts drowned out any exclamations of my father's, and that she had hushed him as I'd come on air, as if he were the one squealing and not her. With a long commanding "*SHHHHHHHHHH*," she'd silenced him (and herself) just in time for their screams of joy not to mute my first words, holding an arm out across his chest as if protecting him from going through a windshield, her way of non-verbally saying: *Hold on, here she comes.* I could picture both of them breathing shallowly until the moment they'd burst into a rousing double-cheer at first sighting me on screen. And then, mid-cheer, they'd quieted again, to hear every word.

My opening lines on the show that evening had been, "Well good evening to you, Antonella," and then, looking to the cameras, "And to *you*, viewers!" (thereby creating the three-way "casual conversation over a backyard fence" ambiance that we as guest designers had been trained to do). I knew that these opening lines had thrilled my parents, perhaps every bit as much as my very first spoken words had, uttered as a baby. "Ball" and "cold"—my first utterings—were delivered to their eager cheers. My tiny mouth pursed into a small circle, drawn out pronunciations of "baaaaaawl" and "liiiiight" were my first experience of the pleasure I had the power to give them; my parents were simply ecstatic at whatever I had to say, from that moment on.

Later, after my first show had wrapped, my first phone call had been to my parents, even before calling my husband Richard, or my daughter Marissa. Making my parents proud was the stimulus for most everything that I did and theirs was the reaction I cared about most. They were not particularly hard to please nor difficult to impress; they loved each of us—my brother, my sister and I—every bit as much as we did them and it seemed to each of us kids that their pride and joy at our achievements knew no bounds.

"You could have *hosted* that show, Naomi!" they'd insisted. "The camera *loves* you, Nomeluh!" my dad had gushed, using one of his loving nicknames for me. "You were simply *made* for TV!" they'd both said.

On twin extensions of their phone line, they'd answered almost before the first ring when I'd called from the green room after the show. Their audible joy was all I needed to hear, even before my sales were revealed (we'd done $750,000 in one hour, not bad for a 'new designer'). No doubt they'd have kept me on the phone indefinitely had it not been for my deliberate mention of celebrity Joan Rivers being in the next green room; which sent my mother straight into super-star mode. Immediately imagining we'd somehow all become fast friends, I knew my mother was already envisioning future *Shabbat* dinners with Joan Rivers, and hence, her focus shifted at once to the task at hand. "GO MEET HER!" my mother commanded—in a tone not unlike God's to Moses on the mountaintop; and then she'd repeated it for good measure: "For God's sake, go *now!* Go talk to Joan!"

And *go* I had, exiting my assigned greenroom and feigning an accidental stumbling into Joan Rivers'—and, oops, as long as I was there—introducing myself, then asking casually if she had a water bottle in her fridge she could spare, as mine (I claimed) was stocked with every sort of soft drink, but no water bottles. I did not actually know whether I had water bottles or not, but the temptation to name drop—"Joan Rivers gave me this water"—was just too great. She could not have been nicer, cracking a couple of jokes that for the life of me I cannot remember, and in the haze of adrenaline over the whole scenario I patted her little dog and told her about my little Gigi at home. I wish I could say exactly what happened after that, or recall the rest of the conversation, but everything else about that evening blurs in my memory, except for the phone call to my folks, which was like an elixir to me.

I was drunk with their joy, which had hit me through the phone lines like warm shots of whiskey down my gullet. I was floating that evening, *in prime time, no less*, my mother might've added, and in my exuberance, I'd forgotten to go by the production desk on my way to the green room, to remove the small microphone which was threaded down the neck of my dress and clipped to the waistband of my pantyhose. Just in time, a production assistant followed me into the lavatory.

"Hon, you're still on mic," she said.

"Oh gosh, I'm so sorry about that! I'm new here," I said. "This was actually my first show."

"Really?" the young lady said. "I wouldn't have guessed it, you seemed like a pro! Honestly, Naomi. Great job."

Had I actually heard this with my own ears? I couldn't wait to share this addition to the story with my parents. "You seemed like a pro, Naomi," thrilled me, no doubt, but a line like this could keep my parents going for at least another week. *She was an on-air pro, even the producers said so!* my mother would repeat with a triumphant smile.

I had not aspired to television or to one day sell 'more affordable' (home-shopping lingo for 'cheap') versions of my high-end diamond designs on national home shopping; and I wasn't sure how my Orthodox Jewish grandfather would have felt about it. After initial meetings with buyers and on-air trainers, I'd traveled from Dallas to QVC's headquarters in West Chester, Pennsylvania, several months before my first show. The head buyers had liked my jewelry and had warmed to me, and they were most interested in my story of the five generations of my family in the diamond industry, which I'd learned about from my grandfather. He had told me about our ancestors and their travels to faraway places in search of diamonds and gemstones for the Czars and Czarinas of ancient Russia; travels that most Jews of the time were not allowed. His stories were real-life oral histories, disguised as bedtime tales, told in a voice muted by age, with vestiges of an old-world accent still left. Listening to him, I'd close my eyes to visualize the fantastical tales and their exotic settings.

I was proud of this family history, but it had taken a long time before I had assumed the mantle of diamond dealer or jewelry designer myself. Like most little girls, I'd dreamed of being a ballerina or a mommy when I grew up, or a nurse or a schoolteacher. My younger sister Sara and I spent endless enchanted hours playing dress-up, the two of us donning all sorts of oversized attire and stepping into many a pair of our mother's high heel shoes; we'd scuff across the basement floor of our family's Chicago apartment, imagining ourselves off to very important places, none of which were very far from our back door. We practiced doing the things that grown-up women did, knowing it was only a matter of time before we did them for real one day.

With a pillbox hat tipped jauntily to one side, strands of faux pearls dangling to our knees, we were anyone we wished to be on those dress-up afternoons, but never did we dress up as a diamond dealer like our grandfather. Neither Sara nor I ever asked our father for an old fedora we could borrow, or a pocket watch like the one our grandfather carried—an accessory we assumed went with the job. We were familiar with the long black wallet he was never without, and knew that it was stuffed with folded papers of diamonds, of all sorts and shapes and sizes. Though this fascinated us, our mother's cast-off rhinestone baubles were all the bling we needed to play make-believe.

Playing 'diamond dealer' interested me little and my sister even less. As a toddler, my sister Sara—younger than me by 14 months—had spoken early, and even then had an uncanny knack for imitating dialects and inflections she had heard on TV. She could have put on a decent old-world European accent like my grandfather's, but she did not. Neither of us feigned broken English or wore a jeweler's loupe like his; our preference was for fantasies of the female kind, practicing for future adventures as fancy grown-up ladies.

I was shy then, with an expanding collection of fears, and no intentions of traveling beyond the confines of my cozy little world. Every persona Sara and I could dream up and dress for was able to happily exist right there in our little town of River Forest, Illinois. The very thought of being anywhere else—without my mother and father, and my brother and my sister—was as formidable to me as any dark and tangled forest that a forefather of mine might have roamed in search of gemstones.

The five generations of family in an old-world profession might well have stopped right there with my grandfather, since my father had already broken the chain by not following *his* father into the business. A writer at heart, my father said he'd tried working with his dad in the diamond business, but he hadn't liked it. He had dreams of his own, and dealing diamonds had not suited him, so he'd donned his writer's cap and embarked upon a career as a journalist, continuing what he'd loved and excelled at while on active duty aboard a Navy aircraft carrier during the Korean War. Later, as a young executive with Sears Roebuck, he'd become editor-in-chief of their in-house publication, *The Sears Parent News*, and as director of publicity, he had happily dedicated himself to his career until a massive coronary hit him at only 39 years old.

He had always encouraged my brother, my sister and me to follow our *own* hearts in our education and careers, and hence, I was never pushed or prodded into the diamond business, nor expected to gravitate to it on my own. If it had crossed my mind, I might have assumed that a woman in the male-dominated diamond business might have been as welcome as a stripper accidentally stumbling into a sanctuary full of Orthodox Jewish males, all deep in prayer—which is to say, not at all appreciated.

Nonetheless, the family business found me instead. Following my father's promotion at Sears, we had moved from River Forest, with its ivy-covered houses and lovely shade trees, to the sprawling ranch houses of Dallas, Texas. Eventually my grandfather joined us, bringing his diamond business with him. On that first summer after he had settled in—while my sister and brother were planted in front of the TV most days—I'd accompany my grandfather to his office, only later recognizing it as loosely veiled free childcare for at least one of us kids. But at that time, cleverly disguised as a job offer, it had been the only game in town for an otherwise unemployed ten-year-old, and I'd accepted the offer happily. With little else to do during the hot, dry Texas summer season, 'working' with my grandpa offered a daylong respite from bickering with my siblings. Sitting beside him, watching him sort diamonds, I listened to his comments on the qualities found deep inside of each stone. Then he'd pass the jeweler's loupe to me, where, through my child's eye, I saw the minute details that made each stone unique.

All the diamonds he showed me sparkled and danced under the fluorescent lighting. There was not an ugly one among them, but from my grandfather I learned that despite their outer brilliance, each gemstone could be vastly different on the inside. Like snowflakes, each was unique; but the dissimilarities in diamonds were *internal* and microscopic: tiny but complete worlds lived inside of each diamond, unveiled only upon eagle-eyed inspection. Magnified ten times through an eyeglass, like a Viewmaster toy with slides inserted, scenes came to life.

The inclusions inside each diamond were birthmarks left by nature, my grandfather said; markings assigned by the good Lord himself, for the convenience of telling one of his works from another. As I learned more about diamonds, there were other elements of a stone's intrinsic qualities that paralleled the differences in people, and these analogies I grasped, even at ten years old. They were also evident in the terms commonly used to describe diamonds; personifications such as: 'she's a beauty of a stone,' or 'this stone has spunk' or 'she's got a lot of personality.' Diamonds, like human beings, possessed unique traits, along with distinct individual essences within.

The mere fact that a diamond could bluff an observer was perhaps what made the most profound impression on me. This type of diamond, referred to as a 'bluff stone,' was the snake charmer among gemstones, somehow able to dazzle a crowd in spite all sorts of inclusions and glitches inside. Whether dots of carbon or white bubbles or feathers, none of the inherent imperfections inside these 'bluff stones' affected their outer brilliance. I thought of them like clever little magicians of nature. They might have been all wrong inside, but when expertly cut and polished they would emerge with the ability to reflect light back to the observer. As if by sleight-of-hand, a diamond that "faced up well" *worked around* its inner blemishes, shining bravely anyway. Failings and foibles aside, these profoundly *imperfect* stones were the champions in my eyes; doggedly determined to gleam in the sun, staunchly refusing to allow something as insignificant as an inner niggle of soot to snuff out their right to shine.

Diamonds without any imperfections whatsoever are rarities indeed. A "perfect" or internally flawless stone falls into a scant 2% of all the world's diamonds, and thus perfect diamonds are often locked in safes, rather than worn on a finger. These lovely, lonely diamonds sometimes never saw the light of day; for even the slightest scratch or nick could affect their 'flawless' status. How much fun was that? I wondered, when all the other diamonds danced full tilt in the light, wise to their issues but uninhibited by them. These slightly mottled ones shown as brilliantly as the more perfect ones did and I made the connection, even as a child, that nurtured, chiseled and carefully cut, we could all be the best versions of ourselves, blazing on, in spite of weaknesses or shortcomings. I'd seen this with my own eyes.

Sitting beside my grandpa, I'd unintentionally begun my future career at the ripe old age of ten. He was a well-respected diamond dealer of his time, and the importers who supplied him with stones, as well as the jewelers and artisans he used, would one day work with me, solely because they'd known me as his granddaughter. Back then, it had just been something to do on a long, hot, Texas summer day but in hindsight, it was essential training that would serve me well in the future.

In the years that followed the deaths of my parents, I felt as if I were drowning in swirling seas of loss and unwanted change, weighted down with a heavy heart. Slowly I began to write about my grief; about my mother and my father and all that I'd lost. And from the pages, something noticeable happened. My parents reappeared.

At first I wrote with pen on a yellow pad of paper, sometimes scrawling wildly, sometimes more deliberately, allowing scenes to unfold in which my parents spoke again. A sentence here and then another, a chapter at a time of things remembered. Significant memories mingled with the stuff of everyday life, engrained in my soul. My parents' expressions and mannerisms remained surprisingly intact and alive in my memories when I wrote of them. They came back to me one story at a time and I began to look forward to these visits as much as I had enjoyed time with them when they were alive. And in the end (which was also a beginning, as endings always are) they were there with me again, as much as they had ever been in life. Both of them had been so much larger than life that the memories of their brilliant souls turned out to be just what I needed to find my way without them.

When all else failed, each remembrance glowed enough to light the way for me, a few unsure footsteps at a time, until at last I found I could walk with conviction, and then with some momentum. And finally, with a whole new stride. Following a map I found written on my heart, a backpack of memories was all I took with me. But with the best of them, I kept moving and remembering, walking straight in the direction of home.

PART ONE

CONDOLENCES

ONE

The only hint of what was coming was an almost-indiscernible twitch of a single flower at the outer edges of the arrangement draping her casket. Just a jiggle, no more—before the spray of lilies, chrysanthemums and carnations leaned dangerously to the left and then slid on to the carpeted floor of the synagogue's pulpit, landing with a thud. Surprisingly, the whole arrangement remained mostly intact but for a few of the carnations that snapped off and rolled in different directions.

In my fantasy, this is exactly the moment when the heavy lid of the casket begins to rise slowly. The mourners gasp, but I am not as surprised as they are because I know it is not magic or hocus pocus, nor do I think that the heavy lid is rising of its own accord. I know—because it's my fantasy, after all—that the lid is rising slowly because my mother is pushing it *from the inside* and she doesn't want to break a nail.

When my mother sits up and the gasps from the audience turn to a shocked silence, I'm first impressed with the fact that her hair is still perfectly coiffed and her manicure looks fresh. I note her silk blouse and wonder how she's managed not to perspire in such close quarters, but this is my mother for you. My front-row seat in the synagogue's sanctuary allows me an unobstructed view of her casket; the ideal focal point from which to continue building these elaborate daydreams I've been escaping into periodically, ever since my mother died.

They're a bit like private movie clips in my mind, each fantasy a better version of reality. In them, I am like James Thurber's imaginary character Walter Mitty, who spends time envisioning that he is somewhere else, doing something impossible. I feel like I have a leg up on him, somehow more entitled than the fictional Mitty to my own particular fantasies. My daydreams have better reason to exist, because my mother really *did* these sorts of extraordinary things in life. For me it was not a stretch of the imagination, by any means.

If anyone could actually not be dead after death, it would be my mother. Walter Mitty was born in Thurber's imagination, but my mother had been *real*. And in real life, for an entire lifetime, every single morning that she had stepped outside her front door, she'd done so with the absolute certainty that something remarkable was waiting to happen; and so indeed it did. In my latest fantasy, I suppose I'd been hoping for one more surprise; this head-trip fueled by the absolute inconceivability of her sudden death, the very fact of which had thrown off my whole understanding of what could—and could not—happen in real life.

Meanwhile, in my flight of imagination, of the half dozen carnations that had broken off, one rolled down the steps of the *bimah,* and landed near our feet; close enough for me to see from its underside that it had been dyed an unnatural color not seen in nature. I knew this would not have escaped my mother, who like me would also have silently judged the carnations. They were strictly "filler flowers;" bunches of them wrapped in cellophane, readily available at the grocery stores and even gas stations, for heaven's sake; appropriate for gigantic homecoming corsages but my mother would have expected better for her funeral. I made a mental note (on the wall of my daydream) to apologize sincerely for including a couple dozen carnations in the arrangement draping her coffin, but covering the length of it was a tall order. Besides—I'd remind my mother—at the time, we'd all thought she was dead, after all.

I'd be dead before I'd order carnations, she'd quip, and both of us would giggle. *Oh, we're just terrible, Naomi! Aren't we awful?!* she'd comment on our floral snootiness. We knew that we were, but these were the sorts of things that humored my mom and me; so what was the harm in a bit of botanical humor, just between us girls?

It had been exactly 3.5 weeks since our nightly phone calls had ceased. Typically, if I hadn't called my mother by 7 p.m. or so I'd know that my ringing phone was her; more times than not, she'd have some wild or ironic story burning a hole in her proverbial pocket until she could share it with me. Depending on the hour, if her call came in after around 6 or 6:30—my brother Joe's evening commute time, an hour in his car from downtown to far North Dallas—I could assume she'd already told my brother the story. If so, I'd have the benefit of Joe's clever quips and reactions, added to her story; my brother's comments and commentary always witty and worth hearing.

Most every phone call from my mom began the same way: "*Oh, Naomi, you simply will* not *believe what happened to me today!*" This was her standard evening greeting; unnecessary really, because I would believe whatever it was and that 'it' had indeed happened to my mother. The stories she told of a regular day's events, all had fantastical or coincidental endings, but the point was that they were *true* tales. They were the stuff of every day, elevated to higher levels of interest *by the way she told them*. My mother was a born storyteller.

Even if she exaggerated some small detail or another slightly exaggerated, it never mattered. My mother often jumped at the opportunity to embellish upon a few points; something I believed she did for the sake of the listener, more than for herself. Her true aspiration was always to share a story *worth hearing*; and hers always were, even if it meant stretching the truth just a hair. To my mother, *real life* was of her own making.

I often wondered when her remarkable storytelling habit had begun. Was it something she was born with, or had she developed it as a survival skill? Whatever the case, amplifying a thing or two for the sake of the listener had in time become my mother's trademark. She had made an art of mild magnification and because she used it wisely—although not necessarily sparingly—she did it efficiently enough that her oh-so-slight elevating of things was never objectionable. Eventually, over the years, it became as endearing a habit of hers as any other.

I only rarely remember it backfiring. One time, I'd told her all about an elaborate Indian wedding that Richard and I attended, sparing none of the details. As usual, my mother had hung on every word as I'd described the extravagant wedding ceremony and reception. She loved to live vicariously through her children. So much so, in fact, that more than once, having become familiar with every detail, she would inject *herself* into a story. Though in truth she had not attended the glorious Indian wedding herself, when the subject of it came up one evening around a restaurant table, she jumped right in. It was a family dinner, early evening on a Sunday, and my brother, Joe, and sister-in-law, Debbie, and the rest of our usual group were passing trays of sushi around the restaurant table when my mother began to gush about the spectacular Indian wedding she'd attended with us; the beginnings of her usual attempt (typically successful) to trump everyone else's stories with hers. Sitting next to my brother, I poked him under the table—our usual signal for 'watch Mom, something funny is brewing'—and I leaned over to whisper in his ear: "She wasn't actually there." My brother's eyes widened; my mother was now describing in great detail, with grand gestures, the beautiful and authentic Indian food served at the reception and the high time had by all, including her. This of course, was the ideal set-up for my brother to egg her on for a bit, before expertly blowing her cover. Poker-faced—as only Joe can do—he took over, and I leaned over to alert my sister-in-law, Debbie, so she was completely on board, adding a couple of 'Wow Mom's' and other exclamations known to send my mom into exaggerating overdrive.

By now, my mom was happily gesticulating as she spoke; pantomiming the height of the ice sculptures and grandeur of the decor and even breathlessly recounting the age-old Indian marriage rituals (which she hadn't seen); all details she'd heard me describe, and had hilariously hijacked for her very own. My brother let her go on for a minute more (me squelching guffaws with some deal of effort) before finally saying, "So Mom, what did you wear to the wedding?"

My mother stopped mid-sentence and paused, cocking her head like a puppy. "Well, I...well let's see. What was I wearing?" she asked, seemingly perusing her closet in her mind, a puzzled look on her face.

"Ohhh...well now, wait a minute," she said. We waited, me trying as best I could to imitate Joe's deadpan expression.

"Was I?...Did I not...Okay, now wait," she said. Her expression was priceless; she was an adorable deer caught in the headlights. Then the corners of her mouth began curling up slowly. She knew. Realizing she'd been lovingly busted, we all guffawed, laughing out loud for a good three minutes, but none of us laughing harder than she did, at herself. She was extremely cute and she knew it. She thoroughly enjoyed any gag or joke—especially from my brother or I—and if she were the object of the humor, all the better.

When my mother told a story, daily happenings were transformed. It was her way. A previously unknown acquaintance was *her new best friend.* A loud noise or a crash was *deafening,* and a car driving too fast was *careening out of control.* In this case, one wouldn't be at all surprised to learn that the speeding driver (who'd slowed down at some point and perhaps ended up parking next to her) had, in some ironic twist of events, also become her *new best friend.* In fact, regarding her death, I knew that she'd have corrected me (if she weren't dead) for saying that she had 'died rather suddenly,' because to hear her tell it, she had, more accurately, *dropped dead.* She'd have boiled down the three weeks she'd lingered in the ICU into something much more short and sweet: *I just dropped dead.* It was also infinitely more dramatic.

In the same vein, she would refer to a very cold day as *bitter cold,* and food served lukewarm as *ice-cold.* Never would she have summoned a waiter with a simple: "Excuse me young man, but I would like my fish a little warmer." Oh, no, she'd have gone with: "Waiter, this fish is *ice-cold,*" encouraging said waiter to feel it for himself if he needed further verification and demonstrating with the press of her own manicured fingertip atop the fish filet.

Sitting at her funeral service, I could hear her always-animated voice in my mind. But halfway through the Rabbi's chanting I began to slip out of my fantasy of her 'not being dead,' which I'd been doing with regularity since she'd passed. I considered closing my eyes, but I knew I'd look like I was sleeping; so instead I stared at my mother's casket. And as I did, a truism began nudging its way into my head-trip, causing the image of my mom in a silk St. Laurent blouse to fade. The fact abrading my figment was that she had been buried in a shroud. Something she'd have agreed to over…well, her dead body.

We had not realized that being buried in a shroud was a requirement of the Orthodox synagogue that owned the section of the cemetery where both my parents had bought plots decades before. My mother would have strongly objected to the ritual washing of the body and wrapping of the deceased in a shroud. But she had wanted to be buried next to my father, and whatever needed to facilitate that would be done. Daydreams aside, I knew my mother would be the last person on earth caught dead in a shroud. Deceased or not, she believed in proper attire. With no exceptions.

TWO

Immersed in my fantasy, after the lid rises and my mother sits straight up, I see that she has not a hair out of place and thankfully, there is no shroud. As expected, always chic, she is dressed head to toe in Saint Laurent, and she faux-fans herself, appearing otherwise unruffled as Rabbi Paley turns around to offer her assistance or at least a glass of water.

Standing, she brushes imaginary lint from her year-round gabardine pants, and insists she's fine, thanks very much, waving off any help. The mourners' stunned silence erupts into laughter and then applause. *My god,* they'll say later, *she didn't even need a drink of water!* I'm as excited as anyone, but I make a mental note to scold my mother for turning down the water. She's simply terrible about hydrating, and she and I have discussed this many times before. "I'm just not a big water drinker," she's been known to say, and I always point out how ridiculous this is for someone who is otherwise so health conscious. She won't say so, but I suspect she does not drink water during the day because she doesn't want to mess up her lipstick.

Meanwhile, the congregation is buzzing, some of the mourners cheering and shouting out to her. Rabbi Paley, in his flowing robes, approaches the microphone to settle the excited crowd. The mood of the funeral has lifted, which may call for a change of prayer or two; but things must be done by the book, regardless. *Don't think the service is over, folks!* the Rabbi indicates, clearing his throat.

The crowd hushes, and Rabbi Paley announces the continuation of the service, offering Mom his elbow, so he can escort her to a seat next to me in the front row. She accepts, looping her arm through his, and together they step down the risers of the *bimah* where she joins her family in the front row; but not for long, because none of us stay for the entire service—we never do. There are side doors to the sanctuary, and each of us is eyeing one or the other of the exit doors, my brother and sister-in-law Debbie already on the edge of their seats, in the standard "we're getting out of here" position. One of the twins—Haley or Paige—has pulled her cell phone out of her clutch (tell me, what 16-year old carries a Prada bag?) but the other twin has been grounded from her phone and looks annoyed about it.

My daughter Marissa is now holding her Mimi's hand, elated that her grandmother is not, in fact, dead. With nothing but a few sideways looks at one another, we all understand that we will stay only until the opportunity presents itself to sneak out between prayers; something we learned as kids and are still good at, years later. We slip outside one at a time, soundlessly; except for my sister who is still a mess from heavy crying and is fumbling with her things. She drops a prayer book, then forgets her purse and has to go back in to get it. But once we gather outside the sanctuary, we waste no time making a plan: we'll head to a favorite cafe for a celebratory breakfast. We've all taken off of work, so why wouldn't we head to the nearest restaurant?

Unlike my father's Orthodox Jewish family, none of us are big fans of organized worship in a synagogue. My mother knows the least amount of Hebrew of any of us; in fact, she can recite precisely one prayer—the *Shema*—which, with great sincerity, she delivers on any occasion. The Hebrew words of the first refrain of the *Shema* (which is the only part she knows) translate to "Hear O Israel, the Lord is our God, the Lord is One," which, in my mother's mind, says it all.

Grateful? Say the *Shema*.

Hopeful? *Shema*.

Narrowly avoiding near-injury or calamity? *Shema*.

Praying for a loved one's recovery? *Shema.*

Someone with a gun to your head? *Shema.*

In an aircraft plunging towards earth? Same *Shema,* repeated 2 to 3 times; or until, well, you know.

Any of us might have guessed that we'd head straight to the French cafe for a late breakfast; the perfect place for my mother to flaunt her fluency in French. She recites the list of menu items in her perfect French, impressing us all; though in truth we could have ordered from the bold-faced English descriptions. Over steaming cups of French pressed coffee, we'll pull apart flaky layers of our croissants—some of us opting for jelly and some of us not.

A waitress in an apron continually refills our mugs with coffee—my mother covering hers with a hand, indicating she's not ready for a refill; it would ruin the perfect ratio of cream to coffee she's achieved. At one point, we'll realize we're the loudest table in the restaurant and hope that no one minds. My cousin Susie has a big, booming laugh—and it sounds even louder bouncing off the walls of the cafe, but we have reason to be jovial. There's much talk around the table about how easily Mom lifted the solid oak lid of the casket, as if it were driftwood—Mom crediting her strength to her daily exercise regime. And this is where she lifts a finger above the table, revealing what we hadn't known until then: that she'd indeed broken a fingernail doing so. Though we can't see any damage, she assures us that a crack runs across the nail; it can barely be seen, but it's there. She has plans to repair it, in a snap, when she gets home: piece of cake, she says, and with this, one of us says, "Hey, speaking of... let's eat cake! This calls for a celebration!"

A couple of us motion for the waitress to return, and when she does, we order two slices of carrot cake for all of us to share. Mom indicates to the waitress that she's ready for a coffee refill; and afterwards—steam rising from her mug—she sets about adding the proper measures of cream and sweetener, to render hers the perfect shade of mocha. She looks pleased and blots her lipstick on her cloth napkin. Setting it back on her lap, a perfect lip print barely visible on the black square linen, which she requested because white linens are well-known for leaving lint on dark-colored slacks. My mother is one of the people who can rattle off a list of restaurants thoughtful and savvy enough to offer their patrons black linen napkins instead of white; a small gesture she appreciates.

About the carrot cake, my mom exclaims, "Well, carrot is a vegetable, after all!" And no one disagrees. A hearty slice is set on both ends of our table, all of us noting the specks of orange nestled into the golden-colored cake, and feeling no guilt whatsoever for eating a bit of cake at that hour of the day, for the sake of celebration. It is moist and appropriately spongy, and we wash it down with sips of fresh-squeezed orange juice, with pulp. Someone suggests a toast to mom, and we all clink our glasses together in the air above our table, as several impromptu toasts ensue. We are—all of us—basking in the bright sunlight of the cheery café, counting our lucky stars; none of us wishing to be anywhere else than where we are now.

Suddenly, I'm shaken from my café daydream by something sounding like a wail; and I'm sucked unwillingly back into my seat in the synagogue sanctuary. My fantasy melting like the sugar in my coffee, I am as much annoyed by the display of unchecked grief as I am disappointed to be back in reality. My stomach growls, bursting the remainder of my fantasy bubble; didn't I just have a croissant, damn it? Then I see that it's my sister who is responsible for the outburst, and now she's sobbing uncontrollably, which annoys me further. Sara never could pull herself together in these sorts of situations, and I suppose I should cut her some slack—it's our mother's funeral after all—but somehow, I feel that Sara insists on being the most affected or the one more deeply violated by any situation. If I'm sad, Sara's devastated; if I'm angry, she's furious, and so on.

Now even the Rabbi's chanting has begun to sound more like a wail to me and this is here where the worst of reality hits me. The truth is that my mother is not wearing a smart silk blouse and classic black gabardine slacks, but instead is wrapped in a shroud, of all things. With the thought of this comes other details, such as the Tahara—the body-washing ritual required for burial—which means she has been scrubbed clean of any trace of the makeup I might have imagined her wearing, in my fantasy. A natural beauty, my mother never needed make-up, but wore it religiously, anyway; perhaps never wanting to show the world less than all that she was. It pained me to think of her—dead, under-dressed and with no lipstick—but the truth of all of it kept creeping in with every verse the Rabbi sang.

There had been nothing about the Tahara requirement anywhere in the original contracts for the burial plots my parents had purchased some twenty years before. My brother—the brilliant trial lawyer—had pointed this out, in no uncertain terms, doing one heck of a job of arguing my mother's case. But in the end he had not been able to sway the powers that be. If one wished to rest in Beth Torah's section of the cemetery, one had to be certified "kosher" for burial. In an attempt to make everyone happy, the funeral home director had suggested a compromise, offering for purchase other available plots in nearby sections of the cemetery. But we didn't see the advantage of burying Mom amongst the poor souls buried in that section, who had assumed they were going to heaven, but—if the Orthodox Jews were right—had been re-routed elsewhere for wardrobe violations.

In the end, we'd conceded on the shroud. We knew without a doubt that my mother wanted to be laid to rest beside the love of her life, my father. The two of them would lie together, in his-and-hers matching shrouds, for all eternity. Dad had passed away almost exactly three years before she did; and I knew for sure that he was waiting for her. Shroud or no shroud, he'd think her as breathtakingly beautiful as always.

THREE

Fantasy or not, it wouldn't have been my mother's first theatrical-style comeback. My mother had once made a dramatic interpretation in the middle of a museum, and my memory of that day may have fueled my fantasy of her doing it again at her own funeral. On that occasion, my parents had joined Richard and me on a weekend car trip to the Texas hill country. In charming Fredricksberg, halfway through a tour of the Admiral Nimitz War Museum, my mother had risen from a wheelchair as if miraculously healed, at the conclusion of a five-minute film clip about the Korean War. We'd rented the wheelchair from a kiosk near the museum's entrance, for my Dad to use—but as usual, he'd refused, preferring to hobble along on his crutches rather than be pushed in a chair.

For many years, my father's prosthetic leg did not fit him correctly, but he'd always soldiered on without complaint, never accepting the help he clearly could have used. He'd scoff at the suggestion of assistance and wave off a wheelchair. "Let's leave that for someone who needs it," he'd say, hobbling away on his crutches, an empty pants leg dangling below one knee.

With a line now forming at the kiosk, we didn't care to wait for a refund, so we'd entered the area of war displays with the empty wheelchair. Glancing at the empty seat, I saw it as a fine-enough way to view the exhibits from a lower vantage point, so I'd plopped into it. My mom set her purse in my lap and began pushing me happily along.

After a time, she and I switched places, so I was pushing her when we reached a darkened area where a film about aircraft carriers was just beginning. My dad stood in the back, leaning on his crutches for the duration of the film. I wheeled my mom next to a row of seats and sat down next to her. When the short film ended and the lights came up, all of us stood to continue through the museum, including my mom, who noticed people looking at her curiously as she stood up suddenly from the wheelchair.

Never one to miss an opportunity for a bit of fun, my mother wasted no time before taking a few shaky steps and proclaiming dramatically: "I CAN WALK!! LOOK, I CAN WALK!!" to the amazement of those believing they were witnessing a 'healing.' I stifled my laughter and tried to look genuinely surprised by her sudden improvement, while my mom herself skipped merrily away. I had no doubt that we'd laugh heartily about it, back in the car, while my dad would roll his eyes and reserve comment. These were the kinds of things my mom and I enjoyed, but my father did not share our amusement, and he lost no time hobbling ahead of us, pretending not to know his own wife and daughter. My dad had a fantastic sense of humor but drew the line at anything that might have—even slightly—inconvenienced or disturbed anyone else.

All too soon, the memory of a happy outing on a sunny day melted away, leaving me back at the funeral, where Rabbi Paley's commentary—albeit about my mother—was putting a real damper on my musings. Trying to zone out, I attempted to return to my daydreams of happier times, which kept dissipating like escaping steam. By the middle of the next prayer, I knew that after its completion I'd be called up to deliver my eulogy—two typewritten pages, now rolled up in both my hands. My most pressing concern at that moment was not speaking, but walking to the podium. I couldn't feel my feet—or thought I couldn't—and just to check I kept wiggling my toes inside my shoes. Worse than that, my legs suddenly felt weak, and I wondered if I would make it to the podium without incident. Not entirely sure that I could, I offered up a little prayer of my own: "Please God, don't let me fall."

At the very least, I believed God owed me one. I'd prayed like heck that he kindly not let my mother die and either he hadn't heard, or he had ignored my request. Dead mother. Thanks a bunch, God. So I added: Please God, don't let me stumble. And P.S.: I'd also appreciate not passing out. Thanks. *Throw me a bone, Lord.*

I looked up at the Ark housing the holy scrolls of the Torah and squeezed the rolled-up eulogy in my hands a little tighter. I'm an orphan, as you know, God, I added. Wringing the rolled-up speech like a wet towel, I sensed no response from God. So while Rabbi Paley sang the last stanza of the prayer, I unrolled the printed sheets and glanced down, reading the first line to myself.

My grandfather was a storyteller....

I could do this. I'd spoken to crowds many times this size.

Before turning the microphone over to me, the Rabbi gently touched me on a shoulder, and in a whisper, asked if I was okay. Yes, I nodded, while inside I screamed, "*Nooooooooooo, I am definitely not okay.*"

I cleared my throat and began to read the eulogy I'd written, hiding my anxiety as best I could and somehow managing not to cry. I'd gotten through the opening minutes of my first live television appearance by imagining that my parents were watching; so it was a similar vision I reached for then—of them both on the edges of their seats, settled into some heavenly chairs. I wanted to believe they were watching.

"My Grandfather was a storyteller," I began. "My father, too;" and I paused here, as much for emphasis as to swallow any cracks in my voice. And I continued.

FOUR

I assured those listening to the eulogy that having a mother so seemingly perfect had not, in fact, been a tough act to follow and that I had loved every minute of it. Until I was seven or eight, I told them, I'd assumed that everyone's mother was a beautiful princess like mine. Fittingly, my mom had played the Princess in a children's theater production of *The Princess and the Pea*; to the three of us kids, she had not just been playing a part. My princess-mother later became a beloved Brownie and Girl Scout troop leader; and as I spoke I acknowledged some of the women sitting in the audience at her funeral, still friends of mine, as having once been 'her' girl scouts. Later in life, Mom had gone on to become a glamorous and successful career woman; flawlessly reinventing herself for each phase of her life, as many times as she'd needed to.

True to form, a re-occurrence of breast cancer just two weeks after my father died had given my mother yet another opportunity to refashion herself. Twenty years earlier, when her annual mammogram had revealed an early stage of breast cancer, my mother had had her left breast removed. She had not seemed to want any sort of reconstructive surgery, not only because of the expense, but also because my father was also missing a part of himself, ever since his left leg had been amputated above the knee due to complications following the massive coronary he had suffered at age 39. With a prosthesis that never fit him perfectly, we were used to the sight of him on crutches, his left pants leg dangling empty. It seemed that my mother had made up her mind that if he could not 'grow a leg' neither would she gain a new breast. Though they'd both lost a part of themselves, neither impairment had lessened their love for each other. They were always ready to joke about the things that ailed them and after my mother's mastectomy they happily declared that now they didn't just *undress* before bed; instead, they'd say, "We *dis-assemble!*"

Then, after twenty years and the death of my father, I had accompanied her to her annual mammogram. It was a first day out for both of us, after burying my father. We were shocked to learn that my mother's remaining breast had failed her, seemingly at the worst possible hour. Later, I'd consider the irony of the timing and the reality that this terrible news had redirected our grief over my dad's death to something 'positive' to focus on. In my mother's world, triumphing over cancer #2 was an ideal *positive* goal to reach for; and as always, she was *all in*.

In my eulogy, I referenced the story of her second breast cancer surgery and how I'd noticed, standing over her that morning, that she had ignored the part of the pre-op instructions instructing patients to arrive without perfumes or powders—and *sans* make-up or deodorant. When they wheeled her in from the recovery room, I had to suppress a giggle: my mom had followed all the other pre-op instructions to a T, but apparently she had considered 'no make-up' just a suggestion. Waiting for her eyes to open, I stroked her arm and gazed at her pretty face. Her long lashes were delicately curved, making me wonder if an eyelash curler had been involved. Taking in the rest of her face and its delicate yet defined features, I noted how especially lovely she looked for one who'd just undergone radical cancer surgery. Her lips were peachy perfect (hadn't a breathing tube been involved?) and she had a rosy glow to her cheeks. Eventually, she opened her eyes and smiled.

"Hi Momma," I said to her softly. I didn't wait for her to answer before adding, "Mom, your surgeon said that you did great and that they *got it all!*" Such a positive report.

She smiled sweetly and lifted one perfectly manicured thumbnail in victory, looking up at me with lips appearing to have retained their childhood color for over three-quarters of a century. I may have appeared to be leaning in to kiss her, but I was actually whispering a query in her ear, out of the earshot of the nurses standing nearby.

"Mom, are you wearing make-up?" I asked her.

A little groggy but already in possession of her post-surgery senses, she looked up at me with a wink and raised a slender pointer-finger to her pursed lips, her coral-colored nail lacquer gleaming in the florescent lights.

"Shhhh," she said in a small voice. Looking left and then right, to see if a nurse was within earshot (she was) she whispered behind a hand she held up to her mouth, as if to shield her comments from the nurses' view. "Well, they *said* no make-up," she said. "But I did just a touch," she admitted, pantomiming the stroke of a brush with fingers across her cheek.

I didn't want to push her to elaborate, but I suspected more than just blusher had been involved. As if reading my mind, in a moment or two she volunteered what I'd already guessed. "And a little touch of eyeshadow," she said. Ahhh, full disclosure, finally.

"But almost *no* mascara," she added, as if this exonerated her, evidence that she hadn't taken any extreme measures prior to surgery.

I chuckled out loud, standing over her for the next while, as she drifted in and out of light sleep, looking camera-ready even fresh from major surgery.

I knew that my mother's motivation was simple: she never wanted to give the world any less of herself than *all that she was.* To her this included showing up for surgery without looking *sick.*

Most memorable to me was the way my mother used the cancer as a springboard to successfully re-invent herself yet once again. Sitting in the pre-op room in her hospital gown before her surgery, she'd held her prosthetic breast, squishing it gently and smiling. She tossed it to me and I caught it, its weight surprising me.

"Good lord," she said. "I won't miss this ugly thing!"

"I have to ask the nurse where to take it," she added, scowling at the fake boob as if it were a dead rat. "Surely there are women who can't afford a prosthetic and here I have one that I'll no longer need!"

I knew this was her way of leaving the loss behind: the donating of her prosthesis would be the first positive she squeezed out of the reoccurrence of cancer, but not the last.

True to form, my mother emerged after the surgery *better for the experience.* Without her once-ample bosom, it was much more obvious, visually, what a petite woman she was; she was more 'in proportion' now. A mere travel-size of her former self, she actually did look *better* this way; as luck would have it, a lightly padded camisole was all she needed to wear underneath her size-small tops. In the end, darned if this slightly downsized version of herself wasn't even more adorable than the previously busty one had been.

For weeks after the surgery, she appeared in a seemingly endless series of new blouses and tops that fit her smaller frame. The day after she went home from surgery, I came by to check on her and was not surprised to find her fully dressed, with her usual make-up expertly applied. Greeting me with a smile, the only evidence of surgery were the drains she showed me that she'd tucked into the waistband of her pants. Her new, streamlined figure looked more appropriate somehow; as if she'd actually *needed* the adjustment, and thanks to the cancer for pointing it out! The sight of her had me considering my own breasts and wondering if I wouldn't look better downsized, myself.

"Wow, Mom," I said. "You look beautiful. And so...so small!"

Moving to her full-length mirror, I stood behind her, as she ran her hands down her sides, admiring herself, and when she moved on, I stepped up to consider the image of myself. Pressing down on my own bosom, I wondered out loud if I was a bit top-heavy and out of proportion myself.

"Oh hush," she said. "You're perfect."

After her final mastectomy, it was apparent that my mom had not just *survived* the cancer surgery but, as always, had managed to turn it into a blessing of sorts. As with other negatives in her life, once she'd reframed the whole ordeal as a 'good thing,' my mother never spoke of it again. And so, neither did we.

FIVE

My mother was perpetually busy—until the day she suddenly fell ill, following a Saturday night in the beautiful dining room of her retirement community. After compliments to the chef, she'd bid all *adieu* and retired to her apartment for the second half of a Netflix movie she'd started the evening before. She went to bed and woke a couple of hours later in excruciating pain. Unbeknownst to her, an inconvenient tear had occurred in her lower intestine. She waited until 6 am to call for help, by which time deadly bacteria had spread.

Entering her apartment after she'd died, I found what would have been my mom's final grocery shopping list on the counter in her kitchen, with items, sadly, that she had not lived to purchase. On the list she'd written: *Mother's Day Cards, *Naomi and *Debbie—the starred entries indicating importance—Mother's Day was around the corner for my sister-in-law and me. She'd made this last shopping list in April, but had not made it to the store before falling ill. Farther down the list, I swallowed hard when I saw she'd written: ** Birthday Card - Naomi!, this entry garnering two stars and an underline.

On May 14th I'd celebrated' my 53rd birthday without her, as best I could, knowing that she lay in the ICU. Glorifying my birthday without my mother seemed wrong somehow. I'd sooner have forgone it, but at the insistence of my husband, my brother Joe and sister-in-law Debbie, and my daughter Marissa, we'd gathered together at a favorite restaurant. But my heart hadn't been in it. Everything we ordered and ate reminded me of her. My twin nieces turned up noses and pushed pickled beets, served as an accompaniment, aside on their plates. Cool and crunchy and vinegary sweet, I knew my mom would have announced to all in attendance that she *adored* pickled beets; all of us knew it, but she'd have said it anyway.

My husband had ordered the salmon, which the waiter informed him was served medium-rare—a trend in salmon for which neither my mother nor I had ever developed a taste. I could go for icy-cold, raw tuna any day, but no thanks to salmon served bright orange in the center. I heard Richard ask that his salmon be 'cooked through' and I knew that if my mother had been there, she would have touched his arm in approval, saying, "I'm so glad you made that clear, dear. I do *not* like rare fish," this proclamation indicating that none of us should like it raw either.

Thoughtful gifts were pulled from under chairs and pushed towards my place at the round table so I'd ooohed and ahhhed, pulling my favorite perfume, a beautiful scarf, a gift card to Barnes and Noble, and other carefully selected items from decorated gift bags stuffed with tissue. I occasionally used these pretty gift bags, too—sometimes *re*-using them—but I knew my mother would have wrapped her gift to me in actual wrapping paper, eschewing the handy gift-bags others had used. Her wrapping was always outstanding, every gift including one of her handmade bows attached.

Holding up a wrapped gift from Mom, we'd all comment on its splendor and declare it almost too pretty to unwrap. This of course pleased her and supported her claim that she, herself, *wrapped better than a professional!* Her bows, especially, were legendary and she made it look easy; I'd watched her do it countless times but still, I could never make one as pretty as hers.

As a little girl, I'd watched her wrap a gift and make one of her beauteous bows, waiting to be asked for my finger so I could happily perform my 'job.' Pressing the pad of my little pointer firmly on the designated spot, I'd hold the ribbon in place until the bow could be lowered and my finger slipped out. Timing was key; the seriousness of the task would be evident on my face and my finger dead-set against the ribbon. Nothing short of an earthquake would have swayed me from my post. When the bounteous bow was only millimeters from my hard-working finger, *"Now!"* she'd declare, and as if in speeded-up motion, she'd double knot the ribbons that I'd been holding fast only nanoseconds before. My finger removed, hers seemed to be flying; coral-colored lacquered nails a blur as she twisted each loop—either inward or outward—somehow knowing which way a particular loop needed to go—and *voila*, there atop the gift was a bow as fat and dazzling as any other. I remember breaking out of my trance to smile along with my mother as we agreed that it was indeed a properly wrapped gift.

If my mother had been there, she would have chosen the perfect gift (never more than $25 or so) and would have wrapped it with a paper of my favorite colors and finished it with a bow that would beat all other ordinary bows, should there be a competition. I knew this about my mother, just as I knew so many things of her; all of which hung in the balance on my birthday that year. I knew her as well as I knew myself, I thought; maybe even better than I knew myself. I knew her likes and dislikes; and that there was never any gray area between the two. In my mother's world, things were either *divine* or *peculiar,* two of her favorite words. I knew her expressions, her mannerisms; what she adored and what she abhorred.

In the car on the way home from my birthday dinner, I began crying softly, which I knew made my husband feel terrible, as he had no way to make me feel better. I could not hide my tears, nor could I have explained exactly why I was crying. A song on the car radio tugged at one of my frazzled heartstrings, and my soft crying turned to sobbing.

"I'm sorry..." was all I could manage to say. Of course Richard said I needn't apologize, touching my arm lovingly; it was all he could do, really. If he'd asked, I could not have explained the impetus for my now-choking sobs; for it was *all of it* and not just one thing. Everything was changing. Even the small things: none of my gifts had had an actual bow attached. It seemed a silly thing, but I had always had a bow on my birthday, since I was two and the big pink bow tied around the life-size baby doll had been placed on my head. It had been a perfect match to my pink party dress, and a photo had been taken for all time. I was crying for that pink bow and for all the bows that I might never see again.

Mom had no way of knowing that she'd missed both Mother's Day and my birthday that year; they kept her heavily sedated most of the time. When she'd occasionally speak, she made little sense; but even so I stood by her bed and spoke to her, not sure what, if anything, she comprehended. I did not mention my birthday when I stood next to her bed the day after, knowing that if she could hear or understand, she would feel terrible for having missed it, and worse for not having even having bought me a card.

It was right there on my grocery list!" she'd have said. "*BIRTHDAY CARD—NAOMI*," as if proof was needed. A birthday without so much as a wish from my mother; so many things were changing in those days, and I felt helpless to fend off the seismic shifts in what had once been familiar. The changes just kept coming. I still had not shown any signs of what I thought to be 'proper progress' in moving through my grief after my father's death, three years earlier. Now I was facing even more heartache, as my mother's life hung in the balance. We had always depended on her unshakable positivity; but now she wasn't there to surround us with it.

Once upon a time, I'd pressed my child-sized finger against a ribbon to keep it in place—but now, even with all the pressure I could muster and capable grown-up fingers, it was all slipping away.

SIX

Orthodox Jews don't mess around. They are our very own Jewish extremists; generally harmless, unless and until their belief system crosses with yours. My father was raised in an Orthodox family of first generation Americans but former traditional European autocrats. Their lives in Czarist Russia had not prepared them to deal with the pressures of the free society, in which they were to raise their children. As immigrants to the US, my father's parents had 19th-century cultural mindsets; while their children—including my father—struggled with 20th-century challenges. Neither generation could embrace the others' concepts, which led to family tensions that erupted and persisted over the years.

In contrast, my mother's Reform Jewish upbringing was a much more modern affair. The extent of their observance of Passover was stocking their pantry with *matzoh*. They had emigrated earlier and assimilated more favorably, becoming newer, gentler versions of their European ancestors. Born in the USA, my grandparents on mother's side were infinitely more easygoing, and over the years, after the two families had merged, my mother made it no secret she considered a significant number of the Orthodox Jewish requirements outdated and even outlandish.

The contrast was evident even in their looks: my mother's relatives all light-haired and hazel-eyed, compared to my father's dark and swarthy relations. Blonde and beautiful, Mom's heritage had been suspect early on by my father's parents, whose Rabbi supposedly requested the presentation of both hers and *her mother's* birth records before agreeing to marry my parents in 1950. This had bothered my mother then, but it was to be only the first of other annoyances to come. She'd scoff at many of the straight-laced customs imposed on her, but none so much as the news that she'd be going to *mikvah* before marrying my father.

Mikvah, the ritual immersion of the bride into a bath of anointed water (meant to purify her) was offensive to her, even before she was aware that this particular formality was not limited to humans; but also imposed upon inanimate items such as plates, serving pieces, and even flatware. This completely undid her. She, the cleanest individual since her own mother, thought it all completely ridiculous but comparisons to dish-washing and baptism fell on deaf ears. In the end, she'd agreed to the *mikvah,* though the suggestion that she had not been clean enough for a bunch of judgmental Jews understandably ruffled her.

I remembered this story on the day before her funeral, which is when we learned that the Orthodox ritual for burial was required for her to be buried in the grave next to my father. This news came as a shock to my brother and me; just as it had been for my mother when she learned that the *Tahara*—the ritual bathing of a body for burial— had been imposed on my father's body, without her knowledge or consent. In fairness to my dad's sister Maxine, who'd arranged it all, she'd had noble intentions. She firmly believed that Dad's entrance to heaven had depended on it, so her heart was in the right place.

To my mom, the *Tahaha*, was the final invasion of her husband, the last abomination of his withered body. Filled with distasteful visions of superstitious old women wielding washcloths, my normally unshakable mother was infuriated, her hands curled into fists so tight that her fingernails must have made half-moon indentations in the flesh of her palms. Fortunately she restrained herself from going to fisticuffs over it, which was good news for my Aunt Maxine, who, at 4-foot-and-change, would have been at a distinct disadvantage.

But if it had escalated to that, I could imagine a cartoon version of the altercation, like a comic strip with animated representations of my mother appearing in each square, wearing some sort of chic superhero costume and delivering a series of punches to my miniature aunt—who is the tiny villain. In each frame of the sequence, my mom's speech bubbles provide expletives to accompany each blow she delivers, while my Aunt's head rocks like a bobblehead:

Pow. "CLEAN!"

Bam."ENOUGH!"

Punch. "FOR!..."

Ka-zowie. "HEAVEN!"

In the final frame, I see my mother standing triumphantly over my aunt, who's left in tatters and obviously stands corrected, while my mother doesn't have a hair out of place. Victorious, she brushes her hands together, symbolically washing them clean of the whole thing, and as she turns to fly off, we see that her superhero cape is Pucci, the designer of the original Braniff stewardess' outfits; a detail my mother would have told you herself. Even better, when not in use, the cape conveniently rolls up to the size of a small travel umbrella, fitting perfectly in any purse; so there's no danger of it trailing out of the closed door of her superhero vehicle. As the cartoon strip ends, my mother is onto the next Orthodox situation. ...*To be continued,* it says.

My mother rarely cursed, but the 'F' and 'S' words had flown on the day she found out about my dad's after-death wash-up; the *Tahara* ceremony performed on his remains at the orders of my Aunt and her Orthodox synagogue. Until then, she had believed she'd buried him in his favorite navy blue sweater, the one she'd chosen herself; carrying it carefully—along with a pair of gray slacks and a leather belt—to the funeral home in a bright red Saks Fifth Avenue garment bag. The news that he'd been wrapped in a shroud was bad enough, but the revelation *after* the fact added insult to injury.

Fifty-eight years earlier, she had bowed to the Orthodox Jewish requirements for marriage, but after that, she'd drawn a line in the sand. Now, on her deathbed, it felt to us a bit like the Orthodox had prevailed yet again. For my mother, even 'dust to dust' had no bearing on the importance of proper attire. Burial-shmerial, she'd have argued; dead or alive, one could and should dress for the occasion. Later, I'd better understand the ritual of *Tahara* and gain a healthier respect for the custom and those who believe in it, but on the day before Mom's funeral, when we learned of its necessity in order to bury her, it felt like the ultra-Orthodox had struck again.

After she was buried, I donated most of her beautiful clothes, with their Saint Laurent labels, to Dress For Success, an organization benefitting underprivileged job-seeking women. I smiled to reflect that she would have believed 100% that any woman achieving gainful employment while wearing one of her silk blouses or all-year wool jackets had been hired, at least in part, thanks to *her*.

SEVEN

When I think of it now, I wonder whether we might have ordered differently at the diner if we hadn't been so confident. Later—with eagle-eyed hindsight—I'd question whether we should have ordered more simply, perhaps toast and tea or just coffee. Would a simple poached egg on toast have been more appropriate, under the circumstances? Should we have said grace or recited a prayer before eating, taking the time to outwardly express more gratitude for the sustenance of the food we were about to imbibe?

Ruminating later over every minute of that day, I remember seeing a foursome seated at a nearby table, holding hands, joined in prayer. Silently, I'd thought it out-of-place. The public display of table-worship, in the context of an otherwise religion-free, suburban setting, seemed odd at the time, but now I wondered if the four of them had also had a loved one in surgery at the same hospital. Later, I couldn't help but wonder if their publicly-offered prayers had worked, while our failure to pray might have doomed my mother.

Joining the buckwheat pancakes still sitting in my gut, these and other thoughts laid heavily through the rest of that day and into the night; but I wouldn't have slept anyway. The weight of it all overwhelmed me. How foolish we had been to hope, how overly optimistic to order pancakes on such a fateful day. After breakfast, warm and full, we'd walked the relatively short distance up the street to the hospital, under cloudless summer skies. Our footsteps clicked and clacked in unison down the sterile hallway floors of the hospital, sounding more like tap-dancing that day than our usual trudging. We'd stepped lightly, still unaware of the reality of Mom's life-threatening sepsis.

Entering the ICU's surgical family waiting area, I spotted my girlfriend Becky Aft, who looked out of place at first sight, until I remembered she'd been receiving chemotherapy treatments at the same hospital. In messages back and forth, as I'd spent days at the hospital at my mother's side, she and I had promised to meet for coffee. I truly appreciated that she had been checking on my mother's progress each day.

Genuinely pleased to see her, I crossed the sun-drenched waiting area to greet Becky with a hug. A human connection. Her smile warmed me, and it felt good to connect with a friend. Especially this friend; one who had endured a battle with cancer and was still, by all accounts, doing incredibly well.

"Becky! Oh my gosh, hellooo! You look fantastic!" I said as we embraced, and I meant it; she did look great. I lowered my voice to ask, "Becky, how is Brian?" My concern was apparent on my face; I knew that in the midst of Becky's chemo treatments, her son Brian had sustained injuries almost too horrific to imagine; somehow surviving a roadside bomb in Iraq. In one terrible moment, Brian had been literally obliterated from the waist down. Becky's brave and brilliant soldier, her beloved son, had now joined the ranks of his brothers in combat maimed by IUD explosions, and in the middle of her own battle with cancer she'd become her son's primary caregiver, literally carrying him home after extended hospital stays and ongoing rehab. I knew I was standing in front of an extraordinarily courageous woman; a 5-foot-tall powerhouse, who had, herself, stood up to one unfathomable blow after the other, and—unbelievably—still stood before me, smiling. She had risen above incredible odds, right here, *at this very hospital.* It struck me that I was standing in a place where lives had hung in the balance. Becky had ultimately tipped the scales and gone on. So I believed I was in the right place for miracles to happen. My mother had been near death, too, but now I believed that she too was about to rebound. As I leaned in to hug Becky, I imagined some of her 'good luck' rubbing off on me.

"Oh Naomi, how is your mom doing?" she asked, her expression sympathetic, and as I spoke, it felt good—finally, to smile with this brand new, positive news. I had never gotten used to delivering somber news to those who asked about my Mom and for this reason I'd begun posting daily updates on Facebook rather than speaking by phone to all who wanted to know her condition; which had remained virtually the same for three long weeks. I remember thinking that day, that I couldn't wait to post something positive at last!

I'd begun explaining to Becky the sudden, decisive and positive turn in my mother's condition, telling her about the final surgery being performed as we spoke, to remove the last of the infected areas. Becky was thrilled and just as she was telling me so, I heard our name called by the nurse sitting at a front desk.

"Pevsner?" she called.

Becky heard it too and waved me off. "Go…you go, we'll talk later," she said, and I turned to follow my brother to the reception desk. The nurse, who had a phone at her ear, indicated with a wave of hand that we were to head to one of the private consultation rooms, where we knew we'd see Mom's surgeon, fresh from the life-saving surgery he'd just performed on her.

"Your surgeon will meet you…" she said. Only later would we realize that she had finished her sentence: "in the *condolence room.*"

The row of small rooms she'd pointed us towards all looked identical; private spaces for surgeons to deliver all sorts of updates to waiting relatives. Later I'd wonder whether half of them were *Consultation Rooms* and the other half *Condolence Rooms,* and whether each had different decor. We'd missed the clue but it had been there, in the receptionist's reference to one of the open doors that awaited us.

She'd called it The Condolence Room.

Only later would I remember Becky's face, registering what she had picked up, but I hadn't. Still drunk on the optimism from the toasts we'd made at breakfast to Mom's recovery, our ears may still have been ringing from the clinking of the orange juice glasses we'd raised high above our table. Funny, the things we remember and the things we miss.

I had noted some random details: the legs on a waiting room sofa; the industrial ceiling tiles, one of which, I noticed, was off-color from the others; the coffee area that seemed to be permanently out of stir-sticks. I'd even noticed the color of Becky's fingernail polish—a nice neutral. But I had not seen that the sun was beginning to disappear behind thick clouds that would later bring roiling thunderstorms. Walking towards the small room with the open door, I followed my brother, and once inside, we closed the door behind us. Through the tiny window in the door opposite the one we'd come through, I looked and waited for the first sight of Mom's surgeon. The glass inside the little square window was tinted, I noted, still fixating on little things: tinted glass in a window; a swirled pattern on the carpet. A paisley design, actually, a nice touch for standard industrial carpeting, I thought, when they could have gone with a solid. Funny how some minutiae escape us, while other details implant themselves forever in our minds. And interesting how, in certain situations, we consider this temporary blindness or deafness to be a good thing.

EIGHT

Mom would wake up and want to know what we'd ordered, and I'd be especially happy to report that I'd had her favorite pancakes, buckwheat.

"Oh my, how I adore buckwheat pancakes. They're my favorite, you know!" Mom would say—as if I didn't know.

Condolence Room.

Relatively intelligent and detail-oriented people, how had we missed a thing so evident? But we had, and in those few last minutes, waiting for the surgeon, we had been blissfully unaware.

Condolence Room.

Apparently things had not been going as well as we'd believed. Not well at all.

The surgeon sat across from Joe and me, his head bowed slightly, and I noticed a small smear-mark on his pocket. It looked like blood, right there on his surgical shirt. Something of my mother's, I thought. The small smear, curved into a familiar shape—just above his embroidered name—a brushstroke of blood curled into something I recognized. I think I smiled as I decided it looked like an element of a paisley motif, the same as I'd noticed on the hospital's carpet and a favorite design of my mother's and mine. The unmistakably familiar curled pattern, also on many a shirt and tie of my father's; she had shopped for him, and he always looked so dapper.

I assumed it was her blood there, just above the doctor's pocket and that she'd seen to it, somehow. Leave it to my mother to have left her mark, I thought. An inch or so in size—I wondered if it was some sort of seal that my mother had added like the perfect accessory; a last little flourish that she'd tucked onto his pocket before sending her surgeon out to deliver the good news. How many times I'd seen her do this to my dad; pushing a silk square into his suit pocket. The blood smear was a deep red, darkening to almost brown around its delicate edges.

As the doctor spoke, I saw the swirl turning brown in other places and wondered if it was the light in the room.

"I'm sorry," he was saying. Something was not right.

"The surgery could not have gone more poorly...." at this point I heard only snippets of what he said, some of it not registering with me, at least not all at once.

The doctor was gesturing, referring to "a rolled up, wet section of a newspaper" with his hands, pantomiming how he'd attempted to turn each waterlogged page of 'newsprint,' only to have it hopelessly tear away. "Her intestines...falling apart...a layer at a time...."

"We weren't even able to close her up...."

Her physical looks had been ironically deceiving, belying her 80-year-old intestines, which—in the end—did not 'match' her youthful outer self. The miles of aging organs were known to fall short in these sorts of situations, apparently.

"Tearing away...like rolled up newsprint...."

Suddenly, I was thinking of paper-maché and a balloon head I once made in an art class, which maintained its wide smile even after the balloon inside had burst. Carefully, I'd covered a red balloon with strips of wet, pasty newspaper; wadding up other pieces of wet newspaper to make a nose and two ears, and attaching the pasty features to the balloon head where they'd stayed put. A momentary thought made me laugh to myself, though I did not share it: "Have you tried paper-maché, doctor?"

But this was no time for jokes. Although in our family almost anytime was good for a laugh, this was different.

Condolence Room.

We hadn't heard it, though the receptionist had said it.

The doctor will see you in the Condolence Room, she'd said.

Oh, if only we'd gone through a different door.

NINE

We had not had to think for more than a moment about which two songs to play at her funeral service. We knew that "Somewhere Over The Rainbow" would be one of them.

That favorite song, about a place where happy bluebirds fly, was one of the simple chorded ones she'd learned to play on guitar, for the sake of entertaining us as children. Sitting atop a chenille bedspread, she'd tucked one leg up under her and we sang along while she strummed and sang to us about a heavenly place up above, the one Judy Garland dreamed about in her journey through Oz.

Towards the end of the funeral service, lovely images of her faded in and out on a big screen to the strains of "Somewhere Over The Rainbow," evoking memories of times gone by. I had finished my eulogy and managed to return to my seat on unsure legs that had not failed me after all. My fears of bursting into tears while speaking had been diluted by my love for her, and I'd encouraged myself by imagining she was somehow listening to my words. I'd intentionally ended my eulogy on a high note, promising to move forward with my life by emulating her propensity for doing the seemingly impossible while making it look easy. I convinced everyone but myself that I could, but even then I suspected that I might not have inherited my mother's talent for squashing down negative feelings and reframing adverse situations. I'd been able to do it under her direction, but on my own it would prove to be much more difficult.

Returning to my seat after delivering the eulogy, Richard took my hand and squeezed it gently, winking at me lovingly; his eyes, too, were wet with tears. Glancing at my fair hand in Richard's darker one, his suntanned brown from golf, I was glad I'd had my nails done just a few days before. I hadn't known she would die on the day I'd left the hospital to grab a quick manicure, but now it seemed ironic that I'd chosen a nail polish color named "Rosy Future." Irony aside, when I looked at my ten glossy nails shining in the light of the sanctuary, I decided that 'Rosy Future' had been the perfect shade for the outfit I'd chosen to wear. The Rabbi began a prayer that I knew to be the end of the service, and I wondered if I'd brought any hand cream in my purse; my nails were perfect but my hands were a bit dry. It occurred to me that my mom would have some—she always carried the essentials—and in a knee-jerk reaction, I turned to my right—but of course, she wasn't there. I imagined her pulling a pen from her handbag to add the name of the polish I wore to her grocery list; she'd have liked it enough to have written "Rosy Future" right there, in her lovely handwriting.

Without my beloved parents, my future looked anything but rosy, but I'd told the gathered crowd convincingly that 'tomorrow I would wake up, put on my make-up, get dressed as usual and head out into the world to see what adventures awaited me, just as my mother had always done.' But after the funeral was over and life began to move on, I just couldn't seem to find that rosy future.

TEN

It turned out to be the last manicure I'd get for a very long time. Things like 'Rosy Future' and glossy manicures didn't matter to me anymore; I had no energy for things like choosing a nail color or making conversation with a manicurist. Long after the polish had chipped and peeled, I could have cared less what my nails looked like. My mother, of all people, would have noticed and chided me for my lack of interest in personal care. But it didn't seem necessary; I'd begun avoiding social functions and even business-related interactions. My mother had been gone for a year then; and my god-awful nails were just another sign that I was not in a good place.

Her knack for camouflaging struggle of any sort hadn't allowed me to see what was behind her strong façade. My memory of her strength was fading beneath the debilitating weariness I now felt all the time. A fatigue so heavy had set in that it sent me back to bed most days. After a year, when the phase of deep grief still hadn't passed, I'd begun to be haunted by the words I'd recited in her eulogy, when I'd told an entire crowd of mourners that I would be *just fine.* I was far from fine. My constant funk disgusted no one more than myself, and I was at least glad that no one knew that I had not been able to make good on my claim that I'd triumph over the loss of her. I hated myself for the miserable, sad version of Naomi that I'd become. Even my short, split fingernails were an embarrassment.

My estimated timeframe for mourning had been indefinitely extended and I felt I could no longer use her death as an excuse, but it was all I had. Apparently grief had a rhythm of its own; my journey through loss and change had its own schedule, which infuriated me. I had been a businesswoman, a leader, adept at being the 'boss.' My original plan had been to take a shorter route through sadness—to navigate a way *over* it. But as the weeks and months passed, I began to realize that the only way to get through grief was to go straight through it—but I hadn't the energy, it seemed. I felt like I was drowning in swirling waters of hopelessness, pulled down by an undertow of relentless grief, and every day it was more of a struggle to stay afloat. I was dead-tired from treading water with nothing left of my parents but the memories that I tried to push away. Memories of their laughter in happier times taunted rather than comforted me, and as a drowning person is known to push his rescuer under, I pushed the memory of them away. At one point I turned their pictures face down or tucked them into drawers, so I wouldn't have to be reminded they were gone. But the truth was, I could not forget.

PART TWO

TRAINING WHEELS

ELEVEN

At 5 or 6 years old I wasn't afraid of the dark; it was the light of day that scared me most. Usually beginning in the mornings, I remember a creeping sense of something terrible about to happen; growing throughout the day, only lessening in the evenings, when I was safely tucked into my bed at night by either one or both of my parents.

The gnawing concerns that followed me during the day were not for anything specific, and this made it nearly impossible to explain, even to my mother, who merely waved off my fears as passing phases—but pass they did not. As an antidote, my parents began enrolling me in various classes—ice-skating, art, even a stint in 'tea-room modeling,' where I'd curtsy adorably before small tables where ladies in hats sipped tea. All of these pursuits terrified me. I hated every minute of any class or activity that took me away from my parents.

On some days I might, for a time, forget about my worries entirely, but this would typically be on the weekends, surrounded by the four people I loved—my family. The hours spent with them were the only ones where my fears were allayed for a time. School days were particularly frightening. I sensed that I was different from the other kids; no one else but me seemed alarmed by the fact that their mommies and daddies had disappeared after dropping us at school. I imagined my parents facing any number of accidents or calamities and never returning—or at least, not by carpool time. I remember obsessing every single day, especially during the angst-filled minutes when everybody's mommy showed up at once for the carpool. I feared placement into the wrong car, and someone else's mommy discovering me too late, while my mother frantically searched for me in vain, her car left running by the curb. I do not know where these fears came from; only that they stayed for years. I also don't remember wishing to be more like the other kids; instead, I wondered when they would all wise up.

Birthday parties for a kindergarten classmate were a subject of great interest and excitement amongst the rest of the pre-schoolers. But on the day of a party I worried, the whole day long, about an impending party I was expected to attend. The buzz about an afternoon party circulated in whispers throughout the school day: speculations about what kind of cake there would be, or what activities awaited us, were discussed at length, in whispers in hallways and in outside voices on the playground. While all conversations on the day of a party were party-related, for me, they might as well have been sound-tracked by the music from "Jaws." A party loomed like a monster waiting to eat me up after school.

On birthday party days, we girls wore party dresses to school, taking care not to soil them while at play on the jungle gym or swings. For me, the starched skirt of my frilly dress was a scratchy reminder of the birthday party just hours away. If I bailed out, I knew my mother would pick me up from school, but I typically promised to at least give it a try; to go with Mrs. Swartz or Mrs. Forrest in their car to the party. While others ate cake and dropped clothespins into bottles, for me it was two hours of pin-the-tail-on-the-donkey hell, until my mother came to take me home. Even this worried me, though I had no real reason to fear that I'd be forgotten. My mother had never even been late to fetch me, but it was a great fear of mine, nonetheless.

Whether I was born with these irrational fears or my creative little mind came up with what was farthest from the reality, I did not know—and still don't. Aside from my irrational fears, my childhood was a cheerful one, especially before my father became ill. The problem with fearing the loss of my mom or dad was that this, my most dreaded fear, would one day come to pass, though the day was still decades away. Of course, they would both die eventually; it is the natural order of things. But when they did, it would be as if my worst childhood fear was finally realized. I'd be all grown-up then, but I'd feel like a child whose heart has been broken by tragedy, as if I were still five years old. My parents' deaths were what I had feared all along, and thus I'd been right to fear it. Even as an adult, the loss of them would be almost more than I could handle.

TWELVE

In 1963, I wasn't the only wide-eyed kid poring over the endless pages of toys in the thick-as-a-phone-book *Sears Wishbook*. But I was the one pictured in the national newspaper stories announcing the Sears catalog's arrival that year. As the director of public relations for Sears Roebuck, it had been my father's job to arrange the photo shoot that would accompany an article scheduled to run in newspapers nationwide, early that December. Above the story he'd penned, a picture of two fair-haired four-year-olds—a boy and a girl—were delightedly perusing the pages of toys and games of every sort and preparing to make their wish lists for Santa. We didn't celebrate Christmas in our Jewish household, but apparently I looked enough like someone who did; and for all intents and purposes, I could've been making my choices for Chanukah, after all.

Contained within the pages of the catalog were thousands of items of all kinds—from appliances to xylophones and soup to nuts; virtually everything one could possibly wish for in 1963 was between those glossy covers. Prior to the catalog's release at holiday time that year, Sears rolled out a PR campaign led by my dad, then a young executive just beginning to climb the corporate ladder—and who better to bat her long lashes (inherited from his side of the family) than his own daughter?

The photos taken that day were in black-and-white but I can remember the deep cherry-red color of the dress I wore, and its delicately hand-embroidered collar. It had the look of an expensive little frock, and had no doubt been handed down to me from my cousin Nina, who had beautiful things and—as luck would have it—remained two sizes ahead of me for most of my childhood.

I remember most of the moments just before the clicks of the camera shutter, when I sat on a stool in front of a mirror, in which I could see my mother standing behind me, brushing my waist-long hair into a ponytail. I watched her expression in the mirror, utterly intent on creating the perfect pony; her deliberate brushstrokes interspersed with a press from the palm of her hand, to expertly corral every shiny inch of my hair into a coated elastic band with colored plastic balls that interlocked and held everything in place. *There now!* The ponytail was perfectly done, as always. As a last step, for good measure, my mother quickly and elegantly licked her own fingers, slicking back the sides of my head with a bit of herself to assure that not one strand would stray.

My perfect ponytail glistening with her magical spit, I smiled in the bright lights as I lay on my belly next to the friendly boy, both of us feasting our eyes on every possible game or toy a child could want. In a quick change between shots, my mother scurried over to the carpeted platform and, with a bit more moisture gathered from her enchanted tongue, twisted my long pony round and round until it became a flat halo, like a ballerina-style bun.

Click click click, the shutter snapped, capturing a millisecond in time, and then another. In the best photo, which ran in some 400 newspapers nationally, my smile expresses complete content and total gratification, as if my every wish had been fulfilled. Now I know that the girl in the picture was smiling because she knew that she already had something that cannot be bought: love and family. For as long as my mother was near me, ever-ready to tame any stray hair, wipe every tear and make everything okay, I had everything I could ever want or need.

After my parents died, I remembered the day of the photo shoot and even the pages of the Wishbook itself. It took some time, but eventually I began to recall an even thicker catalog of memories of my parents, glossy scenes in full-color, which I could "order" just by remembering.

THIRTEEN

As a child, there were so many things I did not know yet, many of which I could not yet articulate. But I did know one thing: I was aware that I was considered "pretty," because this significant point was conveyed emphatically and often by both of my parents. Their proclamations about my appearance—that I was notably good-looking—were enthusiastically agreed upon by relatives, friends and even strangers, who'd prove my parents' theory every time they exclaimed: "Oh, isn't she a pretty little girl!" To which my mother would, of course, agree and beam with pride at the confirmation of what she already knew.

My 'prettiness' seemed a thing of such importance that I carried it like a fragile china doll that might break if I did not hold it carefully in my arms. I had not done anything to acquire it or deserve it, so I feared I could lose it just as easily as I'd gotten it. According to my parents, my physical presence was a fundamental and essential attribute, which may have been behind my kindergarten obsession with cleanliness. Early in the year I became anxious and distressed about any activity requiring my hands to become dirty. A painting smock could protect my pretty clothes, but what about the rest of me?

One day, after a satisfying session with modeling clay, I noticed remnants of it under my small fingernails and reportedly began to cry. I was inconsolable until the problem was solved, and even then I remember feeling somehow soiled. When I started avoiding art projects that my teachers knew I had loved, my parents were called in to discuss the problem. My mother did not take to heart any of the teacher's suggestions to acclimate me to feeling 'dirty' by practicing at home—and I suspect this may have been because, at some level, she didn't want me to get dirty either.

In my first grade gym class, where we played organized games with the more sizable second graders, one day I apparently had an unfortunate collision in the midst of a circle game. Somewhat similar to musical chairs, this game required we run from one circle to another, moving without pause while the music played, but when the song stopped, anyone not in a circled area was 'out.' Running from one circle to another, I collided with a large second-grade boy who had fared better than I, with weight and heft on his side. I went down—passing out cold and awakening on a cot in the school's clinic. As long as I live, I will always remember the three worried faces I saw above me when I opened my eyes. Two of them looked understandably concerned, and one of them was crying—naturally, it was my mother. By her horrified expression, plus the dull throbbing I felt, I sensed there had been damage of some sort to my face. The nurse busied herself with taking my pulse and adjusting a pillow under my head while the school principal, Mr. Butterfield—whose yellow-blond crew-cut fit his buttery-sounding name—began explaining to me that I'd been unconscious. This didn't sound all that bad to me until I heard my mother saying, "Oh my god, her face, her face!"

Blinking in the light, I wasn't sure what had happened or how I had gotten where I was, but I remember hoping my clothes hadn't gotten dirty in the scuffle. Underneath an ice pack stretched across my nose, I knew something bad had happened there but even so, I was far more worried for my mommy, who looked so seriously upset, than for me and what had transpired before I found myself on a cot with grownups hovering above me. "Do you think it's broken?" my mother asked. I understood her to be asking if my face itself was broken.

An emergency visit to our pediatrician revealed that I had a concussion and the doctor gave my mother instructions to keep me under close observation for 24 hours, which she did as a general rule anyway. Once home, I remember being so afraid to see the damage to my nose, which for now was hidden under the bandages; a fear my mother propitiated by covering the bathroom mirrors with towels so I'd be in no danger of accidentally viewing myself. My mother's willingness to cover the mirrors confirmed for me that the very sight of my damaged face might be so disturbing that only *she* should be subjected to it.

I remember coming home that day to the smell of fresh paint and two painters working at our apartment, their white painter's clothes covered with splatters of paint. I was horrified for even workers to see my face, so much so that fifty years after the fact, I still remember walking up the stairs to my bedroom with my head turned towards the wall, overly-concerned even for these paint-streaked painters to witness the hideousness of my bandaged face, though I did not know these men, nor would I ever see them again. But at six years old, I recall feeling 'ruined' and imperfect in a way that embarrassed me.

In the end, thankfully, my nose had not been broken. For a few days, it remained crusty and swollen, as did my eyes. This incident cemented in me an abiding concern for this all-important aspect of myself—my looks—which had narrowly escaped ruin, by just a nose.

Thus, beauty was ingrained in me as something precious. The most beautiful woman in all the world was my own mother, after all, and I knew from an early age that physical allure was something not just to be admired, but to be protected as well. My mother's good looks would last her lifetime: she was lovely at every stage of her life, and even at 80, her looks belied her age. I never believed that I was as naturally pretty as my mother, though I spent a lifetime making sure I was as appealing-looking as I could possibly be. In my business as a jewelry designer, I created a persona based on my face, which anchored my brand on all of my advertising and business-related materials, perpetuating the perceived "value" of my own exterior.

In my pre-teen years, I struggled with a short period of awkwardness, but to my mother's delight, as much as my own, I'd emerged from a cocoon of glasses and braces to rise like a butterfly from the ashes of only-temporary unattractiveness, marching triumphantly into an alluring-enough adulthood. Whether consciously or subconsciously, I attributed a good part of my success to my looks, as if my mother had been right all along.

But beauty can be fleeting. My mother had been the exception, looking incredibly lovely even as she lay dying; both my brother and I had marveled, standing over her, at how beautiful she was in those moments between life and death. Such uncanny loveliness was difficult, if not impossible, for me to emulate over the years. Only after she died would something begin to shift in me, allowing me to loosen my grip on the quest for unattainable physical perfection that had been planted in me at an early age, when I'd almost lost my looks to a broken nose.

Looking my very best at all times was a tiring full-time job, to which I remained committed for many years. After all, I had been raised by a mother who made beauty look effortless, literally until the day she died.

FOURTEEN

May 14th, 1965, dawned bright and blue-skied. Still foggy from sleep, wearing my Cinderella nightgown, I padded into the front room of our apartment on the morning of my 6th birthday and there, in all its glory, I saw it: a cobalt blue and shining silver Schwinn bicycle leaned casually on its kickstand like we were old friends. It was a sight so glorious that I turned away momentarily, as if what I saw was too unbelievable to behold. Turning my head, I saw both my parents standing in the hallway behind me, beaming.

It was the very bicycle I'd dreamt of, though twice the size I'd imagined it would be when I spied it in a picture in the Sears catalog. I had noticed that the child standing next to the bike looked a few years older than I was, but I didn't care that I might have to grow into it a bit. With a chubby finger, I'd jabbed at its image.

"That's the one, Daddy," I'd said. That's the bike I want."

Later, some of our neighbors would notice the bike's size, too, making comments like "good heavens, that bike is entirely too big for that little girl"—gossip that made its way back to me via other children. I immediately took what I heard to my parents for commentary, and they explained that the negative comments were just 'sour grapes' from kids with small bikes. I thought my large-sized new bicycle was perfect, even if I had to grow into it a bit, which was what my parents intended. As a young couple just starting out, they were not in a position to buy the three of us bicycles in various sizes as we grew. So 'too-big' or not, it was mine, and after me, it would be my sister's.

Shortly after breakfast, I saw my father zipping his 'weekend jacket' over his tee shirt and khakis, and I ran for my sweater to button over my favorite white tee shirt. My mother waved me over, and while I stood in front of her, she buttoned the top two buttons of my sweater and leaned down to tie the laces of my red sneakers into double knots. It was just a bike ride, not some dangerous mission on wheels, but you wouldn't have known it by the safety checklist my mother rattled off, like an airline pilot preparing to take off. At one point, leaning down to meet my gaze, she eyeballed me up and down as if memorizing the sight of me, should I not return. These were the days before helmets, so I have to wonder if she thought my fat pigtails would protect me if I fell on my head.

"Now pleeease, listen carefully to your father," she told me, in a tone as severe as the Wright brothers' mother just before the first flight of the Kitty-Hawk.

And then, just before I left with my dad, she uttered the first of what would become an oft-repeated phrase of hers, well into my adulthood: *"And keep your wits about you."* For the next fifty years, whenever I'd get into my car to leave my parents' house, my mom would remind me where to keep my wits; I'd be reminded to *keep them close.*

That morning, my father stood next to me in his white zipper-front jacket with its red and gray striped elastic trim. When Dad was wearing that jacket, my siblings and I knew that good times would ensue. I sat atop my bike, listening and nodding my understanding of all the basics, as my dad reviewed them. My small hands were placed on either side of the silver handlebars as my dad raised the kickstand slowly with his foot, holding the bike upright so I could get the feel of it.

Sitting high in my seat and looking up the long sidewalk ahead of me, I was as ready as I'd ever been.

"Feel good to you, Nomi?" my father asked. His expression was a mix of confidence in my abilities and fatherly fear, inspiring me to action. My confidence level was in high gear and I was all buttoned-up and ready to go.

"Now, begin to pedal slowly," Dad said.

Gently, moving slowly at first, I began to pedal while my dad continued to walk alongside me. Holding the bike, he was observing my pedaling skills; and periodically he'd direct me to brake, just making sure I had not forgotten how to step backward on the pedals to bring the bike to a stop.

When I'd brake successfully on command, he'd say, "Good girl!" I relished his praise.

At this point, I believed I could go it alone. My father was moving fast now, and he was smiling, so things were going excellently, and we continued on that way—him jogging and me pedaling, until halfway up the sidewalk, I felt the laws of physics take over. My Dad released his hold on the bike, and I pumped my child-size-thighs as hard as I'd ever done. The knowledge that I was on my own was every bit as exciting as I'd imagined it would be. I pedaled on; wishing I could see my dad's face but not daring to look back. I was holding tightly to the handlebars when suddenly it hit me: Darned if that bike wasn't sailing...with me on it! I. Was. Riding!

I had one of those unforgettable, turning-point-moments then, when one knows one has mastered the art of something-or-other and can coast for a bit. So I did just that. My hair blowing back, I was sailing on the sweet wind of a victory lap. With the wind rushing past my ears, I wouldn't have heard it if my Dad had been cheering me on. Basking in the sunshine on my face, warming me in spite of the whipping wind, I continued proudly along the sidewalk; cruising confidently over cracks and crevices; experiencing alternating periods of pure coasting joy, the payoff for periodic bursts of thigh-pumping and purposeful pedaling. It was bliss.

I continued all the way up the block to North Harlem Street, which I knew was the cross street to take me to the next corner of our neighborhood block. It was also the street that ran past the back door of our apartment, so I knew that if my dad wanted to intercept or reroute me, that he'd have cut across the empty lot to meet me outside the back door of our apartment. There he could stand—wildly flagging me down if need be—waving both arms or putting himself in my path to stop me. But passing our back patio, I glanced left, and he wasn't there, so I envisioned him waiting just where we'd launched my maiden voyage; both of us sure that I'd soon be there soon. I was halfway around the block!

I continued for the rest of a half block, to reach the corner of Thomas Street, which I knew would lead me back to the start. Soon, I'd have navigated an entire block of our neighborhood, on my first journey from home; sitting proudly above the two wheels of a bike I'd only just met. I may have weighed a mere 40 pounds, but I was puffed with pride at what I'd accomplished and was about to complete.

In the final few feet, as I continued to pedal towards the finish line, I finally saw my father standing in the distance, just where I'd left him. I'd imagined this scene four corners ago, and now, here it was in real time. My smile must have been ear to ear in those moments, as with every sidewalk crack, I rolled closer. As my father got larger and closer, I began to slow down in anticipation of braking soon.

An entire square block—solo!

I was coasting triumphantly when I noticed that he was not standing straight, but instead leaning over with his hands on his knees, as if trying to catch his breath. I slowed and then braked to what I thought was a perfect stop beside my dad—just in time for him to grab the frame of my bike and hold it upright, compensating for the fact that my short legs did not quite touch the ground.

Only then did I see that he was not smiling. My own grin faded. He was out of breath, and it took me a moment to understand why. He had not waited in place for me to cruise around the block; instead, he'd run after me. When he realized that I was not going to stop, he must have bounded back across the empty lot to wait for me at the place where we'd started, his heart no doubt in his throat until I returned.

It had not dawned on me, not for even a moment, that my father would not share my enthusiasm for my maiden ride. I had no idea that he had been yelling for me to stop, while I, deafened by the wind, had not heard his cries. I had assumed I was supposed to keep going; had I been wrong?

In a flash, realizing my error, my joy turned inside out; it happened in a heartbeat. I felt a nauseating combination of embarrassment and defeat, and my smile faded into shame. The worried-sick expression on my father's face told me that although I might have succeeded in rounding the block on two wheels, I had failed him. Utterly horrified, I was speechless.

"Never, never do that again, Nomi," he said, still wheezing from the exertion of sprinting after me.

I did not know what to say. I could only blink in response, which also helped to discourage the tears pooling in my eyes from escaping down my wind-flushed cheeks. After a few moments, they did anyway. I was deflated with the knowledge that I had not made him proud, but had *disappointed* him instead, the exact opposite of my intentions. This realization was like all the air escaping from my two new tires.

"I...I didn't know...." I stammered. It was all I could think of to say.

"You must never do that again," he repeated. "Never...ride... like that...without me," he stammered, swallowing and catching his breath. "You're not ready yet."

And only then did I know this to be true. What had I been thinking? How could I have imagined that I was old enough to ride around a city block without him, on a bike twice my size?

I'd intended to ride home from where we were, but my dad took hold of the bike and walked beside it, so I followed on foot, heading towards our front door with my head hanging. Two of my steps equaled one of his, and I soon fell behind a few paces. All the while my mind reeled with the mixed feelings of triumph and unexpected defeat; two opposites I'd felt all in the same moment.

My dad reached the door of our apartment before I did and steered my bike to a place beside our front door, parallel to the side of the house. I watched as he engaged the kickstand with what seemed like a harder kick than necessary. We left the new bike there, leaning on its kickstand for another day. More than the memory of those glorious moments I'd sailed down our street, the expression on my father's face and the words he'd said when I arrived were what would stay with me for a lifetime.

He'd been right, and I'd known it then. What had I been thinking? I couldn't go forward without him. But on that morning, for a few magical moments under a gloriously blue sky—I'd had the outlandish idea that somehow I could.

FIFTEEN

At six or seven years old, our weekends together as a family were the very best days, but time alone with my father was what I loved best. He and I had our 'Daddy and Naomi' jokes, and there were enduring nicknames he called me by, all reserved for just me. When it was my dad and me, I was the only little girl in the world; though I have no doubt both my siblings had these special times and nicknames, too.

One warm and breezy spring day in our suburb of Chicago, I sat in the passenger seat with my dad at the wheel, both of our elbows crooked over the top of the car doors. We were matching bookends, as we drove along and I'd been looking at my dad, able to admire his profile from where I sat. Studying his face—the weekend stubble, his easy smile—I hadn't seen whatever it was that had prompted a long, loud honk from a car to our right.

It was loud and startling, but in response, I saw my dad do a little wave with his right hand, pantomiming with his expression that he was "SORRY," mouthing the word while he waved. I expected whoever had honked to wave in response, but as I craned my neck to see who it was I saw the person make a hand gesture I knew to be aggressive. For some reason, my father's apologetic response made me feel badly for him; I couldn't imagine he'd done anything wrong and did not know why he had waved an apology.

"Gee, I wonder what crawled up his pants leg!" my dad said, looking at me, and I giggled; the thought of something creeping up a driver's leg, causing a fit of honking, tickled me. My dad smiled back, and the honking car drove ahead; now a car-length ahead of us while both of our vehicles approached a traffic light. Rolling to a stop, I saw that the car had pulled up to the right of us and that the driver looked to be a teenage boy, with another boy—his same age or younger—beside him in the passenger seat. Both boys wore menacing expressions that caused my heart to begin to beat faster, though I wasn't exactly sure why.

Sitting at the red light, I wished my dad would roll up his window but he did not. Another loud horn blaring from their car made me jump, and I looked at my dad, who sat expressionless, staring straight ahead and ignoring these troublemakers. So I did the same. Decades away from driving myself, I knew enough to know that a green light meant to go, and if the power of my fixed-stare could change a red light to green, I willed it to do so right away. The boys had their window down, too, and after another painfully long hoooonk, I heard one of them yelling something and I turned in the direction of the voice to see the boy, who looked too young to drive, sporting a crew-cut, with a sprinkling of freckles across his nose. He was yelling something I couldn't quite make out, but I knew it sounded hostile.

Looking over at my father, I saw to my amazement that he was still looking straight ahead, ignoring them. Yell back, Daddy, I thought to myself, but he didn't.

I was angry, but felt my outrage turn to something different, and even more uncomfortable. It surprised me, as it wasn't something I remembered feeling before. An inexplicable sadness took the place of my anger, and I swallowed hard.

"Hey, old man! Learn to drive why doncha?!" the young driver yelled. The question was directed at my father, but it made *me* want to cry.

"Nice lane-change grampa!" the other kid yelled; leaning over from his passenger seat towards the open driver's side window and shouting loudly enough to be heard over the idling of both cars. This confused me, as my father looked nothing like any grandfather I knew.

Angry voices coming from a car within arm's reach was frightening to me, and instinctively I pulled my arm inside the vehicle. The two of them continued to shout at us, but my father ignored their insults until finally, in a moment that felt like slow-motion, he turned towards the boys in the car, and I waited for him to deliver the best—and last—verbal punch. To my amazement, my father smiled at them.

My jaw may have dropped. In response to what had been the most outrageous, all-out attack on my darling father, his *smiling* at them in response seemed inadequate.

Do something, Daddy, I silently willed him.

He had been untouchable, in my mind, until these boys' verbal attack. My daddy could do absolutely anything; and as a man possessing endless skills and talents, I believed him to be the world's best driver, too. More than any of it, he was a sweet and tender man, something I knew even at a young age. Certainly, he was the last soul deserving to be the target of two rowdy strangers' fury; and as they delighted in hurling verbal daggers at him, I felt wounded, too. Their comments, traveling through the air between our opened car windows, had crossed me to reach him, each word cutting a line across my heart.

"Idiot!" one of them spewed. "Hey, why don'tcha get that heap off the road, mister?!" the other one yelled.

The light may have changed in the next 60 seconds or so, but to me, it felt like an eternity. Released by the green light, my dad drove ahead, and, as if an answer to my prayers, the still-honking car turned the next corner, the driver making hand gestures as they rounded the corner and drove out of sight.

My heart was beating wildly, but my father appeared to be unscathed—as if the whole thing was forgotten as soon as the light changed. We drove on, but something had transpired in that moment that had never happened before; it felt like an invasion of my world as I knew it. My father, who had been inviolable and untouchable in my eyes, had just changed. I had assumed him to be beyond the reach of a couple of loudmouthed delinquents—"jerks" he'd call them later—but they'd attacked him in a gross invasion of the space and safety of our family car. As I saw it, they might as well have thrown rocks through our open window. I carefully studied my daddy the rest of that afternoon for any signs that the incident had hurt him. If it had, he wasn't letting on.

It was the first flagrant injustice I'd ever witnessed, and as it unfolded, on an otherwise perfect Sunday afternoon, I had wanted desperately to save him, but I hadn't known how. This was the first time I experienced being acutely aware of wishing to save my father from pain or distress. It would not be the last time.

The same helpless feeling would come over me, just a few years after that day, when my father suffered a massive coronary at 39 years old. We were told then that "he'd fainted in the principal's office" of our grade school, but later we learned it was much worse than that. On that day, too, my heart would feel like it was breaking, and I would be filled with the same unspeakable sadness. Unfairness, suffered by a man so dear—this torment seemed to me like a grand error of the universe. Hey, you've got the wrong guy! I wanted someone to realize.

Over time, I learned that that most things were out of my control; and worse, that they were out of my parents' hands, too. After Dad's initial illness—which would plague him, in different variations, for the rest of his life—I became secretly prayerful. For years, in the evenings, standing in front of my dresser mirror, I recited every Hebrew prayer I knew. Many a night I begged the universe—and a God my parents had taught me to believe in—to intervene. Why was *my* Daddy so sick? Why him, and not the father of one of the rude boys in the honking car?

The world was not a fair place at all, as I'd previously assumed it was. For if the very best among us—someone as inherently *good* as my father—could be made to suffer, then my safe and secure world was not impervious to tragedy at all. Without a car window to keep the ugliness out, peril and pitfall could—and would—invade our world, and I'd be as helpless to protect my father as I had been on the day I'd had not been able to save him from the boys in the car and their insults.

In the decades to come, seeing my father endure illness and pain became like the full-length feature movie of the two-minute preview

I'd seen while sitting in the passenger seat of our car at the traffic light. Unfailingly, my father would suffer in silence, never expressing anything but gratitude for the preciousness of every day he survived, against all the odds. Personally, I believed my father had been dealt a bad hand in life, but—just as he had that day in the car—he chose to see it very differently.

SIXTEEN

It was summer of 1966, and River Forest, Illinois—the only place I'd ever known—was fading behind us in the distance. On that day I was only looking ahead, from the back seat of our family car, to a new place called Texas. Though everything I'd ever known was shrinking—becoming a dot and then just a speck before disappearing entirely from view—I saw none of it through the rear window. In my memory, only my brother Joe was looking out the back, when my mom said, "Hats off in the car, Joey," and Joe reluctantly removed his brand new cowboy hat before slinking down in his seat, his misery apparent.

In those days before seat belts, I was standing on the floorboard, stroking the back of my mother's hair, asking her for help with a game my siblings and I were playing. "Was that a bus, Momma? I need a school bus to win car-bingo." While Joe lamented his fate in a new city (a new state even), I rested my head on mom's shoulder with a sigh and whispered in her ear, "Will you tell me if you see a cow, Momma? Now I need a cow."

Looking out a side window for sights of other landmarks or notable features along the road, I had been checking off road signs and VW beetles on my travel-bingo-board while my dad drove, tapping his hand on the steering wheel to the beat of a song on the radio. I had no interest in the sight of all that faded into the horizon behind us that day, focusing only on what lay ahead.

I was six years old, and we were leaving for Dallas, Texas; a place we could hardly imagine but that dazzled in our imaginations (at least my sister's and mine) with all that my parents told us we'd find there. Our family car was packed to the gills, with all the things the moving van hadn't taken. The three of us children had squeezed ourselves into the remaining open areas of the backseat of our family car for the long road trip, each with a few of our favorite toys, books, and pillows. I'd intentionally chosen the spot behind my mother, which allowed a good view of my dad and gave me a window all my own. My brother had claimed his territory by the other window, the better to brood through; and my little sister had settled herself in the middle seat, where—being so small—she could stand on the 'hump' in the floor of the car, which housed the drive-train. This position allowed her to look over the front seat to where my parents were.

I knew that we were 'moving' to a place called Texas that day, but at six years old I had no real concept of leaving a home, forever abandoning it, never to return. My sister and I only knew what we had been told about Texas, and all of it sounded incredibly exciting.

At that age, 'leaving' a place meant less to me than the concept of 'arriving' somewhere new. I had no point of reference for a place only to be returned to in a memory. I couldn't have known then that on a nostalgic trip some fifty years in the future, I'd recognize next to nothing, since most of the places I remembered would be gone.

Joe, older than me by two and a half years, might have had an inkling of what we were giving up. But as far as I was concerned, everything I cared about was right there in that car. For me, 'home' was anywhere these four human beings were; so even as we traveled out of Illinois that day, I was still, home, surrounded by my family.

Before the move, my brother had asked my parents for a cowboy hat, and they'd obliged; so he'd been wearing it that day as we'd driven away—just the right thing for an unwilling transplanted Yankee soon to enter the Wild West! I don't remember seeing Joe's face beneath the cowboy hat, but if I had, perhaps I'd have noticed a tear or two behind his horn-rimmed glasses. "Joey" was deep-thinking and already brilliant at nine years old, so he had some understanding of what 'leaving home' meant. It must have been frightening for him to leave his friends, a Cub Scout group, our close-knit group of cousins, and a bedroom he'd only just begun to grow up in.

Decades later, I would wonder what my parents might have been feeling that day. Somehow I'd never asked, and so, all these years later, I can only speculate as to what thoughts or emotions might have been welling up in their hearts and minds as we left that day. They were leaving friends and family behind as well, in a place they had both lived since they were children. Later I learned that all four of their parents, my grandparents, had tried without success to talk them out of moving. Leaving friends, family and a familiar life behind, they chose to head out for something new and unknown.

At six and a half years old, I only knew the excitement of great anticipation about what was coming closer mile by mile: our future.

SEVENTEEN

I remember it as a sunny summer day—or maybe it is a conglomeration of many of the same sort of days all rolled into one—and I am a little girl of 10 or 12 sitting beside my grandfather, an elderly, white-haired man wearing wire rimmed glasses. His hat and suit jacket hang on a coatrack by the door and a clock ticks, atop a dusty, gray safe in the corner. I am swinging suntanned legs beneath a desk wide enough for both my grandpa and me to sit at and the sun slants through a window behind us, illuminating dust particles in the air, before they settle.

My grandfather's hair is as white as the diamonds he spreads out. Carefully, with a pointed tweezers, he spreads them out in front of me, and they shimmer like a fine glitter as they move. One by one, he brings each of the tiny stones up to his eye, and he speaks as I watch and listen, his voice soft and quiet with age. He is teaching me about diamonds and I'm learning more than I realize at the time. I tuck some hair behind one ear, as if to hear him better, as he explains the different qualities inside the diamonds; infinitesimally minute details deep inside each stone, invisible to the naked eye.

His hair has been white since he was in his twenties and even in early pictures of him and my grandma he looks like an old man. In a picture of him and his brothers as children, the six of them sitting in a group on the front stoop of a farmhouse, it's easy to pick out his face among the others, because his mouth has the same stern expression as it does still. This old picture was taken on his family's tobacco farm, where he and all the brothers helped their parents grow shade tobacco in their first years in America, before they went back into the diamond business. My grandfather's father—and *his* father, too—had been diamond purveyors in Czarist Russia, but as transplants to a new country, they'd spend years farming before returning to the diamond business.

In my memory of that day with Grandpa, I lean over the sparkling lot of diamonds and peer through my own jeweler's loupe. My loupe, like his, is shiny silver, and I've made a lanyard into a necklace that I attach to the loupe so I can wear it around my neck all summer, even when I'm not working at the office. I look through the eyeglass with my other eye closed and my grandpa suggests that I keep both eyes open; when I do, I realize this does indeed help me to see the stones more clearly.

Looking at myself in memory, I see that my childhood face is strikingly different from what I see in my mirror today. It's my face before it knew the expressions for grief or great loss; it's my brow before it ever furrowed with anguish or heartache. In 1969, I would not yet have frowned from the fear a dying parent; I would not ever have cried, my heart broken by a boy. I see my face still rosy-cheeked from love and tanned by the Texas sun, still confident in the invincibility of parents, who are not yet sick. My childhood face is noticeably smoother and it shines in places, not yet dulled with despair. But my eyes are mostly the same.

An oscillating fan clicks back and forth and the shaft of white light behind me shines over my shoulders, illuminating the desktop where the diamonds we sort are glittering. As my grandfather moves the mounds of tiny stones to and fro with tweezers, across a thick, white deskpad of paper, the glittering piles look to me like a million tiny dancers gliding from one side of a stage to the other. Sometimes I squint to imagine that the stones are not just diamonds but fairy dust.

Carefully, my grandfather scoops selected groups of tiny crystals with a square silver shovel, lifting each bunch up and off the pad before pouring the shovelful of them slowly into the bowl of his old diamond scale. This scale, the same one that will sit on my desk some fifty years later, already seems like an antique to me as I watch the sun shining through its glass panels, lighting the two balancing bowls inside. When one of the bowls fills with diamonds, it drops from the weight of its contents and my grandfather places little bronze-colored weights in the opposite basket until the two bowls balance again. Having done this with each scoop of diamonds, he tells me the number—which is the weight of the stones. He repeats it twice to make sure I've recorded it in the ledger correctly. I always get it right.

Finally, lifting one basket off the scale, he pours a glittering stream of tiny diamonds into small, unfolded white papers, as thin as onion skins, and folds each paper up around the stones with precision, never losing even one of the pinpoint-sized diamonds. He does this as many times as he needs to, until the white desk-pad is clean and cleared of diamonds. Then he winks at me, and by then it's usually time for lunch.

Although he smiles when he looks at me, he is known to be a tough and hard-shelled sort of man. I can see love in his grin, and when our eyes meet for a moment I think he is proud of me. My father, his only son, is his favorite, and as his granddaughter I feel important because I work for him. Finally in possession of almost all of my permanent teeth that summer, I smile back at him; I'm glad it's lunchtime as I'm getting hungry. We head out of the office, checking three or four times to make sure that our alarm is turned on and the door is locked. Once the office is secured we go down the street for lunch; just my grandfather and me.

I stretch my legs to match his stride, but everything else about us is as different as though we were from different worlds. He wears a summer fedora and checks his gold pocket watch as we walk. I wear my favorite lavender shorts and white summer sandals that make a flapping sound when I walk, and I'm already salivating with thoughts of the thick sandwiches and sour dill pickles we'll eat at nearby Wall's Delicatessen. We'll sit across from each other in red leather banquettes, where crumbs have been brushed off the table to fall in the cracks, and I'll wonder how long ago the crumbs landed there. The leather seat is cool from the air-conditioning, and as I slide into the booth it catches the bare skin on my thighs. I'll pull my legs up under me to make me higher up at the table. There are booster seats stacked by the entrance, but I'd never dream of asking for one. On our way in I see that the booster chairs are full of crumbs too.

In spite of its size, I finish *all* of the sandwich I've ordered, and I can tell that this pleases my grandfather. My brother and sister are "picky eaters" but I am not. My parents point to my appetite as an attribute and for the next couple of years I'll be proud when they say: "She's always been an eater!" as if it's a good thing. But later, at summer camp, a boy will call me fat, at which point I will decide that eating a whole sandwich isn't such a good thing anymore.

Between bites, only snippets of conversation go between my grandfather and me; he concentrates mostly on his food, chewing carefully. Between bites he might say, "It's hot today, sweetheart," and I'll agree; or he'll ask about my *Bat Mitzvah* studies. "You're studying for your *Bas Mitzvah?*" he'll ask, using the old Ashkenazic pronunciation for the Hebrew words, which is slightly different from the modern way of saying them. Somehow, the way he says it sounds more authentic to me. We call it *Bat* Mitzvah, and he calls it *Bas* Mitzvah but it's the same thing either way.

"Yes, Grandpa," I say, proud that I know almost my entire *Haftorah* already, despite months still ahead for studying. It was difficult to learn at first, but once the notes of the *Trope* are mastered, they're easily applied to the Hebrew words of each *Torah* verse. I know I am supposed to *read* the Hebrew verses that I'll chant from the 'family *Torah*,' rather than sing them as a song, from memory, but I am inadvertently memorizing it. When you sing a thing over and over, you can't help but learn it by heart, and as I have studied, a melody has emerged from the notes of the *Trope* arranged in a certain way. Once it did, I began to know it by heart—the song and the words, too. More than a half century later, I'll recite the first few verses of my *Haftorah*, and my future husband's jaw will drop at my ability to pull up this long-ago musical memory. I'll be surprised, too.

"I know the *Kiddush*, also, Grandpa," I say, and this pleases him, too. It's the prayer for the wine—a blessing I will lead the congregation in—and so I must know it well. He tells me (but I already know) that for the occasion of my *Bat Mitzvah* service, our family *Torah* will be shipped in a special box to our Conservative synagogue from its last stop at an uncle's *Shul*. This is how it was for my brother's *Bar Mitzvah*, and will be again for my sister's *Bat Mitzvah*, a year after mine. On that day, I will see the holy scrolls of our family *Torah* up close, and I will even be allowed to touch it, but not with my finger; only with a special silver pointer called a *Yad*, whose tiny hand points its miniature finger to follow along beneath each hand-scribed word. Even though my hands will be clean that day, human hands are never clean enough to touch the holy parchment of the scrolls of the *Torah*.

Our family's *Torah* is almost like an esteemed relative or an ancestor, having been brought here from Russia under vague and undoubtedly dangerous circumstances. No one says exactly how it made the journey from *Niezen*, in old, Czarist-ruled Russia; as if the true story of the *Torah's* travels might elicit its eviction or deportation if revealed. The story of the *Torah* is like a family secret, kept so well that none of *us* even know it.

We finish lunch and leave a dollar and change under the glass ashtray for the waitress, who winks at my grandpa. He hands me a ten-dollar bill, which I hand to the woman at the cash register, who owns the delicatessen. Her name is 'Miss Rose'—easy to remember because she smells like flowers in a place otherwise scented by garlic and coffee. While she scoops out our change, my grandpa sees me eyeing a *Halavah* bar by the register, and tells Miss Rose to add it to our bill. I'll eat half of it while we walk back to the office and take the rest home, where I know my brother and sister will tease me about it, but I don't care. I am the only one of us who likes the uncommon 'candy bar' made from ground sesame seeds covered with dark chocolate. My siblings think it's gross and poke fun at me about it, but I will secretly enjoy the half-eaten bar's evidence of a day spent with our grandfather that they did not share.

When we return to the office after lunch, a man comes to pick up a diamond, and later a lady comes in, who tells my grandfather I am pretty. My grandfather sits behind his desk, and I move to a smaller desk in the front room, where I draw pictures of fanciful jewelry like that of the Russian Czars and Czarinas. Grandpa tells different stories to each visitor who sits in front of his desk, and they listen and usually laugh at the end. He's both a diamond dealer and a storyteller, I think. Sometimes the story he tells is one from the Bible and sometimes about other subjects, but he never runs out of stories for people who come by, and I like hearing them, too.

At the smaller desk in the front room, I answer the phone each time it rings; always saying "Pevsner and Associates" and then, "Hold, please" when they ask for Mr. Pevsner or 'Borie,' which is short for his name, Bernard. Some, including my dad, call him "Mr. B." but all of his grandkids call him Grampa. When we leave for the day, I tear my drawings off the thick white paper pad, and bring them home. Later, I show my parents the sketches of the jewelry I've imagined in my head, and they say I'm an artist, or even a *jewelry designer*; they notice that there are always diamonds in the designs that I draw. I think that the tiaras and rings I dream up and draw might be as lovely as some of the real ones I have seen in photos of *actual* royal jewels: intricate crowns fashioned from gold, set with emeralds, rubies, sapphires and diamonds; or bracelets wrapped around the wrists of the Czarinas my ancestors provided with diamonds. My parents say that one day my grandfather will surely make one of my designs, and I say maybe so, acting casual but hoping he will.

Around the time that the shaft of light from the window begins to shift to the left, we start to 'close up shop' for the day, with the same series of rituals we did before lunch, but repeated more times in the evenings—just to be safe. Decades later, I will remember these rituals: the double and triple-checking and jiggling of locked doors. My grandfather twirls the numbered dial on the gray safe as many times as it takes to convince him it is locked; each time he does, he marks a line in pen on his finger. Once his pale skin is marked with a series of lines, we go through the front door to the office, where he turns a deadbolt and then turns the locked door handle and jiggles it, sometimes ten or more times, just to be sure it's dead-bolted. Every so often, he worries that he may not have done this enough times, and sometimes we go back up the elevator to the second floor office to try the door again. In later years I'll wonder if this was an obsessive-compulsive side of my grandfather. I think it may have been.

My father picks us up in front of the building; he's been at work, too. My father knows a lot about diamonds, and I've been told that my grandfather wanted his son to work in the business with him. But my father is a writer and wanted to pursue his own passion, which he reminds us kids that we must do, too. I don't know what my passion will be yet, but I have plenty of time to decide. In the car, my dad and his father talk about the customers and the diamonds that came in and went out. I listen, lazily; there will always be more to say about the diamonds the next day.

From my grandfather I've learned that there is more than meets the eye lying deep inside of each diamond. Within each stone lies an entire world; and like snowflakes, no two diamonds are ever exactly alike inside. Facets are cut into the crown of each stone, to reflect not only light, but also to camouflage the tiny imperfections hiding deep inside, which can be seen upon closer inspection— under a ten-power loupe—*if* one knows how to look. Sometimes, I look through the loupe as hard as I can—keeping both eyes open— but still I cannot locate a single dot or carbon spot. When I hand the locked tweezers holding the stone to my grandfather, he can always locate these inclusions. His eyes are old, but he has been looking at diamonds for so long that he can still see inside them like a younger person.

One of the most interesting things he's taught me is that the tiny imperfections inside of each diamond do not necessarily affect the *outer* brilliance of the stone's surface.

He says it is important to know about the internal differences in each diamond, but not necessarily to dwell on them. He shows me how brilliant a diamond can be in spite of all that's happening deep inside it, which makes me think of someone who looks happy but has sadness inside; or someone who is frightened but doesn't show it on the outside. When I tell my grandfather this, I ask him if it's a good comparison, and he nods his head and smiles.

After I grow up, many years beyond those summer days at my grandfather's office, I'll be a diamond dealer, myself. I'll find myself peering deep into an extraordinary diamond, one I know to be larger and more exquisitely cut than any my grandfather ever handled. Feeling humbled in the presence of a true gemstone, privileged to hold such a masterpiece of Mother Nature my own hand, I'll wonder what he would think of *my* office, with its glimmering chrome and sparkling glass. Jewel-toned pillows of silk and velvet are plumped and propped up against mirrored walls running the length of custom-upholstered banquettes, curving along a rounded wall, below crystal chandeliers that catch the light with their dangling prisms, illuminating the diamonds—vast improvements over the florescent lights that flickered above my grandfather's plain wooden desk. At the memory of his dusty office, I smile at the photo of him on my desk, taken on a formal occasion. He is wearing a tuxedo jacket and bow tie, but I know that below the dress pants he wore that day he had bedroom slippers on his feet.

As time has gone by, it has become harder to imagine how it actually felt to be the little girl who once sat beside her grandfather in his office. In the frame of memory I can still see my bare legs swinging beneath a wooden desk, and hear the squeak of the chair as it swivels left to right. I know that it *was* me, in those last years before *Bar and Bat Mitzvah* parties, before socializing with *boys* and girlfriends began to take up more of my time and attention. Looking back, I'll understand that in spite of our deepest wishes to the contrary, most everything changes, except the memories we hold close. Though the building that housed my grandfather's office still stands on the same named street, now a beauty salon and a vacuum cleaner repair store occupy the space where his office was. The red leather banquettes of Wall's Delicatessen, with crumbs lodged impossibly in their cracks, have been replaced by a new furniture store, which smells more of leather than of coffee and garlic pickles. These images, which still shimmer around the edges when we think of them, are the precious reminders of the way things once were.

EIGHTEEN

Although Texas was different in so many ways than what I'd known before, I settled in easily, while my brother Joe longed for our old home. I liked Dallas. Everything was indeed bigger in Texas, as we'd been told. Big western hats, a big new school, even the three of us were growing taller; but we also found smaller things in Texas that held great interest for us as newcomers in those early years.

We were fascinated by the southern drawls we detected in everyone but us, and were tickled by the wide range of new expressions and long, drawn out vowels. Each of us delighted in bringing home examples of new, twangy-sounding dictions and colloquialisms. Much like others gathered shells at the beach, for us each new day provided funny or strange new expressions to bring home and share as our nightly entertainment around the dinner table.

In Texas, *slacks* were *pants,* and *bags* were *sacks*; these and other odd-sounding regional expressions provided fodder for many lively conversations at home. We laughed heartily about the Texas way of describing of putting a thing *up* instead of *away*: as in, I *put up* those toys you left on the floor. Over Texas-sized steaks at dinner, we'd pose rhetorical questions such as: "He put it up where???!" and "Well, why didn't he just put the darn thing *away?!*"

Some of our favorite 'Texas-accent' examples were culled from visits to a family-friendly neighborhood cafeteria we frequented, the now-defunct *Luby's*, where diners in a line pushed their trays past steaming food selections, with servers standing behind each item loudly identifying each dish—or food group—with a shout-out. Most of the entrees and side-dishes were identifiable and needed no formal introduction, but there the servers stood anyway, shouting out dinner choices like a farmer calling in his hogs. What was clear to all as creamy mounds of mashed potatoes was clarified by a woman in a hair net repeating, "...mashed potatoes and cream gravy, ma'am (or sir)?" on an endless repeating loop. I found this helpful when it came to things a seven-year-old might not be familiar with or recognize—such as slabs of calves' liver layered with grilled onions—but otherwise, the culinary shout-outs seemed mostly unnecessary. Nonetheless, we'd slide our trays past each bubbling bin of steaming food, loudly identified as: *fried okrey for ya?* or *pinta beans ma'am?* We'd memorize the strong southern pronunciations and repeat them between giggles later at home. "*Cheese grits, ma'am?*" we'd ask in put-on accents as thick as the Texas toast, laughing as if they were the punchlines to jokes only we could have found funny.

At a self-serve area towards the end of the line, one was meant to help ones' self to a drink, but a server stood with a hose in hand, squirting tea or water into glasses filled with ice. Informing diners to *help themselves* (lest they be left drinkless) "*Heppa Sef*" she'd say, repeating again and again what was supposed to be "Help Yourself." This phrase, "*Heppa-sef*" became a favorite of ours and we used it in all sorts of situations. If, for example, one of us might ask the other if they could borrow a hair ribbon or a particular toy, permission might be granted by saying: "*Heppa-sef!*" before tossing the ball or offering the hair tie.

"*Brad odor suh?*" we were asked, a question that might have stumped us if not for the steaming bin of rolls and buns, over which the server stood brandishing stainless-steel tongs and expertly lifting squares of cornbread and knotted rolls onto small white plates. The cornucopia of warmed wheat, spreading across a heated area with shelves of baked goods, was heaven to us Wonderbread kids, and the happiest of us to belly up to the bread bar was my pint-sized sister—all 30 pounds of her. When Sara's nose, with its sprinkling of freckles, took in the scent of warm bread, she simply glowed with happiness in the light of all that golden gluten. Sara would reach her little arm across her already-full tray for a hot buttered roll, while the rest of us would roll our eyes, fully aware that she would be prematurely filled to capacity by the bun or biscuit she'd chosen. Ignoring our parents' predictions, she'd swear she'd eat the bread *and* everything else on her tray—but this never happened.

"Sara, your eyes are bigger than your stomach," one of our parents would tell her; and she'd continue to dispute this, though her case would be weakened by the other selections of food left congealing on her tray afterwards. I'd watch her artfully push food around on her plate with her fork, trying to make it appear as if she'd eaten some, when in truth she had not.

While Sara's appetite remained birdlike, I was, at the time, unknowingly entering what would later be known as my 'chubby phase,' a kinder-than-accurate description of my pre-pubescent years that would complicate my pre-teen experience. With my appetite in full swing, it worked out well for me that I could happily pluck uneaten items from Sara's tray under the guise of 'helping her out' when it was obviously for my own benefit. Sara and I were a perfect pair: me and my suddenly insatiable appetite, alongside Sara and her limited capacity for anything but bread and macaroni.

As we'd leave the cafeteria after dining, the cashier by the door would invite us to return again soon: *"Ya'llComeBackNow,YaHear?!"* a question spoken like four words melded together as one. We knew this didn't mean that we should literally *turn around and come back*; but rather, that we should come back *again,* sometime in the very near future. Nonetheless, this gave us something to laugh about on the way home.

Without computers or handheld video devices in those days, discussions and conversations about things as small as funny phrases and notable accents were what occupied many of our hours as kids. Perfecting our imitations of a proper Texas drawl kept us busy in the back seat of the family car when our mother took us along on the various errands she might run on most days.

So it was on the day my mother drove through a *Jack-in-the-Box* fast food restaurant for the very first time, not long after we had settled in suburban Dallas. Drive-thru fast-food itself may not have been completely foreign to us in those early days, but the concept was fairly new and certainly much evolved from the familiar red and white tiled benches of one of the very first McDonald's, near our home in a suburb of Chicago. There, we'd sat as a family on summer evenings, waiting for my dad to come out of the restaurant with the bags of burgers and fries we kids considered special fare. By the time we migrated to Texas, 'driving through' a restaurant had become the preferred—and certainly most convenient—way of feeding hungry kids, especially for a busy parent, and we kids cheered the concept of *dining while in a car.*

So, as my mother drove up to *Jack-In-The-Box* for fast food that day, needless to say we were all in good spirits. At the sight of the giant Jack in the Box, we kids slid over on the back seat to the window nearest the illuminated menu, to get a better look. Brightly colored photos of burgers, tacos, and milkshakes were almost as exciting as a movie screen and our collective mouths simply salivated at the sight.

"Do you know what you want, kids?" Mom asked. She seemed anxious that we make our minds up quickly, perhaps before the giant box spoke.

Raised images of burgers were lit from behind with ketchup oozing from under sesame seed buns; ice-cold Cokes beaded with condensation looked real enough to reach out and touch. Every sort of soft drink imaginable promised to wet our whistles, including thick shakes in all our favorite flavors. It only took us a minute before we knew what we wanted; and relaying our orders to Mom, we waited for directions to come from a speaker inside the giant jack-in-the-box. All beady-eyed and smiling, "Jack" sported a pointed hat and clown's collar, his head and shoulders looming above the menu.

Mouths watering, the three of us had been too busy climbing over one another towards the outdoor menu to have noticed our mother's sudden unease as she maneuvered the family car into the narrow confines of the drive-thru lane, and up to the metal speaker. She seemed unusually hesitant, and manual windows notwithstanding, it seemed she was rolling them down more slowly than was natural. Once the window was opened, she sat there staring into the silver speaker as if waiting for some sort of direction or something to happen, which was slightly amusing to us kids.

"Uhhh..." my mother said, in a smaller than usual voice. "Um, hello?" she added uncertainly.

"We'd like to order now, please," she said and then, covering her mouth with some of her fingers, as if embarrassed for asking, she added, "Am I in the right place?" I heard my brother stifle a laugh.

Our mother was incredibly skillful in most every field and quite adept in all kinds of new or unusual situations; so to see her acting otherwise was a novelty that brought us some degree of interest; and perhaps oddly, some pleasure, too. Catching her off guard, or having an awkward moment, provided an opportunity to tease her lovingly about it, which of course, we did. At some level she was aware she could be extremely cute and even when she'd feign annoyance at our teasing, it was she herself who often said, "Tell Dad that silly thing I did today!" encouraging us to repeat the story of a situation where she had looked endearingly helpless or temporarily inept, but how she'd pulled whatever-it-was off anyway, in the end. She was typically a good sport and probably not unaware of her own ability to be even-more-adorable in such situations; so as much as we welcomed an opportunity to 'make good fun' of her, the pleasure was hers, too.

Meanwhile, after the slow-motion approach to the speaker, there she sat, uncomfortable with the growing reality that she'd be required to order food from a giant googley-eyed Jack-in-the-Box with a speaker in his mouth. This was a woman who could ably converse with absolutely anyone—she'd have chatted up the Queen of England most royally, but speaking to a giant box was apparently out of her comfort zone. Catching wind of this, we kids waited for whatever was coming, knowing it would be good for laughs.

With the unblinking eyes of the Jack-In-The-Box upon her, its mouth upturned in a creepy metal smile, my mom must have decided it best to stick her head out of the car window to be closer to the speaker, so at this point she was leaning precariously out of her window. The juxtaposition of the formality in her voice with the sight of our mother—half hanging outside of the vehicle while her other half stayed put—was plain old funny to us kids. In our eyes, there was an obvious level of lightheartedness about a talking clown's head that didn't warrant our mother's oh-so-serious behavior, which was in such extreme contrast to the jack-in-the-box's idiotic smile. The whole thing begged for peals of laughter but we three were quiet as mice, quite a feat for us. Practically holding our collective breaths, we watched from our ringside backseats for whatever came next. Our mother was our own real-life Lucille Ball—funny and pretty enough to have played any Hollywood part; but she was all ours. This was as good as any episode of "I Love Lucy." Clearing her throat, it looked like she was about to speak to the clown head, but he spoke first.

"YES MA'AM!" the speaker blared, startling my mother so that she jumped.

"*Ummmm...Okay...so, um, hello there?*" our mother asked.

"Yes Ma'am!" the enormous toy boomed again; repeating his first greeting and confounding my mother, as he hadn't offered any clear direction in either case.

"Yes sir..." (Had she actually just called him *sir*?! We three were dying from repressed laughter.) "We'd like to order...So...Are you ready?" she asked politely.

By the look of the rust in his speaker mouth, it was obvious he'd taken an order or two and had been down this road before. Was she expecting him to brandish an order pad and lick a pencil point to jot down our order with automated hands?

"Mom, just order already," my brother piped up from just behind her, snapping her out of her daze. Getting down to business with the clown head, Mom began to communicate our orders to the speaker-mouth, in a voice notably higher-pitched than her usual one. Although just inches from his giant head, for some reason she was speaking more loudly than necessary and enunciating each word as if the clown might need to lip read.

"UH, YES SIR," she said. "WE WOULD LIKE *THREE* (pausing here to make sure he heard the number three) *THREE* JACK-IN-THE-BOX KIDDIES' MEALS...*ONE WITH A TACO AND FRENCH FRIES*...AND TWO, NO... MAKE THAT ONE, WITH A *BURGER*

AND *NOT* A TACO...AND WITH *NO* CHEESE... AND *ONE* WITH A BURGER *WITH* CHEESE...OH MY, WELL I SUPPOSE THAT'S BASICALLY A CHEESEBURGER, RIGHT? YES, OF COURSE... BUT WITH ABSOLUTELY *NO* PICKLES WHATSOEVER."

And then, pulling her head back into the car, she became as quiet as we'd ever see her.

Silence.

"Hullo?" she said then, in a small voice.

Static came from the speaker, and turning to us in the back seat, she said, "Did you hear what he said? I couldn't understand." She was wearing an expression of mild panic, as if she'd missed survival instructions on a sinking ship. Was she asking us for help? This was epic.

"Oh my, I'm not sure he heard the part about the pickles..." she whispered, her voice trailing off at the end.

"Sir?" she said. More crackling.

"YES?!" boomed Jack.

"Um, sir, you see, we simply cannot have pickles on that one sandwich that I mentioned."

"Do you think he hears me?" she asked us nervously.

"YES MA'AM!" the speaker boomed, causing my mom to jump as if the voice of God had entered the car. "No pickles," the voice said. My mother looked as relieved as if she'd narrowly avoided strike by lightning.

She continued on, ordering with exaggerated enunciation of each word, as you might do when speaking English as a second language; and oddly, at a sound level you'd use at an outdoor sporting event. When she needed to pause to ask one of us to clarify a drink choice, she would first formally excuse herself to the voice in the box by saying, "I'm terribly sorry, would you excuse me for one moment, please? I'll be right back with you," before she'd turn to one of us in the back seat and lower her voice to a whisper. This struck us as hilarious.

"*Cheese or no cheese?*" or "*Did you say Coke or Sprite?*" she'd whisper and then, returning to the box, she'd announce that one of us would have a "SMALL SPRITE, SIR," or what have you. Mom's seriousness in the face of—well, a clown's face—was what tickled us most that day. Certainly, we three weren't exactly aficionados in the 'art of the drive-thru,' but that being said, it hadn't struck us as all that complicated. Our mother, on the other hand, was acting like the whole thing was a scene from some futuristic space-world, like we'd landed on another planet without helmets. She seemed genuinely intimidated by a fiberglass clown's head.

Order finally completed, she sighed as if she'd just finished a marathon, and lowered her head and upper torso back into the vehicle. To those of us in the back seat, it was obvious that the next step would be to drive up to the window ahead, where money would be exchanged for food. *We* knew this, but somehow it had not yet dawned on our mom, who was typically a quick-study. She had rolled up her window halfway, but was just sitting there. As we struggled to hold in any giggles or laughs (some of the latter escaping as snorts) we waited for a chance to laugh out loud at our otherwise capable mother and her uncharacteristic confusion, which pleased us in a naughty sort of way. In that moment, we felt we were smarter than her, a novelty we relished because it so rarely happened. We waited with glee, in anticipation of what would happen next.

For the next few moments, absolutely nothing happened. Mom's head was still cocked in the direction of the jack-in-the-box, as if waiting for something to come out of its mouth. Ketchup? Salsa, maybe? It was fascinating. Another minute passed. And then another. From where we sat, the anticipation was as thick in the air as the smell of grilled meat wafting from the window up ahead, until finally she spoke.

Leaning her head close to the speaker, she cleared her throat. "*Hellooo?*" she said, looking up at the giant Jack-in-the-box's lit-from-behind-eyes, as if to see whether they registered her message and whether a response was pending.

"*Hello?*" she said again, and in those seconds that followed, it was so completely quiet, that we'd have sworn not even a bird chirped.

And then, to our delight, our mother uttered words we would remember and tease her lovingly about for decades to come: "Are you there, Jack?" she said.

Two questions were on the minds of us three: Did she think there was actually someone named 'Jack' inside the box? And how much longer could we hold in our laughs?

After another moment, a crackle and then a voice that rumbling from the speaker said: "MA'AM?"

"Uh, yes, Jack?" our mother replied meekly.

No answer.

And then in a small voice, she said: "Well...what do I do now, Jack?"

And at this, the three of us collapsed into the kind of belly-laughter that cannot be contained; any more than the joy of the memory of it can be properly explained or described. We were doubled over in our seats even as our mother drove up to the pick-up window for our food. Without a doubt, she was our best entertainment. With her, it was always like lunch and a show.

NINETEEN

Summer days in Dallas were best spent in a swimming pool, where it was cool in spite of the burning heat rising off the surrounding pavement. In those days, private pools in backyards were not common, so most days we gathered at the Olympic-sized pool at the Dallas Jewish Community Center, along with most everyone we knew.

Poolside at the "J," our mother sat with the other stay-at-home moms in a semi-circle facing the pool where we kids bobbed, splashed and invented games in the cool water. Slathered with Bain de Soleil, the moms shared recipes and idle chit-chat from underneath wide-brimmed straw hats, occasionally opening paperbacks to read for a while. We children were too busy in the water to worry about what the moms in their circles were discussing; in those days, there was nothing much for a kid to worry about, other than the occasional thunderstorm, at which time a lifeguard's series of whistles would tell us to get out of the water.

Gazing up at one of the teenage lifeguards perched on their chair high above us, I dreamed of being one of them myself, one day, wearing a shimmering tank suit like theirs. I'd imagine myself with smears of white zinc oxide cream on my own nose, expertly swinging a whistle around a finger and then back again. I'd gone to great lengths to find my blue swimsuit, the one I thought most closely resembled the ones the guards wore. My mother had taken me to countless stores in search of the one we'd finally located, and once we arrived home with it, I sat behind her on the couch while she affixed the cloth badge I'd earned for reaching "Minnows" swimming level to the right hip of the swimsuit, in just the place where the real lifeguards flaunted their Red Cross badges. Every late afternoon I'd lovingly drape my wet suit with its official-looking patch on a towel bar to dry; and each morning I'd step into it, pretending I was dressing for my important lifeguarding job, ever-ready to save a life.

Long, sweltering summer days would pass this way; we children only lured out of the pool water long enough to eat sandwiches packed by our mothers at home, waiting impatiently for the time required for food to settle (lest we be racked with some sort of life-threatening cramps for getting in the pool too soon). By the end of the season, my sister and I would be brown as berries, our hair streaked with blonde from the chlorine and sun. I can recall the scent of the bronzing butter spread over the arms and legs of the mothers, but I don't remember any of us kids being covered with sunscreen by our mothers, the way I'd obsessively cover my own daughter with sunblock years later. Our noses burned and peeled, then burned again; in those days it was more a rite of summer than the health risk we know now. By the following morning our blood-shot eyes and pinked cheeks would have faded and we'd pull on our air-dried swimsuits, grab fresh towels, and do it all again.

When I wasn't in the water, playing endless rounds of Marco-Polo with friends and diving for pennies, I would head toward the diving boards to practice. The three of us kids had not learned to swim until our arrival in Texas, as swimming hadn't been popular in the colder climes of the Midwest. I had taken to it like a fish to water, further encouraged by a coach, Don Lehew, who said he'd seen some sort of natural talent in me. Under his instruction, I began practicing dives with increasing degrees of difficulty, including one in particular that he and I did in tandem off the three-meter board. In the days before liability became a concern, a coach like Don could convince a kid like me to attempt all sorts of daring dives. For the tandem dive, I had to find my footing by straddling both his sturdy shoulders, one small foot firmly planted on either side of his head. I'd dive out, in an arc—and he'd follow, just after I'd left his shoulders; both he and I entering the water at the same time with barely a double-splash.

I'm certain none of this would be allowed today, in our modern, litigious society, but in those days, apparently the sky was the limit and my water-logged, seven-year-old wet head was right up there, doing whatever he asked of me.

Coach Don told my parents that I was bound for the Olympics, and the confidence he had in me meant everything, boosting my dedication to practicing and improving. Don Lehew was a popular figure around the JCC pool. A young athlete, 27 or 28 at the time, he was not Jewish; and only later did I understand that he—with his sculpted physique and microscopic black Speedo—was the object of all the housewives' attention. From behind their Jackie-O sunglasses, the moms snuck peeks at Don Lehew's dark tan and muscular build, and he'd oblige with every slow-swagger he made across the pebbled concrete, leaving a wet trail from the deep end to the pool office and back again, stopping to scatter compliments among the admiring women. If he'd just emerged from the pool, he'd do an odd dance, first on one foot and then the other, to clear his ears. He'd cock his head and tap on the side facing up—purportedly to clear water from first one and then the other of his ears. The women seemed to marvel at this, all of them closely observing the head cocking and bouncing as he sprang up and down on one foot at a time, this two-step no doubt accentuating his long, sinewy muscles, in addition to clearing his ears. He looked like an Olympic athlete and several times a day he'd perform impromptu diving exhibitions, announced by the distinct sounds of repetitive springboarding, which meant Don was at work. Reaching ridiculous heights and landing back on the board, he'd even turn front and back flips and land right back on the end of the diving board, leaving the board this way 6 or 7 times before finally performing a heart-stopping dive into the pool, featuring all sorts of inverted twists and turns added to multiple flips. He always managed to straighten himself out just in time to enter the water on-point and clean as a knife. Oooh's and ahhhhs abounded, and then a moment of silence until his head appeared above the water. Don would exit the pool, shaking his head and doing the dance on one foot and then another, to clear whatever water may have sneaked into his inner ear. Then he'd do his strut around the perimeter of the pool, adjusting his Speedo to release the water it held and stopping to chat with each group of ladies along the way.

Some of the kids took diving lessons from Don, once a week or so, but because he was always at the pool (and because, I now know, my parents had no budget for things like private lessons) when Don wasn't teaching badminton and squash to adult members of the JCC, I'd dive with him informally. His nickname for me was "Chief" and though the nickname was never explained, I liked it; I sensed that I was special to him, somehow. He seemed to genuinely get a kick out of me; standing tall—to my 3 feet—he'd cover the entire top of my wet head with his large hand, to turn me towards the deep end where then we'd walk together to the diving boards.

"C'mon, Chief," he'd say, leading me by the top of my head, though I'd have followed regardless. "Let's see if you've been practicin'," he'd say with a wink.

Always eager to show him what I could do, I'd keep my toes perfectly pointed and my legs together. "I don't wanna see no frog legs now, Chief!" he'd say, and for him I'd exhibit my most excellent form; his positive critique of each dive I did like a little song sung to my heart.

"That's my girl!" he'd say in his low-throated east Texas drawl. "It looks like someone's been practicing!" He'd always manage to add the bit about my being bound for the Olympics, a sentiment my parents repeated proudly and often.

Hoisting me onto his sturdy shoulders on some of those afternoons, I remember the excitement I felt as the board bowed slightly beneath the weight of the two of us. High above the sparkling pool on the three-meter board, we were a tower of two. My small, wet feet firmly planted onto both of his sturdy, wet shoulders. Don's firm grasp of both my ankles was all the support I needed to rise slowly to my full height. Then, unfolding my three feet above his six, I looked down from a giant's height to the sparkling water beckoning below. Once steadied, Don would walk—me teetering above him, but secured by his grip—as he'd make his way, one wet step at a time, to the end of the high board, his exaggerated slow gait adding to the drama.

Pausing at board's end for a moment or two—I suppose to assure all eyes were upon us—we'd commence our well-practiced double-dive; which began with my headfirst dive towards the water from off of his shoulders. I'd bend slightly at the waist before falling into my miniature swan-dive, no longer held by the grip he'd had on my ankles. Because I dove first, I never actually saw Don do his part of the dive, but I knew that just after I left his shoulders, he'd follow suit, making a curve just below the arc of mine, timing it precisely so that he and I both entered the water at the same time. I knew it was impressive and felt great pride as I'd walk around the pool after one of these dives, feeling more visible than I had before and basking in the complimentary comments from the grownups I'd pass.

In those days, liability and lawsuits weren't on the radars of parents or pool managers. Diving with Don Lehew during these simpler times was acceptable in a world where nothing 'bad' ever happened—at least not at the JCC pool—so it was a great climate to grow up in. I had no fear of diving then, and thus I became good at it. The daredevil high dives Don and I did never resulted in any sort of injury or even a near miss, until one Saturday afternoon when my 'safe run' came to an end.

On the weekends, when the dads finished mowing their lawns and other chores, they often joined their families at the pool for a few hours, until the sun would begin to set and everyone would head home for burgers or steaks on outdoor grills. My father had pulled up a chair to join two or three other couples, and someone had asked about my budding diving skills. In response, my dad asked me to do just one more dive before we left for the day, and I worn out but happy to oblige. Coach Don wasn't there that day, but I often dove by myself and enjoyed it, especially when one of my favorite life-guards, Steve Olshwanger, sat at the deep end. Only just beginning to be aware of cute teenage boys, I knew the three boards were Steve's to watch, so I enjoyed doing my best dives when he was on duty, in case he was actually observing and not dozing behind his mirrored aviator shades.

"I'll meet you over at the boards, Nomeluh," my dad said, pulling off his shirt and entering the pool. He swam from where my mom sat with the other couples to the deep end, and as I stepped up to the board, I could see him on the other side of the rope, smiling with pride even before I'd done any dive at all. If I was somewhat tired after the long day in the sun, my father's smile gave me new energy. For him, I could have been half asleep and would have willingly stepped up to do any trick I knew.

Recently, I'd learned a new dive called a gaynor, and according to Don I had aced it many times before. I thought it my most impressive dive, and so, perched up on the balls of my feet, backwards at the end of the board, I arched and then straightened my back, lifting my hands up in a dramatic sweep, then bringing my arms down on either side of my body in a proper pre-dive. Facing away from the water and preparing to jump backwards, I needed to leave enough clearance from the end of the diving board to allow the execution of the flip I'd do before entering the water feet first. Piece of cake.

Unfortunately, I had not given myself enough clearance from the board, something I only realized when the top of my head made contact with its surface, the force of all my weight landing on my head and neck. The hit on the head must have befuddled me so much that I remember having no idea why a lifeguard had gathered me in his arms and was lifting me out of the pool. When I saw it was Steve Olshwanger whose arms I was wrapped in, I was in no hurry to reach the side of the pool and could have stayed just where I was indefinitely. I saw people running my way but did not realize I had been injured until a towel held to my head came away bloodied.

I was embarrassed. I felt it was my fault, but my father had already taken the blame and he'd forever insist it had all been his fault; though I'd argue it was *not*, year after year when the story was told. A long row of stitches later, after it healed the accident would leave only a narrow bald spot running across the top of my head—a place where even today no hair grows—but afterwards, I knew for sure that where my flesh had opened up, a bit of *fear* had been allowed in. Even after it had been closed up tightly with stitches, that fear began to grow along with the shaved hair around it. I had been an apprehensive child in other areas of my life, but before that accident I'd had no concerns about diving. After that incident, I lost the bliss of ignorance, and fear sat on my shoulders when I dove. The reality of stitches—or worse—followed me up the ladder to the boards, as did the look on my father's face that day and the memory of how terrible my mistake had made my dad feel.

"She was *exhausted*, poor thing, we shouldn't have asked her to do it!" my father would say, sounding guilt-ridden even decades later when he'd speak of it.

"There was my Nomeluh" my dad would say. "She was ready to do one last dive for her daddy…but I shouldn't have asked her to. Oh, God, I'll never forget that moment…." And he'd cringe and shudder when recalling the scene, his words trailing off as if he simply could not finish the thought, so that one of us would have to tell the rest of the story.

Once learned, my fear of diving was something I had a hard time *un*knowing; and so the window of my diving days would soon close. But a few years later I'd become one of the lifeguards I'd admired sitting around that very pool—high upon a stand, under a red umbrella—finally, myself, one of the guards I had worshipped all those summers as a child.

Fear of injury joined the list of other things I was afraid of, but it was not at the top of my list. I would have listed it at Number 3, below fears Number 1 and 2: *losing my mother and my father,* the parents I adored. Though a remote possibility in those days, the fear of being without my parents far outweighed even a headful of stitches.

With a half-century of life's experiences under my belt, the deaths of my parents would affect me as if I were a child whose father—and then mother—had tragically died too soon. In my long-ago stitched-up head, the memory of them sitting poolside glowed as though it had happened only moments before. As if they'd been cheering me on, and then suddenly they were gone, in flash as quick and hard as a skull crashing against a graphite board. Somehow I'd pull myself from the water in their absence; but with a deep, open wound running the length of me; too wide and gaping to be stitched back together. A hundred stitches without anesthetic would have pained me less than the ache of losing my parents.

TWENTY

With another school year nearly under our belts, we knew that summer was not far off. But something else was approaching, too. That morning, I'd awakened before my mother had come in to our room. I lay quietly, knowing that any minute she'd pop in, singing her cheery 'good morning' song to my sister and me, to wake us up. I lay quietly in bed, listening to the sound of the sprinkler heads popping and hissing, sending water over the neat rows of pansies outside our windows—pansies being one of the few seasonal flowers with any chance for life in the relentlessly summer months in Texas. Waking before Mom's entrance, something about the day already felt different.

We'd moved from our yellow brick house to a modern apartment building two years earlier; the trade-off of smaller rooms offset by the complex's amenities, most notably a crystal blue, oval-shaped swimming pool just steps from our door. In the wake of what was coming later that day, fond memories of the yellow house on Brookshire Drive would give rise to an ache for all that we'd left there. Visions of the five of us running the length of our old front yard, tackling my father for a football, would fade so far as to seem impossible. Those carefree days were soon to be the 'before' to an 'after' where my father no longer had two legs. But in the first moments of that morning, as I yawned and stretched, I didn't know this yet.

I knew my parents' morning routines by heart. About the time the sprinkler heads popped and began spraying, my mother would have finished her coffee and light breakfast before moving to the master bathroom to apply her make-up. At this point in her routine, still wearing her floral-patterned robe, she would awaken the three of us. When I woke up by myself that morning, I knew something about the day was different. The mystery deepened when the scent of her signature perfume entered my room just before my mother did, and I saw my dad standing behind her. "We'll be leaving shortly and you kids have to get ready by yourselves today, so up and at 'em!" my mother said.

For both of them to be dressed and ready to walk out the door just as we were waking up was not the normal routine. More awake now, I remembered that my parents were going to a serious-sounding conference at our grade school, in hopes of having my brother reinstated into his seventh grade class after a suspension for some offense or another. Joe's hi-jinx were perhaps typical of a brilliant, sometimes bored young mind. This time though, his behavior had been serious enough for my father to have had to cancel a business trip to Chicago in order to attend the meeting with Joe's teacher and the school's principal.

Joe's quick wit and his penchant for class clowning were nothing new. His class had been studying regimes led by dictators, and in an outburst meant to entertain his classmates, Joe had let a comment escape that had reduced the classroom to peals of laughter. He'd compared the position of their seventh grade teacher, Mrs. Haiter, to the reign of Mussolini; an analogy that delighted the rest of his class, but that his teacher had not found humorous. Joe had been sent to the principal's office and when the verdict was a one-week suspension, my parents had been called in to meet with all involved and assure them that proper measures were being taken at home to reinforce the school's efforts at instilling discipline.

That week, seeing Joe planted in front of the television while Sara and I left for school, the punishment did not fit the crime, it seemed. A pass from school did not seem like a punitive measure, but at least his suspension had kept our dad from leaving town, and that pleased me. Later, we'd see the irony in the cancellation of Dad's trip; knowing that if he had been aboard an aircraft bound for Chicago, instead of in the principal's office of our school, he would not have survived the massive coronary he had that morning.

As my parents stood at our doorway to wake us up, I remembered that I had been informed the night before that I was to help my little sister dress and organize herself for school. Somehow this official position—'being the boss of her'—didn't hold the joy that it usually did. Everything seemed a bit off that morning, so I shouldn't have been surprised when Mom admitted that she had forgotten to make our lunches, which meant that we could either make them ourselves, or buy our lunches, the latter not an option I considered. We were only given 25 minutes for lunch at school; and the thought of spending 10 of those minutes in the lunch line meant less than 15 minutes to eat—when factoring in the clearing of one's tray and the knowledge that I had to make a run past my locker for the books I'd need for the second half of the day.

Sometime earlier that year I'd begun harboring a silent angst that revolved around a constant concern about time 'running out too soon.' So even before the task of keeping my sister on track that morning, I fretted over things like how many hours I needed for sleep in order to feel rested, how long it took my long, thick hair to dry, and a collection of other very serious-to-me concerns that I spent a good deal of time ruminating over. In hindsight, this may have been something akin to OCD; whatever it was, constant worry complicated my thoughts most days.

Heading for the kitchen that morning and taking a peek at the clock there, I decided I had enough time to make lunches for Sara and me. Mom and Dad were gathering their things to leave as I spread jelly on slices of bread, and then peanut butter. Cutting the crusts off the sandwich I made for Sara took extra time, and this further agitated me. Would a couple of crusts kill her? I wondered, silently cursing Sara for her particular eating habits, as well as my mom for forgetting to make our lunches.

Adding to my annoyance was the sight of Joe, planted in front of the TV with a bowl of Cocoa Puffs and the cereal box he'd left open on the kitchen counter. Its inner bag had been needlessly torn, leaving cereal to escape its only hope for freshness. I grumbled as I worked to salvage the torn inner bag and roll it closed, and closing the box, I carried it to the pantry. No surprise he'd left the milk out, so I returned it to the refrigerator and grabbed the kitchen sponge to wipe up a puddle of milk he'd obviously left for someone else to deal with. Eying the stack of brown lunch bags Mom kept on a pantry shelf, I plucked two of them and dropped in a couple of apples. I knew Sara wouldn't eat hers. What I did not know just then was that it would be a very long time before our mother would make our lunches again.

Returning to our room to check Sara's progress I found her still in bed. I knew she heard me but was pretending not to. "Get up!" I ordered her, repeating this a few times while she groaned in protest before finally I thought of the one thing sure to get her up: "You'd better get up and say goodbye to mom and dad cuz they're leaving." And with this, she sprang from her bed, pulling with her the sheets she'd been wrapped in half way across the room. Sara was a tiny thing who woke up most mornings tangled in damp bedclothes with her dark hair disheveled and sweaty head. Our twin beds, with matching white scrolled rattan headboards, sat two feet from each other, on either side of a two-drawer nightstand; one drawer for each of us, to hold our most important items. Every morning it looked as if Sara had gone to battle with her sheets, while I barely disturbed my covers, which made it easy to make my bed each morning; a task I did without prompting every single morning, without fail. I couldn't stand the sight of an unmade bed, and I usually made Sara's, too, for that reason.

My parents liked to say I was a 'gifted sleeper,' and that I'd been a dream of a baby; happily eating whatever was offered and promptly falling off to sleep as if I were a doll, programmed this way. As small kids, the announcement of the arrival of "naptime" was music to my ears; and before my brother aged out of the requirement, he and Sara unsuccessfully protested the need for rest during the day, while I'd happily trotted off to my bed; merrily sucking my thumb, curled up under a soft knitted throw that my grandmother had made.

Sara, in her little dotted panties and damp tee-shirt, ran to give my parents hugs goodbye and I followed her to do the same; planning to shadow her after that until she dressed and ate in time for the car-pool's arrival. Mrs. Weinstein was driving that morning and she was notoriously never late. My mother smelled as nice as she looked and my father's scent was familiar too, a mix of aftershave and left-over cigarette smoke. He was a smoker in those days, and cigarettes would take the blame for what happened later that morning.

"We'll call you after the conference, son," my father told Joe, who'd come into the living room as they were leaving. "Bye-bye girls," Mom waved to us. "Bye!" Sara and I chorused, speaking together as we often did. And then, "Goodbye, Princess," my Dad said to me. Looking at Sara, he added, "...and my little Princess," touching the tip of her freckled nose. "Bye Daddy," Sara and I said in unison. Neither of us could have known that these would be the last words we'd say to our father for a very long time.

With minutes to spare before Mrs. Weinstein arrived, I padded into the den to put my shoes on. Joe had moved to Dad's lounge chair, setting his empty cereal bowl on a side table; somehow I knew it would still be sitting there when we returned home. In the beginning, I'd felt a little sorry for him after his suspension from school, but my compassion was fading as it began to look more like an at-home vacation than a punishment. Sara entered the den and looked to be mostly ready for school, so I could breathe a sigh of relief; but after the stress of motivating her to get ready on time—while doing so myself—I was feeling more anxious and annoyed than I'd have liked.

Something about my brother being able to lounge around in his pajamas and eat cereal irritated me. Some punishment, I thought. I knew I'd never have such luck, because I was shy and would never dare the sort of shout-out Joe had been penalized for. Besides, I liked school.

"Get your lunch, Sara," I said to my sister, glancing at the clock in the den, which I knew to be 5 minutes fast. "Bessie will be here in a few minutes."

Although we addressed her as Mrs. Weinstein, 'Bessie' was our private nickname for her (her first name was Bess). She was as much a character as we'd ever known; she spoke loudly and with a heavy New York accent, and much of what she said, while we were riding in the back seat of her car, made excellent material for us to imitate later, at home, to great peals of merriment. Her son Russell was almost as entertaining. He also 'talked funny'—to us—and had a smart-mouthed way of responding to his mother's remarks that we found shocking. Russell and his mother seemed to bark—more than speak—to each other and always at high volume, which was so different from the way we spoke to one another at home. Especially unusual to us was how freely Russell—only a year older than I was—used *curse* words in the presence of, and even directed at his mother. This shocked us most of all on many a morning drive. He'd cussed at us before, too.

"What the hell took ya so long?" he'd say if we were more than a minute or two emerging from our door, after the series of long honks from their car. I always doubted it was Mrs. Weinstein doing this honking herself; I imagined Russell leaning over to contribute, after his mother's initial toot-toot.

"Sorry," one of us would mumble, hastily arranging ourselves in the back seat while Mrs. Weinstein tossed a cigarette butt out her window, though the over-stuffed ashtray bulging with burnt-out butts, made it clear she'd light up again soon. When Russell chastised us for our slow response time to the honking horn, Mrs. Weinstein would call him out: "RUSSELL!" she'd yell, barking his name as a one-word reprimand, as if he were ten feet away and not, in fact, within arm's reach. In the beginning we'd been surprised by the yelling, but we'd come to understand, in short order, that the Weinsteins shouted at each other as a general rule. If Russell had forgotten his lunch, on one of the mornings that our mother drove carpool, Mr. or Mrs. Weinstein would stick a head out the door and yell as one might, if, say, the building were on fire. "RUSSELL, YOU FU-GOT YOUR LUNCH!" If it was Bessie, she'd be wearing a housecoat and house slippers; Mr. Weinstein would be in a sleeveless undershirt and boxers, like Archie Bunker in "All In The Family." Even though our car was less than six feet from their front door, with its windows and door open, one of them would yell, chastising Russell as if he were a complete imbecile for having walked out the door without his lunch.

"Damn kid," Mrs. Weinstein would mutter, tossing the lunch into the back seat after Russell, with a lit cigarette dangling from her lips. We'd covertly poke one another, out of Russell's sight, for the humor we found in a grown woman using such an 'outside voice,' and the way her cigarette bobbed and wagged while she walked and talked at once.

The Weinsteins had moved to Dallas from New York around the same time we had. *Pretending to be the Weinsteins* had become one of our favorite games: each of us played one of them, and the object of the game was to yell things at each other such as, "WHAT'S FA DINNER, BESSY?!" and to ad-lib some imaginary response from Bess, like, "CRAP'S FA DINNER; YA GOT A PROBLEM WITH THAT?!" And so on. The three of us could spend a good hour imitating the Weinsteins, all the while howling with laughter, until one of our parents would shut us down. I remember my mother chuckling herself at some of it, before eventually insisting we cease, saying, "Oh you children are not nice!" or "Enough of that, you kids; what if they could hear you?!" But we suspected she got as much of a kick out of our parodies of the New Yorkers as we did.

That morning, I was trying to hurry Sara along to avoid any additional yelling in the car. With only another minute or two until they'd pull up and honk, the sudden shrill from the wall phone in the kitchen startled all three of us. My brother jumped up to answer it, catching it after the second ring, while Sara and I watched him and listened. He stood silently, twisting the long phone cord around a finger while listening to the voice on the other end of the line. Finally he said, "Uh-huh." And then there was another long space of silence, where he said nothing.

"Who is it?" Sara and I asked, to which Joe waved a hand, indicating we should save our questions. "Okay. Yeah," he said into the phone. His expression said nothing; he was neither smiling nor frowning as he hung up without saying goodbye. Sara and I watched him walk back over to Dad's lounge chair and sit down, while we waited for him to speak. I noticed that the milk in the bowl from his Cocoa Puffs had turned brown.

"Dad fainted," he said finally, looking at the TV, not at us, as if that were all he had to say.

"What?" I exclaimed. Though I'd heard what he'd said, it was all I could think to say.

"What's *fainted*?" Sara said, and with this, Joe looked away from the screen at Sara, who I was relatively sure knew what "fainted" meant but had asked anyway.

"Where?" I asked.

"Yeah, where?" Sara echoed, sitting down cross-legged in front of Joe.

"At the *school*," Joe said, as if we were the two dumbest people on earth for having asked; though I noticed he hadn't returned his focus to the television and was looking at Sara and I as if there were more to this conversation coming. I had several questions but didn't quite know which one to ask.

I had never heard of a parent fainting at a child's school, and even if I had, I'd have guessed my dad to be the last person ever to have done so, but regardless, I was wondering just what the procedure or protocol would be for such a thing. Had Dad quickly recovered? Or was he sprawled across the floor of the principal's office after having asked to be excused to go to the school clinic in order to politely faint there? The latter scenario would be more like him, but I couldn't quite picture the scene and wondered if Joe knew anything more. But he appeared to be offering nothing else. He was just sitting there in dad's chair; for a few moments there was an odd silence.

And where were the Weinsteins? I wondered. The show on TV had changed, indicating that the hour had, as well, and it was now past time for the blaring of Bessie's horn. I wondered why they were late, as this had never happened before. Joe got up and padded to the bathroom where he shut the door, and I stood by the front window looking out for the Weinsteins' car. Two or three minutes more clicked by, and Joe emerged (I figured he'd left the toilet seat up) and on his way back to Dad's chair he said to me, where I stood by the window, "Oh, and they took him to the hospital."

That he'd hung onto this detail until now angered me. Bess was now officially 10 minutes late, and this unsettled me as well. Russell was obsessed with being late and liked to be dropped off early, which only happened on the days his mother drove. I wondered if Bessie had gotten a call about my father, too. Maybe she'd have some more information about the 'fainting incident' than we'd been able to glean from my brother. Standing by the window, I surveyed the rows of pansies, and waited in the silence, for a horn to honk.

A full 15 minutes late, finally the familiar car pulled up, but to my surprise it did not honk. Sara, with satchel in hand, joined me at the front door, without my having to yell for her, and just as one of us reached for the door handle to open it, *the doorbell rang*, which had never before happened in carpool history. A doorbell in lieu of a honk? And to add astonishment to my surprise, it was Russell at the door.

What the... Sara and I looked at each other quizzically. Russell moved quickly to the car door, and stood while he pulled the front seat forward as far as it would go, ushering Sara and me into the back seat, a vast improvement over his usual barely leaning forward. I slid in after Sara, as I'd taken a moment to lock the front door with my key. After I settled in, he looked at me and smiled rather queerly before getting into the front seat. Once we were in the car, Mrs. Weinstein turned around in her seat to look at Sara and me. I smiled and fiddled with my house key, waiting for her to either say something or to turn back around, which, in a moment, she did. Pulling away from the curb, she and Russell both looked straight ahead, no conversation between the two of them; the quiet as unsettling as the yelling. Sitting beside my sister, in the stale cigarette smell of the car, no one said anything for the rest of the ride. I carefully tucked the key to our house—tied with a fat orange piece of yarn—back into the zipper pouch of my pencil bag where I kept it. I'd not counted on Joe to lock the door behind us; he'd been too busy watching TV. I'd jiggled the door handle just to be sure it was locked, something I always did. I didn't know it then, but I'd just locked the door to everything I'd known before. For after that morning nothing—on either side of that door—would ever be the same again.

TWENTY-ONE

Dad suffered a massive coronary that morning, in the principal's office of Kramer Elementary; but thankfully not aboard an airplane to Chicago, where he'd been scheduled to be. Forever more, my brother Joe would blame himself, though he was continually told he'd actually *saved* our father's life by having kept him from flying out of town that day.

During the three months he was hospitalized, we were told that children were not allowed in certain parts of the hospital. Later, we'd question this, and eventually it was revealed that this 'keeping us away from Dad' had been Mom's doing. When he finally came home, three long months later, he was almost unrecognizable to us kids. Weighing a mere 98 pounds, he was a virtual skeleton of his former self. Sometime during the long hospitalization, his left leg had to be amputated above the knee due to clots that caused gangrene. Finally, recovered as best he could with permanent severe damage to his heart, he came home.

As frightening as his appearance was then, we could only assume it had been worse in the hospital, and that *this* was what our mother had wanted to protect us from: the sight of him. For my mother, appearances were everything. On the day she brought him home, I'd have taken any version of my father, legs or no. I had missed him desperately and recognized him immediately, in spite of his sunken-in features. His deep brown eyes were unmistakable.

For 20 years after that, he somehow managed to survive one medical setback after another—all associated with the initial heart attack. Year after year and time and time again, he'd barely make it, narrowly surviving countless episodes, even when his doctors would warn us that he wouldn't. More times than we could count we had been prepared for his imminent death by a grim-faced doctor or surgeon or by our mother; but somehow he had always managed to hang on, against all odds.

Doctors' efforts aside, I've long believed that it was my mother who kept my father alive. They truly adored each other and were the loves of each other's lives; so I was sure that my father rallied each time for the love of my mother. Every single day that he was hospitalized, she showed up each morning in his hospital room with a smile and a positive attitude that never faltered. She told me later that she purposely wore bright colors every day because she believed it helped cheer him. And as always, her signature bright coral lipstick was expertly applied; which is what I remember most about the day my mother sat the three of us kids down and told us that *it would just be us four now,* but that we would be all right.

On the day she told us this, my father had not been expected to survive the night and my mother had come home with the ominous task of telling us this. I remember the scene still, all these years later. I can see the three of us terrified kids leaning forward in our chairs. I remember staring at a brooch on her yellow dress while she spoke, and to this day it is my mother and her coral lipstick, and the bright yellow dress she was wearing, that I remember most. The three months that he was hospitalized remains, in my memory, the most agonizing time I ever lived through. Losing my father terrified me—I feared it to my bones—and every day we returned home from school was another day we'd have to ask if he was still alive. I honestly don't know now if seeing my deathly-ill father in the bed of an ICU would have been a vision I'd have forever been unable to shake; and I'll never know, because it is a scene I never saw. Nor did Joe or Sara.

On the day he came home, I would have accepted anything left of him; even this one-legged, emaciated version. I loved my father profoundly and having him home, as weak and sick as he was, some-what eased the constant fear I held of coming home to find out that he'd died in the hospital that day. Finally, he was home and somehow I believed he would never die on my watch. When my mother would leave to go to the store, I'd creep into the bedroom where my father slept to see if the blanket covering him was moving with his breath-ing. As long as he was breathing, I could breathe, too.

PART THREE

HEARTS AND DIAMONDS

TWENTY-TWO

It's the new millennium and I'm sitting behind my wide, glossy white-lacquered desk below several framed articles hung on the walls behind me with headlines like: "The Queen of Bling" and "There's No Place Like NAOMI." A recent newspaper article—beautifully framed for me, as a gift from my friend Sharon—talks about the five generations of my family in the diamond industry, going back to the 1800's when my ancestors were purveyors of gems to the Czars of Russia. The article hangs close enough to my desk to allow me to read the captions underneath the photos of me smiling, surrounded by some of my jewelry and looking quite successful, indeed. I wonder what my grandfather would have said about all of it. Diamond dealers of his time traveled as far under the radar as possible—as much for safety as humility—and I suspect my grandfather might have frowned on articles about a diamond designer winning a design competition. After all, my ancestors were not the ones who *wore* the royal jewels, but rather, the stewards of the gems they procured, the finest stones worthy of the grand and regal ornaments made for heads of countries. I understood from the stories my grandfather had told me as a child that my family had *served* the Russian royalty but were not themselves the kings and queens.

Another newspaper article on my office wall talks about the business I "inherited from my grandfather." But the truth was that there was little to acquire after he passed away at nearly 90 years old. The article suggests I took over when he retired but this isn't exactly true, either, as he had worked until the day or two before he died. Still donning a fedora, with his gold pocket watch attached to a chain and tucked into his trouser pocket, he'd head out to his office or on a road trip to call on his jewelry store clients. One night he went into the hospital for some pain or another and the next thing we knew he had died. The truth about what I inherited from him is revealed when the article mentions his old gray Rolodex, stuffed with dog-eared business cards taped to the Rolodex cards. This dinosaur-age system of storing contact information was the most valuable thing he left me; and that's assuming he meant for me to have it, as he never actually said so.

Searching for the right path after college, I taught pre-school for a while, but I knew that was not my true calling, even though I though I was good at it. I enjoyed using my artistic skills in the classroom, but I wasn't supporting myself very well financially and I knew I needed to find something else; but I wasn't sure what. After my grandfather died, I kept thinking about my days working with him, and I kept seeing the old gray Rolodex file that sat on his desk, bearing his lifetime collection of contacts. Each card told a story: the names and details of jewelry store owners across the southwest; the names of the sons who had followed them into businesses and even *their* sons after them, whole family histories truncated to fit on a card. In my grandpa's pen, notes on the fronts and backs of each card detailed each jewelry store owner's life and preferences. *Lonnie's a Bass fisherman...bought the store from 'ol man Hershberg when he retired...* one note read. Or *Buys mitziahs* ('good deals' in Yiddish) *in September for holiday...Don't call before 11.* He shared tidbits about each longtime customer, all of whom who could have bought diamonds from hundreds of other sources, but chose to deal with my grandfather because of the relationships he forged with each of them. When he died, there were only a few thin, folded papers of diamonds locked in his safe; the thing of most value, his priceless collection of cards, had been left out on his desk. He had *known* these people; had traveled miles of roads to sit in their stores and listen to their stories. He'd known their joys and sorrows, and had provided them diamonds in both their good financial times and their bad. Some had invited him for dinner in their homes, when he'd traveled into their towns. My grandfather had known many of them in the days before their children were born; now some of those children were grown and running their family's jewelry stores with access to bigger diamond houses than my grandfather's modest operation. Nevertheless, they called him for stones. These were his *connections* and in business these relationships were as valuable as the diamonds themselves, even though they weren't locked away at night.

So I decided to try my hand at the diamond business. I started one morning with nothing much more than my name on crisp new business cards, eager to succeed at my new job as an employee of a Dallas diamond firm that had hired me because the manager had known my grandfather and had supplied him with diamonds over the years. Sitting in a large open area with five or six other young phone-sale-trainees, I showed up every day hoping to sell at least one stone to a store, just as my grandfather had done. I was the only female in an office full of men who, it seemed at first, had much more luck than me when it came to calling stores and making sales. To say that I got off to a slow start would be an understatement.

On a good day, a store might request a particular stone, which we would then send them on consignment. When this happened, it was always exciting. Carefully I'd make up the precious package with a diamond or two tucked into it, just as I'd watched my grandfather do countless times. Sending a stone to a store with a good credit rating was not a guarantee that it would be sold, but at least we were half way there. I'd mail each small package out with a little blessing, hoping the jeweler might keep the diamond inside. Some did, but some did not, and then the package would come back, never packed up as nicely as I had sent it out.

On the many days when no one wanted or needed anything, it always seemed that the guys I worked with were able to take the rejection better than I could. We'd all been hung up on, but the guys were able to brush it off, sometimes cursing the rude store owner who had refused their attempt at conversation. They would simply pick up the phone again and call another store. But for me, especially in the beginning, each "No thank you" was like a little heartbreak. A hang-up without a goodbye was a personal affront.

Territories to call were divided up between me, Eric, Lance, Rich and Joe, but no one had been covering Texas, Oklahoma or Arkansas except for Ben and Yair, the Israeli brothers who owned the company, and they were beginning to turn some of these accounts over to us in preparation for their early retirements in Israel. One day when I was feeling brave, I asked if I might call on stores in these areas, knowing that they were all within the territory my grandfather had once traveled to. The brothers agreed and it was around that time that I remembered the old Rolodex I'd been given from my grandfather's office.

I brought the Rolodex to work the next day, and began cross-referencing the stores he'd called on, which were also listed in the thick red JBT (Jewelers' Board of Trade) that we used. The 'red book' was like our Bible, each store listed with credit ratings from 1 to 4, along with the names of the owners and other pertinent financial information. But the real treasure was my grandfather's notes on each Rolodex card, where I could see—for example—that the owner wasn't necessarily the buyer or that *they bought good deals on one caraters* or that someone might *prefer to chat in late afternoon.*

"My name is Naomi *Pevsner,*" I'd say, emphasizing my surname before I could be brushed off by a busy jewelry store owner with little time to talk to yet another diamond broker on the phone. I'd look at my grandfather's notes and quickly add something like: "I remember my grandfather saying that your father was quite a bass fisherman!" Whereupon a relationship, both personal and professional, would unfold. With my grandfather's Rolodex at hand, I'd not only know who the go-to person was, but also a little bit about him or her, which I soon found was key to striking up the all-important conversation that might result in an eventual sale. The other sales guys began to notice when I'd make a 'cold call' and after chit-chatting like I had an old friend on the other line, I'd end up with an order. Springing from my desk, I'd be up and running; scurrying around the office collecting the diamond I needed and materials to make a package, while the rest of them were still making calls.

"Must be that lilting voice!" they'd tease me. Or: "Wish I could sound like a girl on the phone." But I'd discovered that with my last name, I could call a store, make an introduction and spark a conversation in the time it took another diamond dealer to be hung up on. I knew it wasn't necessarily me; it was the relationships my grandfather had forged and cultivated with these business people that brought me luck. In truth, I hadn't "inherited his business" so much as I had begun to follow in his footsteps. After two years, I started to think about going out on my own and even discussed it with the owners of the diamond company, Benny and Jerry Abramov, who encouraged me to follow my heart and give 'going-it-alone' my best shot. That was more than 25 years ago, and to this day both of them remain important business contacts and cherished friends of mine.

I rented a small space in a nearby building and though I didn't own one diamond, I knew I could get whatever I needed from Ben-Gil; or, if they didn't have it, from any number of dealers who had known and respected my grandfather. In these days, before I knew much at all about business, I did not take the time to come up with an official 'business plan,' but nevertheless my business began to grow. Making phone calls and running out to pick up a diamond to ship could be monotonous, so I began seeing private clients who wanted engagement rings or diamond ear studs. These visits from customers not only broke up the solitude of my day but also began to grow another aspect of my business. Even though I had no actual inventory of either diamonds or engagement rings, when I sold the center diamond for a ring, I also got to design the ring to hold it, and as an artist and an illustrator, this is where I could really shine. Once I'd imagined and drawn a ring design for a customer, I would employ the jewelers my grandfather had used to make up the ring; some of them still do work for me today, thirty years later.

One early sale, to a customer whose name I still recall, gave me the profit to afford business cards, invoices and stationery with my new logo on all of it. My parents were so excited and proud to see my first business cards; I remember my father choking up at the sight of my name as a logo. While my mother was squealing with delight, my dad was sniffling, "Look at that: NAOMI!" he said, reading my business card. "Oh, wouldn't your grandfather have been proud of you, Nomi..." he said fondly.

For the first time, I felt like I was doing what I was *meant* to do. I was single then—I had not yet met my first husband, Cass—and before selling diamonds I had long felt a sense of restlessness. I had never been sure what I wanted to do with my life, and I was secretly scared that I'd never figure it out. It was a great relief to no longer feel that low level of anxiety, which I'd always tried to push down when it would rise in me. The feeling of being 'where I was meant to be' was a new and welcome one. I forged ahead, and in just ten years, my once-fledgling company, Naomi Designs, would be named one of "The Top 100 Fastest Growing Businesses in Dallas" by the Southern Methodist University Cox School of Business, recognized in an awards ceremony I'll never forget. I hadn't planned to win any contests, only to make enough money to support myself. I felt the spirit of my grandfather shining through my success. As he had told me since I was ten years old, 'the crown of a good name'—his own, *Pevsner*—was something valuable, indeed.

TWENTY-THREE

By the early '90s, my father's damaged heart had become so weak that he could no longer attempt to climb stairs. Nevertheless, he remained optimistic, sure that one day a new heart would arrive for him. The idea of organ transplant still seemed like sci-fi to us, but we knew my dad would not last much longer without a new heart. His age was not in his favor; he was almost 60 then, and although he'd learned to walk on an artificial leg, his heart function was greatly limited. Finally, he fell so ill that he was hospitalized again, this time tethered to a heart-lung machine because his own heart function had dwindled to the point where he could not breathe or expect his heart to continue to beat. Sixty-one at the time, he was 'old' to be a transplant recipient, but by the grace of God, he stayed on the transplant list, eventually rising to the top, where he waited, praying to stay alive until a donor heart came for him.

With no cell phones in those days, my mother and each of us kids were given pagers or "beepers" by Baylor Hospital, to alert us if and when a donor heart became available. We were intrigued by the new technology; in the beginning, we would "beep" each other just to see if it worked. Eventually, each of us had given out our pager numbers to enough non-emergency friends that the constant triple-beeps became bothersome. In the Baylor family waiting room, when one of our beepers would go off all four of us would look at the pagers hooked to our belt loops, to see whose had actually done the beeping. Eventually my brother Joe found the humor in the situation, and, tongue firmly in cheek, created a dance move schtick that he called "The Beeper Shuffle." Moving his coat jacket away from the pager with a swing of his hips, he repeated the move back and forth to a tune he made up, which we all began to perform together. *"C'mon, let's do the Beeper Shuffle!"* he'd sing, and all of us—even my mother—would do a swish-swish-swish, in unison, revealing our pager on the downbeat, as if checking its message, and then returning to center. At the time we found it funny; as kids who'd spent countless hours in hospital waiting rooms, we knew how to entertain each other and laughing, even over the silliest things, was our go-to. Others in the waiting room might not have understood how we could be so merry in perhaps the gloomiest place earth, but my siblings and I had become waiting room regulars, and we knew that finding humor in the bleakest moments kept us sane.

When my father was officially wait-listed on Baylor's transplant recipient list, we were introduced to Dr. Peter Alivasatos, an early pioneer in heart and lung transplantation who would perform Dad's surgery. A world-renowned surgeon from Athens, Greece, Dr Alivasatos (or 'Dr A.' as he was known to all) was a strikingly handsome, distinguished figure. Standing 6 feet tall, he spoke with a deep but gently authoritative voice. He chose his words carefully, leaving listeners hanging on his every sentence, and I will never forget the most beautiful line he ever spoke in our presence: "Yes, Barry will get a new heart." Those words, delivered from the surgeon who held my father's life in his highly-skilled hands, were spoken as if by an actual Greek god. This man could—and would—*save* our darling dad. It seemed to us, as time and Dad's life-clock ticked on, that 'Dr A.' had also taken a personal interest in Dad. Years later, Dr A. told me that my father had reminded him of his own. "They were both 'men of letters,'" he said in his commanding Greek accent. "Your father was deeply intelligent, as was mine...and I very much wanted Barry to live."

By this time, my father had lived a good part of his lifetime in constant pain and ill-health, but you'd never have known this from him. Every day he woke up beside my mother was a good one, he said; he counted his blessings and never lamented the lot he had been given in life. As humble a man as any I ever knew, his selflessness was as genuine as everything else about him. It was this quality of his—his selflessness—that made it difficult for him to accept the fact that in order for him to live, *someone would have to die.*

At one point, when a heart had become available, Dad had been shaved and prepped for surgery, and we'd blown him kisses as he was wheeled into surgery, the reality of a heart having come for him seeming almost too good to be true. And it turned out that it was. The heart had been damaged in the motorcycle accident that had killed the donor, and was not suitable to be transplanted, so my father had woken up in recovery with the same old heart he'd had before. "It was a bad heart," Dr. A. told him. "Like hamburger, it was." At this news, my dad had looked up at Dr. A., shrugged his withered shoulders, and said, "Well, I've already got a bad one, doc...I sure don't need another!"

So back to ICU he went and we returned to our prayers for a donor heart to come through. Then on April 18, 1992, as we sat at our Passover *Seder* table on the second night of *Pesach,* a call came in. There was a heart for my father. It also happened to be the evening before Easter Sunday; and from then on, my father delighted in telling the tale of his new heart's arrival on both Easter and the second night of Passover, proclaiming happily that he was "one of the blessed few who could celebrate BOTH the Exodus and the Resurrection, at once!"

In those days, the identity of an organ donor was kept sealed, but by the time the heart had arrived from somewhere in East Texas, an angel must have been ushered into heaven. To this day all of us hold a special place in our own hearts for this nameless and faceless donor whose beating heart my father received on a bright, blue-skied glorious Easter Sunday. There was an indication—a slip of a comment from a surgical nurse—that it had been a woman's heart, which would have made sense, as my father was not a large man. Whether a man's or a woman's, that heavenly heart beat splendidly in my dad's chest for the next seventeen years. Though a gifted writer, my father could never find the words to express his gratitude. Instead, he lived every moment of every day—until his last—with an undying belief that he was, truly, the luckiest man alive.

TWENTY-FOUR

One Sunday when I dropped by my parents' house, my mom met me at the door clutching a letter she'd received in the mail, which she began waving in front of me excitedly.

"Look, look at this, Naomi!" she was saying.

"Look at what?" I said. "Who could see anything with you brandishing it like an air traffic controller flag?"

"It's my *fiftieth* high school reunion!" she said, doing a little happy dance as she said it.

"All in that small envelope?" I asked. Oh, how I loved to egg her on.

As usual, she was unperturbed and gushed on, still waving the letter with excitement. "In Chicago!" she said. "Can you believe it?" she asked. Based on her youthful appearance and zest for life, no, I actually couldn't believe it had been fifty years since she'd graduated from anything but nursery school.

"Wow, Mom." I said. "You're gonna go, right?" I asked. Just then I heard my dad's voice coming from the kitchen.

"You and your mom should go, Nomeluh!" he was shouting. "Take your Mother to her reunion! I'll pay for it!"

I headed towards his voice. I knew my parents could ill-afford a trip to Chicago, but I didn't say so as I headed through the kitchen to see my dad seated at the kitchen table in his robe and slippers.

"Hi Daddykins," I greeted him.

"There's my Nomi-girl!" he said brightly. His dark hair was

tousled from sleep—the familiar forelock usually falling in front, now pushed to one side from the pillow he'd slept on. That curlicue in front had always reminded me of the same one distinguishing Superman from Clark Kent, so seeing it lying off kilter to one side of my dad's head, I found myself wanting to fix it or straighten it, but instead I plopped down into a chair at the table next to him.

He'd been working on a plate of eggs my mother had made, and by the looks of the remnants of toast points sitting beside the sunny-side eggs, I could tell he had dipped the corners of each piece of toast into two perfectly cooked yolks—a breakfast tradition he and I shared.

"Mmmmm, dunking the yolks, huh Dad?" I said.

"Indeed," he said and he smiled. I was the only one of the five of us who shared his eating habits. As a little girl, I'd intentionally imitated most of his long-established eating rituals, and eventually they'd become my favorites, too. Dunking toast into egg yolks was one of them; another was a favorite lunch both he and I enjoyed: plunging cold, leftover chicken into a blob of Miracle Whip (never mayo). For dinner, we both loved to mix Mom's meatloaf with garlicky mashed potatoes on the plate, covered the ensuing mash with liberal squirts of Heinz ketchup. The rest of my family, sitting around the dinner table, would turn up their noses at such a haphazard concoction; but the mix was something he and I shared and, a wink from him, as I'd mash my meat and potatoes, made it all worth it.

The usual back and forth ensued then, during which I was offered—and I refused—a plate of eggs or toast or any number of breakfast items, before my parents could be persuaded that I *had* indeed already eaten. Dipping a last bite into toast, my father swallowed the rest of his coffee and looked at me with some seriousness, before returning to the subject of my mom's reunion again.

"Nomi," he said. I think you and your mother should go. Really, I do"

"Go where?" I joked, watching for the expression on my mom's face at the thought that I might have forgotten her big news in such short order.

"My *REUNION*!" she said incredulously, though she knew I was joking and waved me off accordingly. "Oh, *you tease!*" she said.

"Why, just the thought of it all kept me up half the night!" she said, though I doubted this, knowing my mother slept like a baby from 9 pm to sun-up, and had never lain awake for anything less than a royal wedding airing on BBC at 2 am.

"Oh my gosh, my best girlfriend Marcia will be there...and Myra Gold, too!" Her enthusiasm now on overdrive, she continued rattling off Jewish-sounding names of old (or I should say 'aging') friends, still living in Chicago, who would surely be attending Sullivan High School's reunion. Dad and I sat at the kitchen table together while my mom headed off towards their bedroom, still talking excitedly about who'd be attending the big reunion gathering. My mother's delight brought my father every bit as much joy; so I wasn't surprised when he leaned forward, touched my arm and looked me straight in the eye.

"Go with your mother to Chicago, Nomeluh," he said. "She would dearly love to show you off, and the two of you would have a grand time!"

Getting around on his prosthesis had become difficult for my father, though he'd never say so. His fluctuating weight, from constant medical episodes, had made it nearly impossible for the artificial limb to fit properly in recent years. He'd fallen down escalators and found himself sprawled across sidewalks, eventually learning to navigate on just his crutches when the residual leg would become too chafed or tender. Without his prosthesis, he'd taught himself to throw both crutches away from his body in a fall, so as not to be further injured by falling on one of them. All in all, with his special needs, he felt he would have been a hindrance to my mother, and was looking to me to be my mom's travel partner.

"When's the reunion?" I asked. But the date didn't matter; I'd have gone regardless of timing.

As my mother chattered cheerily from the hallway, where she stood on tip-toes in front of the hall closet, the place her infrequently-used suitcase was stored, I looked at my dad and nodded.

A mother/daughter trip to Chicago, decades after we'd left our old hometown, was the stuff memories were made of. And pleasing my parents was enough motivation for me to do just about anything.

So with a nod and a wink, I told my father I was in. I'd go home and ask Richard to book a first-class trip for me and my mother, and together we'd fly back to Chicago for a long weekend that both of us would remember for a lifetime.

After three days away from my father, my mother cried as we pulled into their driveway. She was so excited to see my father, they might as well have been parted for an eternity.

"Oh my gosh, I can't wait," she said, her voice quivering with emotion; I thought she might jump out before my car had come to a stop.

"Oh, there he is!" my mother squealed, at the sight of my father coming out of the garage. They were overjoyed to see each other, and it was touching to watch their reunion, but I was anxious to see my husband, too, so I bid them farewell quickly. My father stopped me just before I ducked back into my car.

"Nomi," he said, touching my arm, "I don't know how to thank you, sweetheart. There are no words...." I thought he might cry.

"Dad, it was my pleasure," I said. "Honestly, it was so much fun for me. We had an incredible time." My dad's immense gratitude was sweet but unnecessary; I wouldn't have traded the time in Chicago with my mother for anything.

The next day, I found an email from my dad in my inbox. I printed it out and have saved it all these years, because it is so full of the love my father felt for me. I didn't know it then, but I do now: that sort of adoration from a father to a daughter was so deep and so complete that no one else could ever love me this way. The loss of a father like him would be devastating.

This is father's email. By now, I know it by heart.

My Darling Nomi:

I cannot properly thank you for what you did for your mother with the Chicago trip. You probably could ill afford the time and expense of it, but going with you did SO much for her on so many levels.

You surely know what a deeply sentimental journey it turned out to be for her. One of the most significant of her life, she says.

Her descriptions of talks with Marcia and Hank and so many other former classmates brought tears to my eyes, and hers too, just in the telling of them.

For her, the trip had even more luster because you were with her; she is SO proud of you and with good reason.

Each time you do something remarkable for your mother and me (and there are so many) we say, "Now this is really something! This time she's really outdone herself." And then you do it again.

There must be a special place in Heaven reserved for daughters like you; and I believe it is at the right hand of the good Lord himself.

Thank you, Sweetheart, from the bottom of my heart.

Your ever-lovin' Dad.

TWENTY-FIVE

When my parents were alive, the three of us kids, even as adults, naturally gravitated to their house on Sundays. I spoke to my parents every day—sometimes even multiple times a day—but by Sunday I needed to relax with them in person. Perhaps they thought I came by for their sakes, but in truth it was as much for me as for them. My parents were my closest emotional connections and time spent with them—in the house I'd grown up in—grounded me each week and was essential to my well-being.

One Sunday, I rang the doorbell and stood waiting as my mother's sing-song rendition of "Cooooming!" grew louder and closer as she neared the door. I had my own key, but entering on my own, without my mother's animated and effervescent version of a grand welcome at the door, would not have been nearly as satisfying.

"Oh hi, honey!" my Mom chirped, swinging one of the double doors wide. "C'mon in, dear!" she said, ushering me over the same threshold I'd crossed many hundreds of times before.

My mom looked lovely as always, but on this day she seemed especially elegant for a Sunday afternoon at home: accessorized with small gold earrings and a smart neck scarf tossed over one shoulder as if there might be a party going on—or at least a small gathering I hadn't known about. Seeing no apparent guests lurking beyond the entry hall, I leaned in for a hello-hug, leaving a bit of space between us to accommodate the Polaroid camera I only then noticed she had hung around her neck on a strap, tourist style.

"Something's come between us," I said, eying the camera. It was a low-level joke, but it elicited a giggle from my mom as she headed to the kitchen. I followed her, heading straight for the coffee pot, which I was pleased to see still had a few inches of coffee remaining.

Reaching for the still-warm pot, my mother grabbed my wrist and gasped as if I were about to drink something vile. "Oh honey, let me make a fresh pot!"

"This is fine, Mom," I said, knowing it would take a mini-debate to convince her, but catching a lucky break when my father called out from the back bedroom.

Passing the den on our way to the kitchen, I'd noticed that my Dad wasn't sitting in his usual easy-chair, where he'd typically plant himself for the duration of a Sunday. My dad would never have stayed in bed this late in the day unless he wasn't feeling well, so my heart dropped for a moment.

"Hey, where'd everybody go?" I heard him say, his voice coming from their bedroom.

He sounded all right, and his voice had had enough strength to have reached us from down the hall, but still I worried for a moment more.

"Uh-oh," I said to my mom. "Is Daddy sick?"

"Oh nooo, honey! He's fine. Just fine!" she said.

Setting the pot back into the coffee maker, I waited for further intel, sure to come.

"I've got Dad all set up for the photo shoot we're doing in the bedroom," she continued, speaking as if 'a photo session in the bedroom' was as common as pancakes on a Sunday morning—which it wasn't.

"C'mon back, you'll see!" she said, heading towards the bedroom. I followed more slowly with my cup of coffee, and by the time I entered the room Mom was already positioned with the camera, paparazzi-style, the subject being my dad. I could see she'd lined up my father up for the shoot, raising the camera to frame him as he sat smiling in front of a white backdrop of pillows. But as I entered the room, my dad looked my way, rather than at the camera, which apparently spoiled the shot my mother had been taking.

"Oh darn, I got the side of your head," Mom said. "Oh well, maybe it'll be a good profile picture!"

Always the optimist, my mom.

"Nomeluh!" Dad greeted me warmly. "Hello, sweetness!"

"Hi, Dad-uh-luh!" I answered, using the silly 'matching' nickname I'd made up for him. "What's going on in here?"

"Your mother's on a mission," my dad said. "Though my ugly mug might permanently damage her camera."

My mom hadn't heard his comment; she was busy adjusting the scarf around her neck in front of the mirror over their dresser. "I thought the pop of color would be perfect," she said, and I had to agree, noticing that her colorful scarf matched her lipstick.

"You know, they do the obituary photos in color now!" she said, giving me the first clue as to what she was doing with the camera. I wondered what had prompted the sudden need for obit pictures, since neither of my folks were showing signs of imminent death. "Obituary photos?" I asked, condensing my longer question to one word.

My dad was seated towards the middle of their bed, leaning casually against the white background of pillows; he had apparently been 'styled' for these photos by Mom, his left hand placed on his lap and his right wrapped around a personalized coffee cup with enough space left between his fingers to allow the word "Grandpa" to be visible in the picture.

"Okay, now me," my mother said to my dad, indicating with hand motions that he should rise and allow her to sit in the make-shift studio.

He rose on command, and she shoved the camera into one of his hands. Looking my way, Dad rolled his eyes lovingly, as if to say: I just do as I'm told; which is something he did actually say quite often. I could see he'd slicked back his hair, and had on pants instead of his usual hang-out-at-home Sunday clothes. He'd even put on his prosthetic leg, though typically on a Sunday he'd 'go casual,' which meant crutches and no artificial limb.

Assuming my mother had 'suggested' he don proper pants for the shoot, I asked: "Do they use full-length pictures in obituaries now?"

"Well, your mother must think so," my Dad whispered, winking at me as he passed, reminding me of the time he'd told the three of us kids at dinner, "If your mother says it's sunny outside, and it's pouring rain...you'd better have your eyes examined." His point was: Your mother is always right.

My mom smiled for her shot, and Dad caught the picture that came slithering out of the camera, and waving it in the air to dry. My mom reached for it excitedly. "Ooooh! Let me see. Let me see!"

"I love it, honey!" she said to my Dad. "This will be a keeper. I don't look too bad, do I?" she asked me brightly.

"Nice," I said, agreeing wholeheartedly. "But why are you...and whose camera...?" I had a handful of questions but my dad started speaking so I figured my queries would keep.

"I'm surprised I didn't break the camera when your mother took my picture!" my dad said. He always said something like this in reference to photos of himself. "But your mother looks as captivating as ever," he added, pointing the camera at her and taking another shot.

My mom smiled demurely, as Dad clicked the shutter and the photo began to emerge from the camera's innards with the familiar iconic sound.

"This one will be perfect!" my dad declared, and as the photo came into view, revealing Mom's lovely image, I agreed. Accented by the bright red lips she'd been clever enough to bring to the shoot, and the scarf with its matching red detail swirled into the pattern, it was, indeed, perfect. I added the photo to a growing pile on the side table.

"Soooo, obituary photos, huh?" I asked. "Now that's an upbeat and positive project for a Sunday afternoon."

"Well, honey," my mom said. "These things *simply need to be done*."

When my mother made this sort of statement, one did not argue. *Simply. Need. To. Be. Done.*

"Lord only knows what sort of unflattering photo might be selected for one's obituary if these things are not considered ahead of time," she continued. "So your father and I just thought we'd go ahead and have ours ready, so we could check that off our to-do list!"

"I see," I said, though I didn't.

"These are the sorts of things your father and I think of and so, well, why not just get them done?" she said. She was not actually asking a question, and I doubted my father had actually 'thought' of any of this. I would have bet the farm it had been my *mom* who'd done all the thinking for them both.

"So where'd ya'll get the camera?" I asked.

"Oh, it's Cynthia's, dear. I borrowed it for the weekend to take our obit photos," Mom said, matter-of-factly.

Before I could ask anything more, the camera was shoved into my own one free hand, my mom suggesting that I take the next shot.

Setting my coffee cup on the nightstand, I backed up and saw Mom pulling Dad back towards the bed, where he was strongly encouraged to sit beside her for a photo of the two of them. I pointed the camera and prompted them: "Say cheese!" My mother needed no direction: she was already smiling gloriously, frozen in a pose she'd have kept for no-telling how long, had I not been a quick shot.

"Perfect!" I said, waving the newly regurgitated photo in the air and referring only to my skills, as the image hadn't appeared yet.

As the image came into view, revealing my two smiling parents, I thought it was a great shot, though I silently hoped my mother wouldn't notice that the 'Grandpa' coffee cup wasn't visible.

"A photo of the two of you together...hmmm, would this be for a 'joint obituary' article?" I asked, in jest.

My mother didn't answer this, too busy bouncing like an excited kid and grabbing for the photo. I handed it to her and quipped, "A shot of you both will be handy if the two of you perish together, like in a tandem skydive gone wrong."

Plucking the photo from my hand and proclaiming it 'very nice,' my mom seemed pleased and with this, I assumed the shoot was over. My dad turned to see my cooling cup of coffee on the night table and asked, "Honeygirl, is your coffee hot enough? We can heat it for you."

"No thanks, Daddy," I said. "It's okay."

This offer to heat my coffee was so 'signature Dad'—as in his mind, he was never doing enough for the ones he loved. We all knew that one had to be careful not to compliment him on a new pen—or worse—a removable item of clothing, or he'd insist on giving it to you. He was always literally trying to give you the shirt off his back; "Please, take it!" he'd insist. Many a time I'd heard him going back and forth with my brother, Joe, saying, "Dad, I don't want the jacket! I only meant that it looked good on you." Later, even as Joe was walking to his car to leave, you could hear my dad yelling after him: "Are you sure you won't take this jacket, sonny-boy? Take it! I'll never wear it...." This was the only time my father would tell a fib. Joe would step on the gas, leaving Dad standing on the curb, wondering if he could send the jacket to Joe in the mail.

Ever worried about everyone but himself, this was my Dad in a nutshell. "No thanks, Dad, my coffee's good. Still warm!" I lied, plopping down on the bed. My mom shimmied over and smoothed out the duvet cover around me as if we were still in photo mode, and the wrinkles might show in a picture. Watching her pretty hands smoothing out the sheets, I knew she did this by habit, always seeking to make every nook and cranny of her world more perfect. On any given Sunday, she could be seen repositioning decorative items and adjusting things here and there; "piddling," as she called it. From one end of the house to the other, she would go, between loads of wash and folding, preparing perfectly plated lunches and welcoming the three of us 'children' when we'd stop by for visits.

Finishing the smoothing of the area around us, she moved to the dresser across from the bed, chatting all the while. "I told your father, we simply must take pictures for use in our obituaries!" she said, in the same tone she would have used for 'we simply must take pictures for our presidential medals of freedom!' I assumed she was waiting for my response, but I was simply unable to say "Good thinking, Mom!" so instead I asked, "Why this weekend? Is a deadline looming?"

My parents were in their late 70s at the time, and though it was true that Dad was constantly facing some health crisis or another, his transplanted heart had been beating happily for ten years by then, so even he had no immediate plans for kicking the bucket.

"Well," she began, and my dad and I reclined as she flitted around us, tidying and talking about the need for decent head-shots in obituaries and all the terrible ones you see nowadays, and so on. My dad and I leaned back and listened contently to my mother, both of us knowing that she was always the star of the show.

A decade after that Polaroid shoot, in 2009, on the day we had to choose a photo for Dad's *actual* obituary, I had long forgotten about those photos. One of us submitted another picture of my dad instead. Three years later, when Mom died too, I had—in truth—forgotten about the pictures they'd both intended us to use.

Years later, when I found them in some old boxes of memorabilia, I smiled until I laughed out loud. I took the stack of Polaroids over to show my husband, telling him the story of the day we'd taken them. He studied their faces: Mom, so happy in the moment, forgetting about the subject matter and its gloom; and Dad, always smiling and happy as long as she was happy. How darling they were, Richard and I agreed, each proudly holding their coffee cups like trophies bearing the noblest badges of all: "Grandpa" and "Grandma." Coming to the last photo—the one I'd taken of the two of them—I felt my heart swell, remembering that moment in time so clearly.

They had been fully prepared to leave this world when their time arrived, and they'd showed me this in even the most whimsical of ways. It was I who simply could not fathom it.

TWENTY-SIX

Soon after his heart transplant, with his new lease on life, my father became an integral part of my growing company. At Naomi Designs, my dad was the 'Senior Jewelry Appraiser,' accountant and book-keeper—and a beloved favorite of both employees and clients alike. If he'd once disliked the diamond business, there was no hint of this now. He passed every certifying exam with flying colors, becoming a Graduate Gemologist, certified appraiser and colored gemstone expert through the Gemological Institute of America, the standard accreditor for our industry.

Beyond his expertise, he charmed all with his genuine goodness, which was evident in even brief exchanges with him. Our clients fell for my father. When he'd congratulate a young man on the purchase of an engagement ring, he'd offer wishes that struck each person as the most sincere they'd ever heard—as they may well have been. Holding one of their hands with both of his, he'd say things like: *I hope you and your bride-to-be will be every bit as happy as my dear wife and I have been for fifty wonderful years.* Or: *A sincere thanks to you, young man, for favoring us with your business.* In his quiet, gentlemanly way, he endeared himself to others and left them feeling touched.

Since receiving the gift of life—the heart of an angel—he'd lived graciously, making the most of every day, every hour and every sec-ond. Having decided to try his hand in the diamond business, which he'd once avoided like the plague, he quickly became an accom-plished expert, integral to our operation. I loved seeing him at the office every day and knowing that he *loved* what he did. He was also my greatest fan, reveling in my success in a business I'd begun with nothing but a book of invoices, a stack of business cards and a telephone atop a borrowed desk in a small, windowless office.

On the evenings when I occasionally worked late, he always made an excuse to stay too, 'coincidentally' having some project to finish. I would always urge him to go home, where I knew my mom was waiting with dinner, but he'd claim he had things to do; I knew the truth was that he didn't like to leave me at the office alone at night. One evening in April when I stayed past 6 p.m., I heard him in his office, though he usually left by 5:00. At around 7 p.m., I finished some drawings and wandered into his office, giving my legs a chance to stretch and hoping to talk him into going home.

"Hi Daddy," I said, yawning and pulling a chair in his office up to his desk, where he was typing something at his computer.

"Nomeluh!" he said, offering me his typical, enthusiastic greeting, sounding as though he hadn't seen me in a week, though we had seen each other all day, on and off. "What's new, Honeygirl?" he asked.

Across from him, leaning on my hands with my elbows on his desk, I sighed. His was by far the smallest office at Naomi Designs, but it was the one he'd chosen and insisted upon, though I'd tried to point out its downfalls. With no windows, and space for little more than his desk and chair, it was not exactly prime real estate. In my opinion, it wasn't a space worthy of our Senior Gemologist and Certified Appraiser; especially when it was my dad who held these titles. At the time, I thought he deserved better, but later I came to see that he'd chosen this office for other reasons.

This small office opened into the hallway that led to the back door, which was the one that all deliveries came through. But more than that, my father knew which of the constant streams of back-door people were ones I did not have time to schmooze with. The double doors of my office were glass, so even if they were closed, I—with my A.D.D.—could be distracted by a person standing there, whether they were pantomiming a knock or wildly waving their hands to get my attention. In the midst of a typically crazy work day, stopping to direct my attention to each interruption was something I dreaded. Although all of them were well-meaning, and some were appropriate and necessary, the constant disturbances were difficult for me to recover from. After years of constantly interrupted concentration, I'd reached the point where each little distraction planted a seed of angst in me that, by the end of the day, grew into a veritable beanstalk in my gut. My dread of distraction grew to the point where *even the expectation* of the next inevitable interruption gave me anxiety. I wondered how I would ever manage to get through the piles of work—the work itself causing a low level of panic to rise in me. That things never slowed down on any given day should be a good thing for a small business, but increasingly, it frazzled me.

The worst 'offender'—if you could call it that—was an elderly, Orthodox Jewish gentleman in our building named Mr. Becker. Sweet-faced, looking like a retired Rabbi out of uniform, Mr. Becker would stop by to *schmooze* each day—certainly no crime, but by the third time he showed up each day I wanted to strangle the poor fellow, until, gasping for air and begging for mercy, he promised never to enter our offices again. He was an old-timer who'd been a diamond dealer and a jeweler in his day, but had not actually done business in some years. Even so, he came to 'work' everyday, after attending daily prayer services with some other observant old-timers. With nothing much else to do, Mr. Becker spent his time visiting the people working in the office building we shared. Many were diamond dealers and jewelers with little time to sit and visit; I wasn't the only one who'd see him coming and pick up my phone to engage in imaginary conversation when he'd appear at my door. But even this didn't stop him; he'd come in, sit quietly and wait. He was a kindly man with an interesting history that I thought I had no time to hear about. But my father did, and this, I realized, was a reason he'd taken the office by the back door. My dad guarded the gate to my office, and even with his own work to do, he always made time for Mr. Becker.

Israel Becker had survived concentration camps, spoke multiple languages besides his native Russian, and had translated top stories from a Russian newspaper, in which my father feigned great interest.

Mr. Becker loved that I was a *Yiddisha maidele,* (a nice Jewish girl) and was always thrilled that I knew some Yiddish, the old and dying language used by Jews in central and eastern Europe before World War II. When he'd come by with a Yiddish comment or phrase, I'd respond in kind, which always sent him into happyland. I'd grown up around my Yiddish-speaking grandparents on my father's side, and even my parents used certain expressions from the old country, adapted to fit into modern American situations. I understood more Yiddish than I could speak; but Mr. Becker got a kick out of my using my limited vocabulary.

"*Vi geyt es?*" he'd ask, when I hung up the phone and smiled at him.

"I'm good thanks, Mr. Becker," I'd say. "*Nu?*" (meaning: *So?* as in: *So, how are you?*). I'd be itching to get back to the pile of work rising on my desk, but I knew he'd planted himself in front of my desk for at least a quick chat. Looking at the assorted jewelry parts and half-drawn designs covering the surface of my desk, he'd comment in Yiddish something about my doing 'too much work,' or he'd recall the days when he himself used to be as busy. "*Az a yor ahf mir*" (*it should happen for me*), he'd say, with a faraway look in his rheumy eyes.

"Mr. Becker," I'd say, "I need all this work like a *lokh in kop!*" (translation: someone who needs something, like they need a hole in their head; *loch in kop*=hole in head,). And with this he'd simply *kvell* (glow with pride or happiness) at the modern American *maidele* in his midst.

But no one knew like my father did how these visitors threw me off, which is precisely why he'd seated himself in that closet-sized office, where he could divert Mr. Becker and other distracting visitors before they reached me. My father made himself into a 'daddy-barrier' of sorts, absorbing much of the distraction that he knew kept me at the office late most nights, catching up.

As I sat across from him that evening, the office phone rang and I assumed it would be my mother, checking on his ETA for home. He answered the phone in his deep, professional voice, perhaps by habit, because he'd have seen by the caller ID that it was my mom.

"Yes, Sweetness. I'm just finishing up here," he said, referring to my mom by one of the many endearing names he'd given her. "Yes, darling, I'm leaving soon. But you go ahead and eat; don't wait for me," he added, knowing full well she would do neither. She never ate before he got home, and as they'd shared dinner every night for the last 57 years, it seemed silly to think that this would change now. "Okay, honey-girl, will do," he said before hanging up. And then, "I love you too."

It always had been this way with them. They were the loves of each other's lives, true soulmates, and I knew I had been blessed to have grown up in the light of such love. I had come into his office mainly to encourage him to go on home to Mom, since I knew I'd be a another hour or so. Meanwhile, with a few minutes to chat, I asked for his opinion on a subject I'd been brooding about. My 50th birthday was coming up, and my sister-in-law was planning some sort of celebration at their house. She was waiting for me to give her a list of invitees, but I'd procrastinated; I honestly did not want to have a party, though I appreciated her offer. I had mixed emotions about turning fifty, and preferred to skip the celebrations.

Sitting across from my dad, my mind was wandering. Maybe I'd wrap it up and go on home, too. It had been another long day. My dad interrupted my thoughts.

"It's going to be your birthday, Nomi," he said. "Your 50th is a big thing and your sister-in-law wants to give you a party, as you know. I think you should be gracious and accept her offer," my dad said.

He knew that I would have preferred to skip my 50th birthday altogether. He also knew that I had been mildly annoyed with my sister-in-law Debbie for a couple of weeks. This was highly unusual because she and I are very good friends, but a recent disagreement had been weighing on my mind, and in those days, I could take an annoyance and hang onto it for longer than necessary. True to form, holding my grudge tightly, I wasn't eager to allow my sister-in-law to 'redeem herself' by throwing me a party. Better I should stew in my hurt feelings a bit longer. Damn my birthday for coming so inconveniently and pushing me to 'a truce' before its time.

"I dunno, Daddy." I scowled at the mention of the party. "It's very nice of Debbie to offer, but do you see why I'm still a little annoyed with her?" Why I asked him this I don't know; my father never said or even insinuated anything negative about anyone and would never have 'taken sides' with any of his 'daughters.' Debbie was just as much a daughter as Sara and I were to him—ditto my husband, Richard, and even my former husband, Cass, Marissa's father, both of whom he called 'son.' That's the way it worked in our family, and so I'd known, even as I asked, that he would not support or perpetuate my grudge against Debbie.

My father also knew my stubborn streak and that I had a tendency to take things personally, whether or not they had been intended that way. Before addressing my question, he looked up at me as if to read my mind, which he had an uncanny way of doing. His response was evident in his eyes, which had grown more expressive since the creeping neuropathy he'd long suffered (a side effect of the anti-rejection drugs he took as a transplant recipient) had spread to the lower half of his face, limiting his ability to show facial expression from the nose down. With or without expression, I could have guessed what he was about to say.

Aware of the situation I was 'mad' about—one so earth-shattering that today I honestly cannot remember what it was about—he pulled no punches.

"I think you can be as stubborn as your grandfather," he said. "Nomi, call Debbie and let's celebrate your birthday together," he said, in a no-nonsense tone, his eyes smiling at me in his frozen face.

Knowing he was right, I was touched by his wise words, but even more so by his inability to smile as he said them.

The neuropathy had begun in his throat, the dying nerve endings eventually forcing him to eat through a permanent feeding tube to his stomach, since he was unable to swallow food or liquids without inadvertently directing some of it into his lungs. For the past two years he'd existed on a diet of thick, milky, liquid sustenance that came in cans; a lifetime of normal eating now just a memory. He'd bring his can of sustenance to the office each day and around noon, amble into my office with his "lunch." If I wasn't on the phone, he'd ask to sit on the couch near my desk or at the round conference table in my office to "eat," and naturally, I always welcomed him, trying not to look disturbed about the fact that my father was doomed to a life without the joy of food. But, ever grateful, before each 'meal' he'd pull the can's tab and as he poured the thick beige liquid through a funnel into the tube, he'd say "Bon Appetit!" as if he actually meant it. "Enjoy, Dad!" I'd respond, joking always our go-to way of coping. It was wrenching for me to watch this lunchtime ritual, though I never said so; had he known it disturbed me, he would never have allowed me to see it.

"So, why don't you call your sister-in-law, honeygirl?" he asked, and I knew my time to be pissed off was up.

"I'll do it," I said, "if you'll go home to Mom. Your dinner is probably getting cold," I joked.

"That's my girl," my dad said approvingly.

He agreed to go home then, and after we hugged goodnight I returned to my office, listening to the familiar click-clicking of his gait: a click of his heel then a pause—and a second click—as he lifted his left thigh high enough to allow the prosthetic knee to bend and the foot to swing forward into the next step. Click, click, pause. Click, click, pause. I listened, always, in the silence of the space between clicks, for the dreaded sounds of his occasional falls. His carefully choreographed step-swing-step-walk was familiar to all of us; he had walked this way for almost forty years. Slow and steady, as always, he walked to the door and through it. Sweet man that he was, I loved him more than I could ever say.

The door locked automatically behind him, and I leaned back in my leather chair and turned towards the windows to see the sunset over midtown Dallas. I smiled as I heard the sound of my father doing his 'double-checking' of the already-locked front door, jiggling the handle just to be sure it had indeed locked; just as my grandfather had done four, five, sometimes even six times. My dad only did it a time or two, but I suspected that sometimes he had gone as far as the elevator before deciding to come back and check our outside door handle just *one more time*. His 'little girl' was inside, after all.

Little girl, indeed, I snorted at the thought. A *fifty-year-old-version* of one, I was. The stress of another typical day falling away, I looked onto the highway below and then back to my sparkling office and the glamorous showroom beyond my double-glass doors. I was happy, I thought; and I knew for sure that I was blessed. Turning 50 would not be so bad after all. I was halfway to 100, true, but had much ahead of me. I watched the sidewalk below my wall of windows to see my dad exit the building, walking slowly to his car on his prosthetic leg. God, I loved him. I honestly didn't know what I'd do without him, but as this thought crossed my mind I shooed it away. *'Perish the thought,'* as they say.

Finally getting to a good stopping point in my work, I put the jewelry in the safe and turned off lights, heading home to my husband. We celebrated my 50th birthday at Joe and Debbie's and a grand time was had by all. I did not know it then but it would be the last time I'd celebrate a birthday with my father in attendance. Eleven days after I turned fifty, he died.

TWENTY-SEVEN

Heart transplant recipients are safe from the threat of failure to which their original organs were doomed; but while a transplanted heart keeps on ticking, other dangers lie in wait: rejection, infection, cancer and more. For seventeen years, my dad fought off countless health crises, including adverse reactions to necessary medications, organ rejection, and even bizarre intermittent vision impairments.

A couple of years before his death, when the dreaded neuropathy first set in, we feared the worst, but Dad, always optimistic, seemed to take it in stride. It had begun as a 'metallic taste in his mouth' that wouldn't respond to treatment and eventually made food tasteless. From his tongue it spread to his throat and began to affect the lower half of his face. It would be another year before he'd lose the ability to smile, but early on the numbness and increasing paralysis made it hard for him to swallow; and worse, made it all too easy for any liquids he drank to trickle down into his lungs. Even solid foods were a choking danger, and after several hospitalizations for fluid in his lungs, his doctors decided that a feeding tube was the only way to keep his plummeting weight up and save him from recurring cases of pneumonia. Food quickly became only a memory for my dad, but characteristically he took the news in stride and learned to pour cans of a thick liquid nutritional concoction into the tube implanted in his stomach.

When we met for family dinners at restaurants, the rest of us ordered aromatic and appetizing entrees, and true to form Dad never bemoaned his fate or acted anything other than perfectly happy to be at dinner with those he loved. He'd feed himself through the tube beforehand and watch us all eat; looking as pleased as if he had a thick steak coming. My parents ate dinner at home most nights, and my mother always set a lovely table, even after Dad became reliant on the feeding tube. She'd set his evening can of liquid food on a china dinner plate across from hers at their table for two in the kitchen, and they'd enjoy dinner this way, together as always. My mother loved to tell us how every evening when they sat down, before Dad pressed the plunger of the syringe to force the liquid through the tube, he'd say, "Bon Appetit, dear!" And she'd respond in kind.

Every night, they'd share the details of their days over dinner. When they finished, Mom would carefully place her knife and fork across her plate as Dad covered his empty can with his unused cloth napkin. According to my mom, at this point Dad would deliver the same line he had used after *every single dinner* my mother ever made for him, since we were kids.

"Good vittles Ma Smalley!" he'd say, a quote borrowed from the old radio version of *Gunsmoke,* originally offered as a compliment to the widow-lady who ran the boarding house in the long-running TV series. To this day, my husband says the same thing to me after dinner, even if I've only picked up an already-prepared dinner and re-heated it. It's our little nightly ode to my dad, and a nod to the dinners my parents shared for 57 years.

My dad's inability to smile was more noticeable to me than the amputation of his leg had been, years before. He had always smiled while he was speaking, and this elevated or accentuated whatever positive or dear thing he would be saying. Even after his signature smile was gone, his eyes still twinkled. After another year, the neuropathy began to affect his speech, ever so slightly at first, but then more noticeably, and I knew this must have troubled him, but he never said so. An eloquent speaker, my father had a command of the English language and a genuine love for it, never 'wasting' words, he always chose them wisely. Sometimes he would pause momentarily before speaking, and without fail, always knew exactly what to say. After his death, I lost count of the number of times someone would share their story of my father touching them with his words, offering something poignant or encouraging, or lifting someone's spirits by reaching out to them just when needed. I adored that people remembered him so fondly, but I knew that in his humbleness their appreciation would have brought him to tears.

"Me?" he'd have asked. "They said those things about me?!" His eyes would no doubt have been tearing up as he raised a hand to his mouth in surprise. "I can't believe they'd remember me," he would have said. At his core he was incredibly humble.

The neuropathy in his face and throat persisted. Eventually we were forced to consider a procedure known to have reversed neuropathy in some patients, as the paralysis would ultimately begin to affect his breathing—which of course, would be the end. The procedure that had helped some patients was a risky one, and he knew this—but he had survived many a hazardous therapy before, so the treatment was scheduled and we were all optimistic, as always.

On my dad's last night at work before the treatment, he and I had both worked late. Chatting in my office, I remembered that he would be out for a few days, and before he left I said, "Oh, good luck with that treatment thing tomorrow, Dad!"

He'd answered in his usual lighthearted way, "Hope it doesn't kill me, honey girl!"

It had long been our way to joke about these sorts of things. But in the end, his little jest turned out to be a premonition. The irony was that quite miraculously the procedure did begin to reverse the paralysis in his face almost immediately—but there would be a deadly flip-side.

Following the treatment, Dad developed a dangerous infection and remained hospitalized for the next several days. Visiting him in the hospital Sunday evening, we all sat around his bedside, happy and daring to sigh with relief because that morning the infection appeared to have taken a small turn for the better. As we bantered back and forth in our family's typical style, we had marveled at the sight of

Dad's familiar smile returning to the corners of his mouth and showing signs of spreading slowly but surely across his frozen face.

"Oh my God, daddy!" I exclaimed, barely able to believe my eyes. "You're *smiling!*" Frantically digging through my purse, I pulled out a compact mirror so he could see it for himself.

"I see it, too!" my mom grinned. "You're *smiling*, honey!" We left the hospital that night, fully expecting him to rally, our collective spirits high. I fell asleep with happy thoughts of my father *smiling* at me for the first time in a long time. But at 3:00 in the morning when the phone beside my bed jangled me awake, I think I knew.

"Na?" It was my brother's voice on the phone.

I shook my head in an effort to clear it and as I did, all my sweet dreams of wide smiles scattered.

"Joe? What's wrong?" I asked anxiously. But it was really just to buy myself some time. I knew what it was, but wanted to steal a few seconds more of *not* knowing.

"He's gone." Joe said. "I'm so sorry, Na..." We sat in silence for a moment.

"He's gone?" I asked; as if I'd heard wrong, but I knew.

Exactly one day after my parents' 57th wedding anniversary, my dad passed away in the night, but not before he had recruited a nurse to purchase an anniversary card from the hospital's gift shop for him, to give to my mother. He'd signed it with a shaky hand, and pulled it from under his bedcovers just after Mom arrived that morning. It was May 24th that day; in the wee hours of the 25th, he slipped away. His was a soul surely headed straight for heaven, to a place reserved for those worthy of a seat next to the good Lord himself; where he'd wait for the love of his life to join him three years later— almost to the date.

Only later would I ponder my mother's timing, passing away a few days before what would have been their 60th wedding anniversary. It comforted me to know that she'd made it to his side with an extra day or two to spare, which she'd no doubt have spent in getting ready: acquiring the most heavenly dress and of course, just the right shoes for dancing with my father.

In my mind's eye, I see him leading her easily, as elegantly as Fred Astaire once did Ginger Rogers, to the tune of the Anniversary Waltz; my father once again on two sturdy legs. Theirs had been a true love story, to which I was so fortunate to have had front row seats. Though they're gone now, their song plays on.

TWENTY-EIGHT

Shoeless in the summer grass on the evening after Dad's funeral, I sat on a willow bench in our backyard and cried, holding my head in my hands. I stared at the long blades of Bermuda grass shooting up between my bare toes. Lawns grow fast in Texas in May, and watching my tears drop to the ground, I could not reconcile myself to the fact that some things continued to grow while others wilted and died.

Through my tears the grass blurred, becoming the same turf I remembered being installed in 10-inch clods, like squares of carpet, around my childhood home on Hillbriar, so many decades ago. The Bermuda grass had arrived on a truck at our then-new house piled high on a wooden palette, to be carefully arranged by our yardman with my father as his assistant. The green squares had been placed side to side, encouraged to grow and become a plush lawn stretching across my parents' lot. The red brick house with its black shuttered windows was the first new brand home any of us had ever resided in and it had been so exciting to settle in as its first residents. Everything felt so new and the corner lot our house was built on was the biggest in our development of modest homes—a fact my parents spoke of often, and with great pride. They never said, but later we learned, that both the house and the new lawn had been barely affordable for them at the time.

Sitting on the bench the evening after my father's funeral, I remembered how religiously my father had tended his new lawn-to-be on

Hillbriar Drive, and how he'd water each area by laboriously moving an old-school sprinkler from one thirsty patch to the next, swinging his artificial leg off-center to move sideways across the lawn, several times a day, all summer long. In a routine that became as familiar as other things of summer, Dad would unscrew the oscillating sprayer from its attached hose, without spraying himself in the process. Once disconnected, with sprinkler apparatus in hand, he'd make his way towards another water spigot around the side of the house, carefully lifting his prosthetic leg in an arc over the grass and repeating this as many times as necessary. Even without the automatic sprinkling system some of our other neighbors had, ours was always the prettiest and greenest lawn in the development of houses.

Staring at the grass underneath my feet, my tears were like the drops that had fallen from the hose my father had held in his hand. But he was gone now and someone else lived in that red house; perhaps they'd installed the automatic sprinkler that my parents had not. Looking up from the grass, I sniffed and wiped my eyes. Feeling a bit foolish, I spoke to him out loud.

"Oh, Daddy," I said. "Where are you?"

No one answered.

Eventually the sun began to sink behind a cedar elm in the distance, and I stood to walk back towards the house, wiping my eyes on the sleeve of the tee shirt I'd changed into after the funeral. It had the words US NAVY emblazoned on its front—a nod to my dad, a Navy man. Raising my face to the vast blue Texas sky above my house, I mused to myself, "Where *is* he, now?"

The concept of heaven as a real, tangible place, at that moment seemed as unlikely as the tooth fairy to me. I wondered how any of us fell for this fiction; it seemed unlikely that his soul could have hitched a ride to a place that had always sounded a little too good to be true. I envied people who truly believed in heaven, but it seemed something dreamed up to comfort the living, a silly fairy tale invented to cover the pointlessness of death. My lack of faith at that moment was extreme, and now I was angry.

"Where the *#@k do we *go*?" I asked the sky. "And what do I do now, without you?" Secretly, I wished he would send me a sign.

My dad would have known what to say, but he was gone and suddenly it seemed silly to be looking to the sky for answers when we weren't the sort to believe in "signs" and had clearly just buried him in the dirt, hours before. That's where he'd gone, *nowhere* else, I told myself. What a bunch of idiots we all were, concocting comforting fairy tales when the truth was simply that one day each of us would cease to exist. Period. End of story.

Abandoning previous thoughts of a soul able to 'rise' from a six-foot grave to a place beyond the skies, above one brick house or another, in Texas or anywhere else, I felt an unabridged sadness I'd never known before. Asking for some sort of 'sign' from my dad now seemed moronic. *Signs,* indeed, I thought. There are no signs.

So it had seemed to me then. But that evening, I hadn't yet seen the next day's newspaper, which would have been just going to press, as I'd stood barefoot in my yard looking at the sky. The next morning, in the light of a new day, I would consider the possibility that perhaps the skies had heard me after all.

I slept fitfully that night and woke the next morning to the day's newspaper, open at the foot of our bed. Richard had taken the sports section as usual and left the rest for me. I saw that the business section had been placed on top, which reminded me of a phone call I'd gotten from my parents on the morning that the front page had featured an article about me and my growing diamond business.

We'd known the story would run on an upcoming Sunday, but hadn't been told exactly which one. My parents had seen it before me and I'd answered the phone to hear them both practically screaming with excitement. Sharing one receiver, they'd been audibly ecstatic, simply beside themselves about the glowing two-page write-up, complete with photos of me, my jewelry and the glittering, glamorous store. To them, to be featured on the front page of the Business Section of the *Dallas Morning News* meant I had 'made it.'

I'd been plenty happy about the news of the article myself, but their joy could not be matched. They were practically screaming excerpts of it into the phone, to the point where I had to hold my phone away from my ear. I had been in a grocery store check-out line when they'd called, and I was sure that even people as far away as the produce section could hear. After a few minutes, they rang off, on their way to purchase multiple copies of the Sunday newspaper from various locations, to stockpile for anyone who might not have seen it. This also gave them the opportunity to show the article to anyone behind the counter of a bookstore or newsstand. "This is our daughter!" My mother must have repeated a dozen times that day.

I remembered this with fondness, gazing nostalgically at the business section on the morning after my dad's funeral. Suddenly a large color photo above an article caught my eye and looking closer, I realized why. It was a story about commercial real estate on Dallas' North Tollway, and right there in the center of the page was a photo with a bird's-eye view of three colorful billboards hovering over the city. Of all the miles of highway a photographer might have captured, I knew this location well. Right there in the middle of the photo was a billboard with my picture on it.

Looming large over the highway, it was the very same billboard under which my dear parents had sat, like dates at a drive-in movie, on the night it debuted. They'd gazed up at it with immeasurable pride, calling me from their car as evening fell, as they wanted to make sure the lights were working. My parents reported from their car that the gigantic billboard was now awash in light, their happy voices tripping over each other as usual.

"Honey girl, your Mother and I are SO PROUD!" My father's voice breaking with emotion. "Your gorgeous billboard! Your beautiful face! It's spectacular, Nomaluh! SPECTACULAR!" he'd said.

Gazing at the paper at the foot of my bed, I remembered the night before, when I'd sat in the backyard and asked for a sign. "How can I go on without you?" I had wondered out loud. I hadn't expected an answer, but now it seemed that I had gotten one.

Go With The Flow, the headline read in bold font, just above the photo of the billboard my parents had exclaimed over. I heard the words of the headline in my father's voice, repeating words he'd said to me many times. *"Sometimes you have to go with the flow, honeygirl,"* he'd say. *"And what will be will be."*

A chill came over me then, but I wasn't cold. *Oh, Daddy.* I thought. Perhaps my father could see me from above my billboard—my sign. Perhaps he had sent me a message from his perch above us all, leaving it for me front and center on his favorite page of the paper, the business section. A sudden image of him crossed my mind: with shoulders shrugged and palms lifted, I imagined him gesturing to the front-page photo of my billboard and saying, "You asked for a little sign, didn't you? Well technically, Nomeluh, it's a *LITTLE SIGN, eh?!"*

Oh, Daddy. *A little sign* indeed: my too-big billboard reduced to fit into a picture under a bold headline on his favorite page, proclaiming *Go With The Flow.* As always, here he was, giving me good advice.

TWENTY-NINE

Thinking routine might save me, I returned to work a week after my father's funeral. Opening the door to our studio and offices, everything looked exactly the same as it had a week before, which seemed impossible when so much was different. The familiar tone of the alarm system began its beep-beep-beeping, and I wondered if my usual passcode would disarm it. Perhaps the code had changed, too, with his death. After all, it had always been my father's birthday. I entered the code, prepared to enter the date of his death as a second option, just in case the universe had reset the passcode. But as usual, the alarm silenced.

Double-checking the door lock, I knew I was alone for the first hour of the day. This was my much-needed quiet time, when I'd typically make coffee for everyone and organize my desk and my thoughts, until I heard my father's key in the door. I knew his timing; walking on his artificial leg, it took him a bit longer to enter the 'mantrap,' the tile-floored area between our front and secondary doors, where he'd hang his cane on his arm for a moment to unlock the inner door. On my phone's speaker I could hear the sounds of his entry, and I always drew some comfort from the familiarity of the click-click sounds of his steps and the creak of the heavy door against his shoulder as he pushed it open to enter. Small routines that suddenly I longed for. Crossing the carpeted showroom towards my office, he'd typically peek into my open double-doors to see if I was on the phone, before greeting me with his usual "Nomeluh! Good morning sweetheart!"

He'd be laden with his briefcase, cane, lunch bag and files he'd brought home, but I knew better than to offer to help him. Often he'd set his briefcase down and fish out a newspaper article from my mother. "Your mother says you should read this," he'd say. Or sometimes: "I have no idea what this is, but your mother wanted you to call her to discuss; when you have time, of course," he'd say. Usually, whatever he brought was something of interest, or something I'd asked my mother for that she'd found and delivered as promised. It might have been a recipe, or an obituary I'd missed, or a list of family birthdays (though she'd remind me anyway with a phone call: "Honey, it's cousin Susie's birthday today so be sure to call her"). My parents' follow-up was typically impeccable; in so many ways, I counted on them to keep me on track.

A sound in the mantrap interrupted my thoughts and I turned my head suddenly, expecting for a split second to see my father. But it was just a magazine that had slid off one of the chairs in the sitting area. I knew he wasn't coming in.

If I could be alone all day, I could get through it, I thought. Without the added difficulty of conversing with others, I could survive my first day at work without him. But it was going to be a challenge to field others' heartfelt messages of condolence and hear their loving memories of my dad. I'd smile and thank each one for sharing, but by day's end I'd be weary from the effort.

A week's worth of unopened mail sat neatly stacked on my desk, waiting for me to go through it. I picked up a fat, padded envelope, seeing by the return address that it had come from the QVC offices in Pennsylvania. My royalty checks came in a windowed envelope, so I knew this was something different, and I sliced through the top of the small paper package to find a CD in a plastic case inside. A note slipped out, and I unfolded it to read:

Hello Naomi!

We thoroughly enjoyed our visit to Dallas, especially the day of filming with you, your staff, and your fabulous operation. All of you were so gracious, we felt right at home in Texas!

Please hug your darling parents for us. They were truly a highlight of our day of filming and both so very interesting and entertaining! Thought you'd enjoy the clips here of your father talking about your family's fascinating history. Your dad is quite remarkable—and fantastic on film, as you'll see here. Your father's narrative is so special I knew it was something you'd want to save. Enjoy!"

~Ellen

I stared at the disc in my hands and re-read the note. Opening my computer, I slipped the DVD into the slot and remembered something I'd said to my husband the night before. He'd seen me crying over a photo of my father laughing, and had come closer to comfort me.

"What if I forget his laugh?" I asked, looking up at Richard.

"You won't forget," he answered.

"But I might," I cried. "And...and...what if I forget his voice?" I said, choking on my tears and the very thought of this possibility. When Richard didn't answer right away, I noticed he had choked up, too.

After a moment he said, "You'll never forget his voice." But I wasn't so sure.

Now, I inserted the DVD from QVC into the computer, and suddenly the screen lit up with my father's sweet familiar face and his voice through the speakers—rich and resonant, his words chosen carefully as always. I caught my breath in surprise; here he was, visiting me right here at my desk, on the first day I knew he wouldn't be coming in. My heart swelled as I listened to my father telling bits of the family history; it was like hearing it anew, even though I knew much of it by heart. I hadn't been in the room when they were filming him, so this was something I hadn't heard before.

I'll be damned, I thought, staring into his eyes on the screen. It felt like he was speaking to me, telling me he would always be there for me. Parts of that interview today, are on my business website; a click on the 'Family History" section brings up a clip of my father, and I still visit occasionally, just to see his face and hear his voice.

That night, I was looking through some boxes of family photos when I found the photo of my father leaving Baylor Hospital after his heart transplant. Someone had snapped the photo just before we'd wheeled him out the double glass doors into the sunlight, and while I remembered that moment clearly, I'd forgotten the moment he'd been shaking his nurse's hand, looking up into her eyes and thanking her, taking her hand in both of his; my father's special way of shaking someone's hand.

I'd seen him do it countless times over the years. With a gentle gesture, he'd wrap his right hand around the other's hand, while his left hand came up to join the already-clasped hands, totem style. It was a sweet salute of sorts, one that somehow elevated whatever words he shared to a level of undeniable sincerity. I had recognized the handshake's effect on those he touched; sometimes, a person seemed taken aback by the unexpected delivery of such unconditional love, wrapped in something as common as a handshake. It was as if this small gesture opened up a portal to between his heart and theirs. "*It is my* great *pleasure, young lady, to have met you,*" he might have said, still holding their hand in both of his; he'd add, "*Indeed, truly my pleasure.*" And when he said it, you'd know he meant this unequivocally.

When a happy and satisfied customer left our showroom with a diamond bauble wrapped in our glittering paper, it was my father who'd come from his office near the door to bid them farewell, always with, "*Thank you for* honoring *us with your business,*" words meant so sincerely that even years after he'd gone, clients of mine would remember him and tell me how he'd touched them. I remember one woman in particular, with tears in her eyes, telling me how extraordinary my father was. She seemed distraught to hear that he'd died and by the way she gushed about him, I assumed she had known my father well so I was taken aback momentarily when she said, "I only met him that one time, but felt connected to him…"

This was the impression my father made on people. A consummate gentleman and a sweet, humble soul, my father had a genuine love for his fellow man that knew no bounds. This small handshake of his was as genuine as it was endearing and when I found the picture of my dad leaving the hospital, his special hand-shake frozen in time, I considered it like a note or a wink from my father. I had begun writing my book then so it felt a bit like my dad was looking over my shoulder. *"I never really thought about that handshake of mine Nomi, but I read what you wrote and I don't quite know what to say, sweetheart! It was only a handshake and I'm touched that anyone noticed!,"* I imagined him saying from heaven. Always so humble, he was.

Finding the photo, it was as if he had taken my smaller hand in one of his, and had gently folded his other hand on top, without needing to say anything at all. The warmth and love in that gentle gesture of his went straight to the very center of my heart—which is where, I would slowly begin to understand, he would always live on.

THIRTY

Long after I was remarried to Richard, we kept up the tradition of celebrating Thanksgiving at Rockport with the Casparys, Marissa's grandparents, on her father Cass's side. Six months after my father died, I brought my mother along for Thanksgiving at the Casparys; her first trip out of Dallas since Dad's passing and her first steps into a life without him. On the first morning after we arrived, she and I had laced on our walking shoes and met at the bottom of the stairs for a one-mile walk that had quite literally been her first walk-about in other ways, too.

Heading towards the bay, we walked through tall beach-grass swaying in the morning breeze, and I noticed tears in her eyes.

"Mom, are you okay?" I asked.

I knew how much she missed my father—her soulmate—but she told me her tears were not sad ones. It was the glory of the morning that had brought her to tears. The sound of the bay waves, the sand under our city feet, the rising pink sun, and the unmistakable scent of the ocean, all had taken her breath away.

In her typical animated tenor, she declared, "Oh my, Naomi! There are whole parts of the world just waiting!"

"Yes there are, Mom," I answered. "And you will see them."

With this, I watched her take her first steps into the future, through a low fog of sadness, stepping towards whatever lay ahead.

True to form, after that morning, I don't remember her speaking of being sad or being held back by heartache or by grieving for my father. Her positivity had inspired me then, and still did, now that she, too, was gone. In spite of my inability to emulate her confidence, I liked to think that my parents were having a heavenly Thanksgiving together this year; along with my grandparents and all their loved ones, whose voices had once rung around our holiday tables. I missed them all, desperately, and now she, too, was gone....

Richard and I spent our first Thanksgiving without Mom with the Casparys in Rockport. Arriving at the Corpus Christi airport for the 40-minute drive to Rockport, the low-hanging clouds matched my spirits, but I was determined to try to avoid moping. Marissa would be arriving from Dallas that evening, and I wanted to have food in our rental house, so, dropping Richard at the house, I headed to the local grocery store for provisions. It was a relief to enter the cool air of the grocery store, but as usual, the aisles of food reminded me of my mother. A self-proclaimed 'foodie,' my mother celebrated good food and spoke of it amorously. 'Simply *gorgeous* vegetables, *plump, fat, fresh* turkeys, *beautiful* baked goods'...her use of superlatives was always in high gear when describing the bounty of any season. I sighed, rolling my cart up and down the aisles, where shelved items on both sides spoke to me of her.

Oh, I adore fresh figs! Is that a new sort of quinoa?! she'd have exclaimed. In a market bursting with holiday fare, the memory of her lurked around every corner. My positive attitude slipping away, I neared the cold cases stocked with the butcher's choicest cuts for the holiday. I remembered that I'd never pinned my mother down on the exact recipe for her famous brisket—and now it was too late. So, *step away from the brisket, Naomi,* I said to myself; sure that I couldn't look at that particular cut of meat without tearing up. *Scared of a brisket, eh?* I thought to myself. My, how far I had fallen.

Since my Mom had been gone, even eyeing a clever or an interesting new food item could be painful, because I knew I could no longer rush to the phone to tell her about it. My mother had been the self-proclaimed queen of 'new products;' one such find could make her day, and the excitement of sharing it with others made her *week.* Often, an alluring new food item necessitated trips to multiple stores, to stockpile as many of said item as she could find, especially if freezing for future use was an option.

My trip through Rockport's grocery store was proving to be just the place to pick up a good case of holiday blues—just in time for Thanksgiving. Cheerlessly pushing my cart, sulking and pining for my mother, I was preparing to turn down another aisle when a commotion caught my eye. An unusual number of shoppers surrounded a refrigerator case full of foil-wrapped honey-baked hams. Coming closer, I saw an adjoining case featuring other frozen Thanksgiving fare: bags of prepared yams, containers of corn pudding, green-bean casserole, stuffing and one or two other side dishes. Bold signage read: 6 FREE SIDES WITH PURCHASE. This explained the gathering frenzy. Every bit my mother's daughter, and no fool for a freebie, I approached the crowd gathered shoulder-to-shoulder around the case, and wedged myself between two women with their heads leaning into the cold case.

With the purchase of a spiral-sliced ham came a jackpot of complimentary accompaniments, and suddenly my gloom lifted considerably. Because nobody can squeeze into a crowd of ham-grabbers like a petite Jew, I maneuvered my cart between two taller shoppers, the women leaning into the cold case far enough to get a good case of freezer burn. Locking my mitts around an ample sliced ham like a steel claw in a carnival game, I lifted and deposited a five-pound beauty into my waiting basket, all gleaming gold foil, reflecting the fluorescent lighting like a giant pork-jewel. After hooking the ham, I grabbed the free sides, plucking them as easy as taking candy from a baby. One after the other, like balls through a hoop, I tossed into my cart cornbread stuffing, cranberry sauce, green bean casserole, and frozen peas and pearl onions, where they settled in nicely, all of them nestled around the mother ham. I was in and out, wheeling away from the free-for-all in record time, possibly leaving miniature tire skid-marks, as if I'd just robbed the local ham-bank.

In my peripheral vision, I could see the women who had filled my spot now actively fishing for the free side items I'd seized in under ten seconds. As I proudly eyed my five free sides, it hit me: Oopsie, I was missing one.

Free or not, there was no way I was voluntarily going back into that feeding frenzy. I remembered seeing the packages of grits, but at this point I made the executive decision to forgo them. My mother had adored grits, but they were not mandatory for Thanksgiving, so I wasn't breaking tradition. Grateful for my booty—even *sans* free grits—I headed towards the checkout, my spirits ascending as I reflected that my mother would have been pleased as punch about my FIVE freebies, for no one had loved a deal like she had. Would she have gone back for the grits, I wondered, frowning at the thought. *Had I given up too soon? Oh stop, Naomi*, I thought; *be grateful you're the next in line.*

So grits be damned, with my dear mother full-frontal in my mind, I placed my selections on the moving belt of the check-out counter where a young lady began to scan my purchases, and hand them off to another young lady standing beside her, who expertly bagged them. They were a good tag-team.

"Do you have any coupons?!" the smiling checker asked.

"No I'm sorry, I don't," I said; repressing the urge to blurt out something inane like: *"I have no coupons. I also have no mother and no father so keep your grits...I'm an orphan!"*

I was thinking absently about how my mother would have pulled an envelope of collected coupons from her purse, when the checker suddenly said to me sharply, *"Ma'am, you're missin' your grits,"* speaking as seriously as if she'd said: You're missing your pants, ma'am.

"Really, it's okay," I said. Wondering if my response had been effectual enough, other possibilities crossed my mind, like: *Most of us in my family are deathly allergic to grits. Or: We're Jewish so we can't eat grits with ham.* But I ended up going with "I didn't see them," a boldfaced lie. Since I was on a fibber's roll, I added, "It looked like you were out of them." The minute it was out of my mouth I regretted I'd said it, as I imagined someone sent to a cavernous storeroom for backstock—or worse, to a refrigerated warehouse a block away—finally returning with a case of grits, glistening with ice crystals while all of our frozen sides would have thawed.

"Really, I'm okay without the grits," I said. "Honestly, I don't need...I mean, we don't really *do* grits at Thanksgiving...." I stammered. *Did someone in line behind me just gasp, over 'no grits at Thanksgiving'?* As if I thought we were *too good* or too citified to stoop to something as 'down home' as grits? *Well la-de-da, fancy Miss Dallas...Excuse us for offering!*

But as it turned out, this was not the problem. The problem was that *six free sides* meant SIX, not FIVE. End of story. You'd have thought a buzzer would go off as I'd exited with my missing side. *Ma'am, step aside, we're gonna have to check your bags.*

"*Oh no, ma'am,*" the checker said; I noticed her expression had darkened considerably, her cheerful smile replaced by a serious look of concern.

"*You* have *to have your grits, ma'am,*" she said, her brow knitted. I could think of no response for this, as the man behind the woman next in line tapped his foot and leaned on his basket like he'd just reached exhaustion.

"It's fine. Really," I said.

Apparently it was not. I considered bribery: *I'll pay you to keep your grits!*

But the checker spoke again. "*You* have *to have them,*" she said. "It's *SIX* free items."

She turned to her assistant, and the bagger-girl spun on her heels, heading fearlessly back in the direction of the traffic jam around the hams. God bless her. Now painfully aware that the whole checkout line was halted due to my missing grits, I did that thing you do when you don't know what else to do, which was to begin jabbering about one thing or another, to fill the awkward void. With my Mom on my mind, she was the easiest subject to grab and go with.

"As a matter of fact, my mother used to loooove grits," I said. Was further clarification necessary? "I mean, she didn't *stop* loving them," I added. "It's just that she passed away last year...."

"Oh, I'm so sorry about that," the checker said, frowning. I welcomed any response, to fill the minutes painfully ticking by. The woman behind me had lifted her head, as if the death of my mother mildly interested her, but I silently hoped she would not comment. My whole focus was now fixated on exiting the store.

"Yup, my mother used to do a garlic cheese version of them that was to die for." This came out of my mouth as if of its own accord as I tapped my foot nervously, hyper-aware that there were now people *behind* the woman and the man behind me; the line was now six or seven carts deep, curving around to the left while the other checkout line went to the right.

"Full of butter, of course," I said, rolling my eyes at the reference to the pools of melted butter (not to mention the cheese) atop my mother's garlic-cheese grits. I was shocked that these thoughts were escaping my mouth unaided, and willed myself to stop speaking. *For God's sake, be quiet, Naomi,* I said to myself fiercely, the music you hear when time is running out on a game show, now playing in my head.

Hurry up, hurry up, hurry up, I was chanting to myself. Now, even the other folks in line were straining their necks to look for the bag-girl, all of us united in rooting for her return. I halfway expected everyone to cheer when she finally came into sight. I could hear my mother loud and clear in my mind, and the way she'd have recounted the story. *Why, the entire store practically ceased operation for my grits to be located!*

Her version of the events, in her signature style, would have been much more interesting than mine. Standing there, I knew my mother would have been delighted with this entire episode, and would have exaggerated certain details in her telling of it, but then no one could tell a story like she could. *Ahhhh, Momma,* I sighed, suddenly realizing that in a way, I had just done my annual pre-holiday trip to the grocery store *with my mother,* after all. And with this thought I smiled.

Finally, the young lady who'd gone on the search-and-rescue mission for my free grits returned with the elusive box clutched in her hands like a Thanksgiving Day football. She came from somewhere in the bowels of the store, practically running the box like a touchdown pass as she neared the now ridiculously long line. Making her way to the front, she stumbled only slightly as she neared the checkout stand, tossing it in a split-second save to the checker, who raised both arms to receive it and brought it in.

In a sweep of sheer scanning greatness, this young lady swiped, scanned and bagged the package of grits in what appeared to be one smooth move. I handed her my credit card, thanking God above that I did automatic bill pay online, as a card decline at this point was almost too painful to imagine. I signed my name in one straight line with a loop in it—nowhere near any actual signature of mine—but it worked.

"Thank you and have a nice Thanksgiving!" I heard, halfway expecting those in line behind me to cheer. Having just witnessed teamwork at its true best, the checker and bag girl in perfect synch with one another, I felt 'thankful' in whole new ways.

This kind of seemingly meaningless minutia of one's day was exactly the stuff that my mother could—and did—skillfully elevate into something more interesting than it was. What might for others have been fifteen minutes of annoyance at the grocery checkout stand, for my mother would have been a hilarious sequence of events worth telling. I was thinking about this as I smiled at the two employees and looked at their name tags. I always liked to thank someone by name, a habit I'd picked up from my father. *No sound is sweeter to anyone,* he'd said, *than the sound of their own name.*

At a glance at the large name-tags pinned to the red shirts of my 'dream team'—the checker-girl and her quarterback, the bag-girl—made me literally do a double-take.

Their names were: NAOMI and SANDI—the same names as me and my mother!

Wondering if anyone would believe this, I sputtered in astonishment, "C-c-could I t-take your picture? The t-two of you?"

The long line of people was momentarily invisible, as the two of them obliged, arm in arm, smiling widely: Naomi and Sandi. I snapped the picture of the two of them. "I'm Naomi, you see, and my mom's name was Sandy...." Fearing stoning from those waiting in line, I left the store smiling.

Arriving at the car with my bags of bounty, it seemed that the air had cleared some since I'd been inside. The cloud-cover had lifted, and a faint bay breeze passed by. I felt sure that though my mother was gone, the pith of her remained. It was there in her love of certain foods; in her joy in discovering a fabulous new edible item or bargain; in the memory of all the beautiful Thanksgivings she'd made for us. It was there, most especially, in her ability to find humor in the ordinary, and then to weave it into a story, always having a last witty word to say or comment to add.

Loading the bags into the car, I spotted the all-important package of grits sitting at the top of one of the bags, noting the words in big bold letters just below the brand name: ALIVE WITH FLAVOR! Mom, is that you? I smiled.

The memory of her was standing there beside me and would have been buckling her seatbelt as I came around to my side of the car after tucking our bags of frozen freebies into the back seat. I was headed down a country road together with the memory of her; though she was gone, *she was still with me*, just as sure as the clouds above us were beginning to clear. Through the half-open car window, a welcome bay breeze blew my hair. A warm whisper of wind that was *her* said quite clearly in my ear: *I may be gone from this earth, but dammit I know a fabulous food find when I see one!*

THIRTY-ONE

M y mom's excitement about a new food product was best when shared, even if it required a trip to the store—or multiple stores—to procure enough of a favorite item to share with all of us. My mother's 'extreme need to share' had been in full swing once over a product called "Ozeery Breakfast Rounds," a breakfast item she discovered and for which she immediately became the self-appointed spokesperson. She'd come across the circular multi-grain muffins—which were flat, to fit in a toaster—and had fallen for them hard and fast. Chock-full of raisins, chunks of apple or nuggets of sweet dates, she'd found these buns to be so good that they'd prompted her quest for enough back stock as would fit in her freezer.

After cleaning out her neighborhood grocer's supply of Ozeery Breakfast Rounds, my mother traveled to various other grocery stores in the North Dallas area to find that they had bagels, muffins and the usual breakfast fare but *not* Ozeery Breakfast Rounds. Frustrated in her search for these tasty treats, my mother had at least four or five of us on high alert for them, and I could scarcely believe my eyes when one day, lo and behold, I stumbled upon them and froze in my tracks (as if they might suddenly disappear): *Ozeery Breakfast Rounds,* in all three flavors, at a Whole Foods store by my home. Expecting to hear angels sing as they came into view, I could barely believe my eyes! As if someone else might swoop in and grab them before I could, I looked right and then left before ducking down to make the call to my Mom, reporting the find. This was big.

Hearing the ring of my mom's phone, I cupped my hand to the side of my mouth, directing my voice into my cell phone so that no one within earshot could hear what I was about to reveal. She answered on the second ring and, I, taking a breath, delivered the big news.

"Mom," I whispered with repressed excitement. "I found them!"

"Found what, dear?" she said.

I couldn't believe it. Had she drunk too much metabolic weight-loss breakfast tea? (This was another 'must-have' product she'd absolutely insisted I try, stuffing several teabags in my purse on a recent visit. A week or so later, I hadn't had the heart to tell her it had given me diarrhea.)

"Found what? Are you kidding me, Mom?" I said. "I found the **Ozeery Breakfast Rounds!**" I said, in the same serious tone I'd have used to deliver a statement like: "I discovered a cure for cancer!"

There was silence.

Maybe she was holding her breath; or pausing to allow this truth to sink in. Perhaps she thought I was joking, and she'd quieted to wait for the punch line—but none was coming. This was the real deal. True, we were a family of jokers, but I would not jest about this. Perhaps she'd paused just to savor the moment: the moment her eldest daughter had found the world's greatest breakfast item, as usual doing my utmost to satisfy her every whim or wish.

Finally, surrounded by buns and bread, I heard her voice. She responded none too soon, as I saw other shoppers turning down my aisle and feared they might be breakfast-bun consumers, too.

"YOU FOUND THEM?" Her voice quivered. "WHERE?"

She sounded on the verge of tears, tears of breakfast joy.

"At Whole Foods," I whispered, as if my location were a secret, though anyone within earshot knew where I was because they were there too. And you'd think I'd said, "The North Pole" rather than "Whole Foods'—as if I'd located them at such an unlikely place that it had been complete serendipity. *A grocery store of all places!* To her it was an absolute stroke of luck or genius, as she had been searching the same stores herself, with no success. All of this became part of her story. As she'd say later, "Well, I tell you, they simply just appeared there! Naomi nearly rolled right past them!" The story of the search and the find would become a decent tale to tell, spun by the queen of turning nothing into something.

I had made her day and I knew it. I heard her sniffling on the other end of the phone.

"Mom. Don't cry. I'm going to get them for you, don't worry. (Turns out she had allergies and wasn't actually crying.) "How many packages do you want?" I asked her.

At this, I received my marching orders. "Get them ALL," she said, her voice low and gravelly, sounding like someone possessed by the gluten-devil, whose head might have been spinning around on its shoulders as she talked. She was crazed with the find.

I knew better than to argue about the practicality of mass quantities of perishable items with my mother, especially in the midst of such an emotion-filled moment. Hence, I began shooting the forty-eight to fifty packages I lifted from the shelf into my cart, an armful at a time. I wished I'd opted for a larger basket, but if my luck held, they'd all fit—which, with a little finagling, they did.

Keeping my head low and looking in all directions, I saw that, thankfully, no one had noticed the hoarder on Aisle Six. I'd intentionally left four or five packages of Ozeery's on the shelf (a truth I would never, ever tell my mother), and in a flash I mixed them in with packages of Mrs. Baird's buns and Sara Lee's English muffins, to cover the gaping empty spaces where the missing Ozeery's had been. If I must say so myself, this bit of free merchandising on my part looked as good as new.

Doing a complete 180 with my cart, I headed to the check-out, mission almost accomplished. I had cash in my wallet, but this purchase was going to require credit. While I was digging in my wallet for my Mastercard, I noticed a woman in line in front of me curiously observing the mountain of muffins in my cart. Her raisin-eyed stare unsettled me, and—sensing her antennae go up—I could not be sure where this was headed. With rising heart rate, I attempted to look as nonchalant as possible, mindfully slowing my breath, keeping my eyes on the prize.

Why was she so interested in the contents of my cart, anyway? I wondered. Was there a limit on number of packages or had I maneuvered into the express lane by accident? A quick look at the signage confirmed that I was not, thank goodness, in the express line—but if I had been, now so close to accomplishing my mission, I might have gone so far as to have feigned ignorance or confusion, claiming I thought the "15 items" sign meant "15 dozen." That's the mode I was in.

"Oh my!" said the woman, staring at my cart.

Oh, dough-balls, she's speaking to me.

"Wow, those things must be VERY good!" she exclaimed. "Is there some sort of special pricing on them today?" she asked, one eyebrow cocked.

Oh God, a coupon clipper, I thought. *Roll along, lady. The muffins are mine.*

My loyalty to my mother rising above any sense of shame, I heard myself tell a bold-faced lie to this complete stranger. "No, they're not very good at all really, but I get them for my mother because they're the only thing she can eat now," I said, these complete untruths coming out of my mouth before I could stop them. And as if theatrics were needed, I delivered this 'overstatement' with an expression of sadness, as if my mother had some condition whereby only baked goods could be tolerated. What a life; my poor mother, cruelly condemned to existence on nothing but bread.

"Uh-huh," the woman said in a skeptical sort of tone. "Well… they look rather nice, actually!" she said. Don't bother looking lady, I thought to myself, these muffins are mine. Grabbing a magazine, I paged through it in order to avoid more conversation and in a few moments, thankfully, the woman paid for her groceries and left. My Ozeerys were safe.

I unloaded them, a few packs at a time, onto the moving belt. Once all 50 or so of them were scanned, bagged and paid for, I rolled the cart out of the store and to my car at a frenzied pace, excited to deliver the goods to my mom; who I now pictured sticking her head out her front door to watch for me. I was high on the find, and the first thing I did when I got into my car was to call my mother; to let her know I was on my way.

Before calling, I had stuffed part of an Ozeery Breakfast Round with raisins and apples into my mouth, so. "Maawm?" is what I sounded like when she answered, but she knew it was me. "Sorry Mom." (I swallowed hard here.)

"Hi," I began again. "I got a few dozen," I said, accidentally spitting a bit of a sunflower seed as I said it. I couldn't hear her response at first; there was some sort of loud background noise on her end.

"What? Mom?" I asked. "I can't hear you. What are you doing?"

"Oh, sorry, hon," my mom said cheerfully, the noise in the background ceasing momentarily. "I'm rearranging my freezer to make room." Visions of my mother force-defrosting tubs of spaghetti sauce filled my mind; leftovers sacrificed for the good of the muffins.

"Come over right away, dear," she said, and hung up.

I'd actually been on my way anyway, but tearing off a piece of a second breakfast round and chewing away happily, I texted Richard to tell him I'd be a little late. Soon, I knew, my mother would be busy, happily giving away 'samples' of the muffins to all her neighbors at the senior living facility where she resided; the smell of toasted multi-grain muffins permeating the hallways as she cheerily shared the story of how she'd come by these treasures.

"Well, my daughter, Naomi—you know Naomi—she's the famous jewelry designer—well, anyway, Naomi found these when they were simply impossible to find anywhere in the city!" she'd say.

She had the ability to find joy in the simplest things. I have always thought that my favorite quote, by the great writer Roald Dahl, applied to her more than anyone else I knew: "For those who do not believe in magic shall never find it." My mother believed in magic wholeheartedly; and more than that, she could make you believe, too. I learned from her that though one might not see the magic at first glance, later, in the telling, it would become clear.

PART FOUR

SOMEWHERE OVER THE RAINBOW

THIRTY-TWO

Nearly a year after my mother died, and four years after I'd lost my father, I was still immobilized by grief. Other than seeing the occasional client I thought I couldn't avoid, I had become a sad version of myself, and a master in the covert 'Art of Doing Nothing,' sometimes staying in bed much of the day. At least I did 'nothing' well, I reasoned.

For, like my mother, if I were going to do a thing I wanted to do it *right*; 'doing as little as possible' was no exception. As her daughter, I'd perfected a routine allowing me to function in the hours my husband was home, or when my daughter Marissa might come by, while doing as little as possible in the interim. I knew that after Richard left each morning there would be hours before he came home; I'd only need an hour to shower, dress and concoct a list of the things I had supposedly done that day—which was not as easy as it sounds because the goings-on I'd claim had to be believable. Dinners could be ordered in easily enough, and dry cleaning delivered, but by the time Richard returned from his office, I'd have gone to great lengths to cover my inability to have done anything productive during the day. Every night before I fell asleep, I'd swear the next day would be different; but come the morning all bets would be off. I'd do it again.

I'd wake with a crushing weight I could not get out from under, telling myself that I'd just lie there for one more hour. And then the hour would become two and then three; as my little dog—my constant companion—nestled into me like an attached appendage. I'd wake sometimes, and reason to myself that if I moved I'd wake her, so I'd purposely stay in one position and fall asleep again. It was a dog's life but only one of us was enjoying it.

Work was easy enough to avoid with my capable assistant, Francesca, covering for me. Tall, pretty and impossibly brilliant, Fran had been summa cum laude at Dallas' SMU, and had headed to New York to become a rising superstar in the investment business. Happily crunching numbers in the second tower of the World Trade Center, Fran had 'escaped' on 9-11, returning to Dallas, but she could not run from the periodic emotional meltdowns one might expect after surviving an atrocity in which thousands of others had perished. Fran understood the sort of emotional coma I'd slipped into and I depended on her. But there was only so much that others could do in a business that revolved around having its designer— me—at the center of things.

Eventually I moved my business phone line to a desk in our apartment, and let the answering machine take messages. After a while, I stopped checking the messages each day and became less concerned about who was calling me 'at work.' Since *work* was now just a phone in our apartment, it was easier to forget about it. Francesca started her own business, and I decided not to renew the lease on my now-too-large office space. In just a few months' time, I downsized a business once dubbed one of the 'fastest growing in Dallas' to a phone on a desk. At some level, I felt as if I'd escaped from the shackles of a business that had consumed me; whereas once I'd loved every minute of it, now I couldn't seem to remember those days.

It would be years before I'd admit to anyone, even my husband, that I finally turned off the phone's ringer, so the customers' calls went to a voicemail I didn't care to check. The only good of it was that even in the deepest days of my grieving, I could still chuckle to myself as I'd pass the living room 'office,' with the phone that now 'rang' inside the wall jack. Like the great and powerful Oz behind a curtain, the veiled screen of the once-great Naomi Designs had been pulled back to reveal nothing but a ringer-less phone. I figured if one day I decided to write a book on downsizing, it would be short and sweet, my sage advice encapsulated in a single line: *Unplug the phone.*

No doubt people had been leaving me messages like: *Naomi, this is the third message I've left. I'm starting to think you don't want my business....* But I didn't care. The person I had been was no longer there. I was out to lunch until further notice. I simply could not stomach one more person distraught over a crooked earring, or concerned about a ring turning her finger black. Jewelry was trivial, and a short-term allergy to an alloy was not a dreaded disease. Since my mother had gone, I could no longer interest myself in such petty matters. She was the one who had made everything *matter*.

My shame was that I knew others who'd lost parents, who'd managed to put one foot in front of the other and continue moving through life. But somehow I couldn't. My inability to function appalled me and I knew my parents would have been disappointed in my failure to thrive—but knowing this didn't help. I had fallen into a cycle that repeated itself day after day and because sleeping all day did not make for restful nights, I'd often lie awake in the dark while my husband slept. During the day, ruminating thoughts exhausted me enough for yet another 'nap,' and I'd lie on my back and think about people I knew who had lost children or limbs, suffering unimaginable tragedies and yet still finding the will to survive and even thrive; but I couldn't seem to do it myself. I was ashamed of the pitiful, sad version of my former self that I'd become.

At least I could give myself credit for one small daily feat: at 4:45 each day I showered, dressed, and at 5:30 p.m. greeted my husband at the elevator that opened into our glamorous apartment, with a smile and a full face of make-up.

"Hi, Hon!" I'd say, sometimes adding a tidbit like, "Woo! What a day!" for authenticity. It was as if I'd become a pretend version of myself. Despite my misery, I'd greet Richard at the door with a lip-sticked smile, blushing cheeks and a sweep of mascara. Even in the worst of circumstances, *never* would I have shown up barefaced, as this, I felt certain, would have been a dead giveaway. Presenting oneself in the best possible light was simply what one *did*, under any circumstances. After all, I was my mother's daughter.

My husband had some idea of what I was going through, but he didn't know how to comfort me. Besides, I never let on how badly I was struggling, so he followed my lead and acted normally, while I suffered mostly in silence. I knew that my siblings missed our parents too, but it seemed to me that both of them were 'carrying on' better than I was.

No one said the word "depression." Even though all sorts of depression had run in my family for generations, somehow I never considered that I might be in the thick of it. Pure, unadulterated grief was what I believed it to be, as I'd never had a loss comparable to the loss of my parents. I was waiting for it to fade, but so far nothing had changed. I was—in a word—pathetic.

In my lowest and loneliest moments, I'd reach for a book. My thoughts seemed scattered most of the time and I moved in what felt like slow motion; some days only from my bed to the couch, dragging a book. I could not focus on simple tasks and didn't care to do much of anything, but reading was the exception. As always, I could get lost in a book and forget, even though I'd often have to wipe my eyes in order to see the words on the page. I could see the traces of where fat, wet, teardrops had dried into sad circles on previous pages, like pitiful little bookmarks marking my progress through the book.

My mother and I had shared books, giving each other 'teasers' and previews with the hand-off of each one. "Oh Mom, you are going to *love* this book!" I'd say after I finished one. "Naomi, promise you'll read this next. I'm dying to talk with you about it!" she'd say.

We were a book club of two but since our exclusive reading circle had shrunken to one, I'd been choosing the books myself without her input and one genre in particular—Memoir—had become my go-to. Evidenced by the stacks of memoirs rising atop my bedside table, fiction or mystery held no interest for me. On the days that I could focus, I needed to read a *real* story, one with a triumphant ending, which assured me that happiness was actually possible, in real life. No fantasies or cliffhangers would do; there was plenty enough mystery in a life ahead without my parents. I imagined myself in some kind of holding pattern, just waiting for a new normal to set in. In each memoir, I found flickers of hope, based on others' triumphs over tragedy or hardship; so I pored through dozens of them, sure that the answers I sought lay somewhere hidden in the stories of the struggles of others.

One night, in the dark, I rolled over and came eye-to-eye with a favorite framed picture of my parents, illuminated by moonlight. I cried quietly, not wanting to wake my husband. The next morning I removed my parents' pictures from various spots in the house so I wouldn't think of them each time I passed. I knew I'd never see their smiling faces again, and it was too soon to look at their images and smile, so I considered this a precautionary measure. Rather than pretty pictures of deceased relatives, I kept only books beside my bed; books that I read religiously, with the faith that one of them would 'save me.'

Eventually it began to look like I'd created a homemade holy place on a two-foot tabletop; building high stacks of dog-eared book-temples that I could enter. My nightstand was my village of sadness, where paperback skyscrapers teetered above a city of coffee cup rings and neon highlighter pens. It seemed to me that right there by my bed sat a crossroads where my two worlds intersected: life without my parents crossing all that used to be. Thinking that I might read my way to salvation, I became a memoir-junkie, inhaling others' memories. When all else seemed lost, I was encouraged to find that I could still swell to a gripping tale of a hero's journey. I hoped that somewhere in the words of one of my favorite authors, I would find myself.

Dozens of memoirs later, I was facing the one-year anniversary of my mother's death and didn't feel any sort of shift in my feelings of loss. I had, however, begun to detect a tipping point in the memoirs of others I'd read; a place in the book where the struggle shifted ever so slightly, or an answer began to reveal itself. In these moments, when the writer suddenly sees a small light up ahead in the dark, I'd breathe a sigh of relief and hold a kernel of hope that someday I would begin to see a light, too.

Halfway through a bold memoir I was reading one day, I recognized the name of an actual *place* where such a shift had occurred and it caught my attention because, coincidentally, I'd read about the same place in a different memoir, just a week earlier. The authors and their stories had been unrelated, but both of them had written about the same place: a yoga retreat called *Kripalu* where truths had been revealed to each of them, albeit in different ways. A week or two later, wide-eyed after reading about Kripalu in yet a third memoir (all three authors totally unrelated), it seemed more than just a coincidence. By the *fourth* mention of Kripalu in yet another book, I decided to Google it.

On Kripalu's website, sprawling green hills framed by snow-capped mountains appeared in glorious splendor across the screen. I'd never heard of *The Kripalu Institute for Extraordinary Living*, but in an instant, I decided to go there. For the past year, I'd had difficulty making decisions, but I had no hesitation about Kripalu. I thought that if nothing else, perhaps I would stumble upon my own tipping point at such a place.

Looking through the site, I read about Kripalu's weekend yoga immersions, soulful spiritual retreats, and healing workshops. I had been increasingly aware of the approaching date that would mark the one-year anniversary of my mother's death and had been dreading it, so I decided this would be as good a day as any to transport myself to Kripalu. At least it would be a new place to cry or a different bed in which to hide beneath the covers. I scrolled down the Kripalu event calendar to the anniversary of my mom's death and saw a picture of a face I recognized from the back of a book cover: a pretty blonde woman with pale eyes, a half-smile and a familiar last name, *Shapiro,* which I recognized from the book spines next to my bed. I had devoured her memoirs with intense interest, so it seemed like kismet to learn that she would be holding a workshop on 'the art of writing memoir' on the anniversary of my mom's passing. I'd especially related to Dani Shapiro's eloquent writings about her deceased father; I hadn't imagined that anyone else could miss their father as much as I missed mine, but her ability to bring him to life on the page made me dare to imagine that through writing, maybe I could bring my parents back too.

I pulled my credit card from my wallet and booked my stay at Kripalu before I even knew where in the world it was. After dinner, Richard and I went online to look at airfares. With the click of a keyboard, I had a ticket and would be headed to Hartford, Connecticut in just two weeks' time. Before we booked the trip, the days ahead on my calendar had been empty squares with numbers in them and little hope for any activities to be penciled in. Now they were filled with a countdown to Kripalu. I began to imagine rubbing literary elbows with other lost souls like me, who wanted to write of their pain. I imagined we'd bond as writers and friends, and in planning my trip, brooding thoughts of my lost parents gave way to new visions of my soon-to-be yogi-sisters; new friends and new hope in a place called 'the Berkshires.'

I hadn't moved mountains; but at least I was out of bed. Suddenly there was so much to do! My frozen brain began to thaw enough to think about the yoga clothes I would need for a place like Kripalu. I booked various appointments to have my hair highlighted, my nails done and a long-overdue pedicure, all things that I had once done on auto-pilot, but had let slide for months. Familiar necessities and high-ranking priorities in my previous life, I was pleased to find that my ability to accomplish these mindless tasks came back to me like riding a bike; I would check them off my list with a flick of a wrist. I didn't know if I'd write successfully, or if I would find yoga as healing as others did, but if nothing else, at least I was determined to *look* the part when I arrived at Kripalu.

THIRTY-THREE

It might not have been the same sort of 'out-of-body' experience I'd heard others describe, but still it seemed somewhere on the spectrum of such a thing. From the back seat of the silver sedan I rode in, I knew I hadn't hovered above the vehicle as a vaporous, airborne version of myself, able to peer through the rain-streaked windows to see myself sitting slump-shouldered in the back seat, wearing dark glasses. If it had been the real deal—a true body-exiting—I supposed I would have observed the driver of the sedan from a vantage point other than the back seat, where I now had a clear view of his constant fidgeting with the rear view mirror and tuning of the radio dial; both of which were becoming increasingly irritating to me. From where I sat—now back in my body—I wished he'd focus on the winding road and pay more attention to driving through the storm. I could see that the hard rain had slowed but not entirely ceased.

Whether it had or had not been a standard sort of an out-of-body experience, I felt a definite sensation of *coming back to myself,* except that I could not remember having been faced with the sort of formidable decision others have described: making the choice between drifting further and further away, or returning to the confines of my skin and bones. No such options had been extended to me; which may have been for the best, as if I had had the possibility of choosing: a) returning to my 50-year-old skin or b) opting for a one-way ticket to the heavens where I assumed my beloved parents were, I might well have chosen the latter.

So I knew I hadn't 'left' myself but still it felt like the blood rushing back to a limb you've sat on too long, as if, with a *whoosh*, I'd rushed back into myself. Technically I knew how I'd gotten into the back seat of that car, but it was more of a vague recollection than a clear or recent memory. Looking at my lap, I had no recollection of buckling my seatbelt, and wondered why I was so thirsty. Had I been only slightly dry-mouthed at the airport and decided not to grab a bottle of water before meeting the car in which I now found myself riding? Or had I slept through drinks I'd been offered on the flight?

Suddenly shivering in spite of the car's heater, I pulled my jacket collar up around my neck and was glad to be a passenger in the car rather than the driver, especially considering the rain. The deluge had slowed to a drizzle, but the road remained wet, so I hoped my driver was taking special care. I'd had enough of a rough ride on the aircraft, as it lurched and shuddered through the storm. A series of long lunges and wild plummets aggravated our approach to the airport, and a hard but safe landing in the rain storm had elicited clapping and cheers from the grateful souls on board. I was hoping for an uneventful ride to Kripalu.

Although once upon a time a flight like that would have petrified me, I now recalled that the extreme turbulence towards the end of the flight had not bothered or frightened me. I'd been a phobic flyer for decades but had finally overcome my fear of flying a few years before. Now my fear of a rough flight was gone...just like my parents were gone. That was how things were, it seemed: going, going, gone. Most recently, I seemed to be losing my short-term memory. But my grief still stuck to me like glue. I had not been able to shake it. As usual, as soon as I thought of my parents, my eyes filled with tears that I had no power to stop.

I missed my parents desperately. This great grief had set up shop in my soul, leaving less room for more recent memories and causing confusion about where I'd been or what I'd done on a given day. I had not just 'awakened' in the back seat of a moving car, and had some awareness of the turbulence I'd flown through to get here, yet I could not remember what seat I'd been in on the plane, or if I'd had a drink. Had I searched the clouds outside the aircraft window for a glimpse of the heaven where I assumed my beloved parents now resided? Had I fogged the small window with my breath and wiped a fallen tear from its surface before closing the shade? Or had I been seated on the aisle, where I'd silently chastised the passenger beside me for snoring?

I wasn't sure how long we'd been driving and yet I was aware that the driver had been adjusting and readjusting his rear-view mirror since we'd begun the trip. I wished he would find an acceptable angle and return his eyes to the road; and I hoped that his fiddling with the mirror was not meant to connect our views of each other so as to encourage conversation. Friendly conversation seemed almost as difficult and treacherous as the rain-washed road. Lately I'd been having difficulty speaking without crying, so I was relieved when the driver's hand went from the mirror back to the steering wheel. For both my safety and my sanity, I wanted him to just concentrate on the road.

Through my window I could see a faint hint of some sun trying to break through the clouded sky in the distance. I saw no parallel for myself; I could not imagine any possibility of brighter days ahead in my life. In my world, the forecast hadn't changed in a year. With exactly 363 dark days behind me since my mom had died, the clouds may have been beginning to part in the distance of wherever-it-was that I'd landed, but there would be no corresponding lightening of my mood. My normal sunshiny disposition had been clouded over by the constant sadness and hopelessness that were my new norm.

I had no parents.

Sighing and stretching out my cold, stiffening hands, I opened and closed them over my lap and considered them as if for the first time. Whose hands had I inherited? They weren't my mother's hands; her fingers had been longer and lovelier. But they weren't my father's either. His strong and solid hands were unforgettable. By comparison, mine suddenly looked almost alien. I had a single freckle on the back of my right hand, between my thumb and forefinger, and I remembered that my dad had the very same freckle in the exact same place on his hand. How this small detail had fascinated me as a child! My dad and I had shared this right-hand-freckle like a little secret and I'd considered it a mark of honor and proof positive of our special connection. Looking closer at my right hand, I noticed for the first time that the freckle had faded a bit as I'd grown older. With both my dear parents gone now, it seemed fitting that even this small speck would fade away too. Just a vanishing pinpoint, a trace of a shadow from a former freckle, was all I had of what had once been a mark of distinction, connecting me to my dad. The cruel irony of it all.

With this thought, I choked on a new batch of sadness rising in me and cursed myself for not having more than one soggy and crumbling tissue with which to dry what must surely have been my 10,000th tear. I sniffled in lieu of blowing my nose and hoped that the winding and weaving of the road would occupy the driver enough to divert his attention from his crying passenger. I feared that if he asked me what was wrong or offered me a Kleenex, I'd start telling him the whole story, beginning with: *"Well, my mother passed away a year ago on Sunday...."* Once I started I knew I would not be able to stop. *"...and my father died before that,"* I'd snivel and sob and continue: *"and...my family has all but fallen apart...I mean, so much is different now...literally everything has changed... I hate the business I once loved ...and I'm the fifth generation in the diamond business, so...."* My crying would escalate here. *"So it's my* legacy, *right?!* I wouldn't pause for him to answer this. *"How can I hate the very legacy left to me? It's unthinkable\ My Dad worked for me and he was there every day....unless he was sick...and he was always sick but he always recovered...until he didn't...and oh my god, how he suffered...such a sweet man to suffer so... But without my father, I don't think I can stand one more crazy customer... someone who thinks her diamond earrings are crooked when it's really her head that's the problem....And it's worse than that...I sleep all day now... I'm worthless...and I miss my mom so much I feel like a grieving child... but I'm fifty-four, for God's sake... I'm not a child...And now I'm nobody's child...."* A new flood of tears would emerge here and I'd blubber on, the floodgates opened irrevocably. I knew it was best that I *not* speak at all, for fear of losing it altogether. Although it was true that neither of my parents had technically died young, and I myself was not a youngster or even a teenager, somehow I felt like a child whose beloved parents had perished tragically in some horrible accident and twist of fate. But I was a full-fledged grown-up, having turned fifty just days before my father died, so this 'childlike' grief seemed inappropriate, even to me. I was old enough to deal with these sorts of losses and to accept life's inevitable changes as they came. My parents themselves had done this time and time again; why couldn't I? But rather than rising from adversity, I'd been sinking farther into hopelessness. I was out of Kleenex and tired of crying.

Closing my eyes, tears ran down the curves of my cheeks, falling in drops to my lap below, becoming salty spots on my jeans. I knew that even these would eventually disappear into the fabric and then into thin air, and I began to imagine that I could vanish too, like one of my pencil sketches rubbed away by an eraser, my image swept away with a brush of hand. Behind my closed eyelids, I imagined myself rubbed away with every swish and squeak of the car's windshield wipers; eliminated bit by bit until I was gone. Each whoosh of rubber across the rain-slicked windshield erased me. I was going, going, gone. Going, going, gone.

THIRTY-FOUR

Lost in this visualization, the click-click-swish of the wipers became a ticking metronome, keeping time, while I closed my eyes and the car drove on. Click, click, swish; click click, swish; matching the beat of my broken heart. Click, click, swish. Click, click, swish....

The rhythm became the metronome once sitting atop my Aunt Ruth's piano. Uncle Leo was a songwriter, and we'd sit beside him on the piano bench while he played and sang. Click, click, swish. The obelisk time-keeper had hypnotized me as a child, just as the sound of the windshield wipers did now, as the car drove on through fields of tobacco, their sturdy stalks waving in the rain. Uncle Leo, Uncle Sam, Uncle Abe, and the others, my grandfather among them, had all been little boys then. They had lived on a shade tobacco farm belonging to my newly-immigrated ancestors, just to the right of the rain-soaked road we traveled that day. Had I known this once and forgotten? My grandfather and his brothers, all my dear great-uncles, had once been new arrivals to the very place I'd just landed in myself. The little Russian boys who'd spoken no English had farmed tobacco until they followed in their father's footsteps to become diamond dealers like he had been, keeping up the family legacy of having served as purveyors of diamonds and pearls to the Czars of Russia.

I knew by heart the stories of their journeys to exotic places far and wide in search of the jewels for Russian royalty. I had heard many times how it had been on one of these buying trips that my great-grandfather had escaped with his family, knowing that the

Revolution was imminent. I remembered the story of their arrival by ship, through Ellis Island—I had even found the ship's manifest bearing all their names! I had assumed that they'd gone directly into the diamond business in New York City. But I had forgotten something....

Had he not been gone for four years, my father would have reminded me when I'd booked the trip: *"You're flying into Hartford, Nomi?! Why, that's less than a mile from where the Pevsner family farm once stood!"* For all of the stories I knew so well, I had forgotten this one. *"Look for the signs that say Windsor Locks. In Connecticut, Nomeluh, you'll see where your ancestors first settled! Your great-grandfather did so well farming tobacco that he was able to own one of the first trolley cars! That's how your Grandpa met Grandma Lucy, my mother—he was traveling to her family's nearby farm, where he proposed one evening and the rest is history, your history, Naomi..."* My father was gone and no one else knew where I was at that moment, but on either side of the rain-soaked road (why hadn't the driver taken the six-lane highway?) the fields of tobacco stood at attention.

She's here! Barry's daughter, Bernard's grandchild, she's come back! To where we began anew once, too. I remembered the stories of my grandfather and his brothers, and how they'd split up a map of the U.S., each choosing a territory to cover as diamond dealers out of New York, and later moving to Chicago. But their story had begun earlier...right here in the tobacco fields, where I was now.

Lulled by the ticking of the windshield-wiper metronome, I began to fall asleep, thinking drowsily about my Aunt Ruth, my dear Uncle Leo and his music—both of them, along with their piano, long gone now. The piquant fragrance of his cigar was just a memory too. He'd been a small boy once, on a farm where great leaves had grown under the shade to produce the wrappings for fine cigars. Perhaps he'd sat in the shade on a sunny day or under a tree on a rainy day like this one; he and his brothers wrapping the rolls of tobacco and beginning a lifetime affair with the cigars that he was never without. I'd only known him as a white-haired man with a cigar, but he'd been a boy once. Right here where I was now.

All the brothers were nothing but memories now; so much else had changed since then, and was changing still. Would nothing remain the same? I harbored a quiet fear of my memories themselves becoming as distant and faded as the once-familiar feel of my uncle's cool hand on my cheek. Thin-skinned and delicate with age, my Uncle Leo's hands had been as much a part of his greeting as his soft and gentle voice had been. Thankfully, I could still recall the soft brush of his fingers on my cheek as he asked: *"How ya doing baby?"* He had a voice like silk and a touch as light as a whisper.

"I'm good, Uncle Leo," I'd say; for how could a child of five or six be otherwise?

"Sweet girl," he'd reply. I'd look up at him from my three-foot perspective—past the cigar that gently bobbed as he spoke, to his gray-green eyes, slightly clouded, that were still fully able to convey a look of complete and unconditional love. He had greeted all of us this way—my siblings, my cousins and me—with a soft touch of cigar-scented fingers and various words of endearment. *"Sweet, sweet girl,"* he'd repeat. And I'd smile up at him and breathe in the smell that I still vividly remembered.

"Sweet like your Daddy, you are...and beautiful like your Mother," he'd add, raising an eyebrow and a finger for emphasis, then touching the tip of my nose for punctuation. At a bump in the road, I opened my eyes. The windshield wipers, ticking like a metronome, had been interrupted by the voice of the limo driver. I wasn't entirely sure what he had said or whether it required a response, so I stalled by clearing my throat.

"Ummm, I'm sorry....You were saying?" It was all I could come up with on such short notice and in truth, even simple sentences required more effort than I could muster lately. I looked down into my lap (did I think I'd find some speakable words there?) and saw that my hands were vigorously wringing each other, as if to squeeze out the sadness they'd been carrying. What had he just said?

We passed a sign that I could read in the now-clearing rain: "Welcome to Massachusetts," it proclaimed, indicating that we had passed through Connecticut on our way to a town called Lenox, in Massachusetts. The driver was pointing out a landmark, which I gathered I was supposed to look at.

"Over there," he gestured to the left. With some effort, I turned my head to see a mountain range in the distance. *Big deal,* I thought. *Mountains. Yes, I see them.* Following his pointing finger, I looked through my window, the glass now drying from the rain. With a crystal clear view, it took me a moment to focus on it, but then there it was. And when I saw it, I understood his insistence.

THIRTY-FIVE

The driver was jabbing his finger at the window, his voice animated and excited. "Well, how about that?" he was saying. I looked through the clearing glass to see two perfect rainbows stretching across the half-darkened sky, beyond the clouds. I took off my dark glasses and squinted as if I were seeing double by mistake—but there they were, unfurling gloriously across the entire length of the blue-gray sky. The clearing raindrops had blown to the sides of my window like curtains opening onto a stage with a backdrop too gorgeous for any set. I opened my mouth to say something, but nothing came out.

It reminded me of the scene in *The Wizard of Oz* where black and white images give way to color, so that we see Dorothy's checkered dress go from gray and white to china blue, and the little Munchkins dressed in every shade in the crayon box. In the days before VCRs and on-demand television, the annual airing of *The Wizard of Oz* was a special night at our house. As children, sitting with our parents in front of our television, we cuddled pillows and wrapped ourselves in blankets, watching year after year until eventually we knew the beloved movie by heart. I always waited for the moment when color came back to Dorothy's world, the Emerald City radiating true emerald green. To me, her being lost was more frightening than even the flying monkeys or the wicked witch. Horror-struck by the premise of a little girl like me being sucked into a whirling vortex, and deposited far from home, *this* was my greatest fear come to life, in Technicolor. I could imagine nothing more horrific than being ripped from the cozy cocoon of my home, and I'd avert my eyes from time to time, to count the four souls I was surrounded by. One, two, three, four...my mother, my father and my sister and brother were all safe and sound; so I could return to the movie, where Dorothy was still wandering, lost. Each year, while the movie credits rolled, we three headed to our beds, content and calm with the knowledge that just as Dorothy had found her way home, and we too would soon be safely tucked into our own beds. My sister and I would gaze at the wall above our twin beds, where a wallpaper border of double rainbows traveled the length of our wall, and thank our lucky stars that we weren't lost.

Since my parents had died, it felt as if everything I'd considered home had been swept away by tornados of change. In the end the black funnel had come for me too, just as it had lifted up the girl from Kansas, and taken her away from everything she'd known and loved. A swirling sickening cloud had sucked up everything I'd ever known and me along with it. And then, just as cruelly, I'd been dropped into a black and white world, devoid of color. Dorothy had awakened to find herself safe at home, surrounded by those she loved, but I would never again see the faces of my loved ones, except in pictures.

Without our parents, around whom we had orbited around all our lives, the three of us kids had scattered. It had been the first time I'd left town without letting my siblings know where I was going. In the past, each of us had spoken to our parents on most days, and thus, we would have heard the news that 'Joe was in California' or that 'Naomi and Richard left for the weekend.' Now the three of us 'kids'—no longer children—rotated around different suns and were directed by the pull of other priorities. Without my parents, I had tried to muddle on, but I had not managed to hold it together as well as Dorothy. Hopelessly lost and far from home, I was no heroine in any beloved old movie. Without the parents I'd loved so much, I wasn't sure exactly who or where I was. I had lost my bearings.

The driver was fidgeting with the radio again. "Pretty rare to see two of 'em," he said, nodding at the rainbows still visible in the distance. "Well, here's a coincidence, dontcha think?" he added as a song came on to the radio. "How about that? The song and the rainbows!"

Did he expect me to respond? I gathered by the widening of his eyes in the rearview mirror's reflection that he must be referring to the rainbows, or the rain, or the song on the radio, but frankly it was overload to me; my brain was slow in connecting all the dots.

"I look for coincidences like this, don't you?" he said. He turned up the volume on the car's radio; I hoped his doing so might save me from a required response. Couldn't I just be left alone in my misery? I wondered.

Just then the swelling chords of *Somewhere Over The Rainbow* filled the car, a perfect match to the backdrop of the two rainbows. It was the very song I had selected to play at my mother's funeral, exactly one year ago. I knew the words by heart. It had been "our song"—mine and my mother's—and I'd indulged myself by listening to it a time or two since she'd died.

"*Birds fly over the rainbow...why, tell me, why can't I?*" My own predicament was outlined in lyrics about a place where troubles melt like lemon drops, above a rainbow-colored scene like the one outside my window. I hoped that my mother had found a place where happy little bluebirds fly; even though it was a place where I couldn't join her, no matter how hard I wished upon a falling star.

"What a coincidence, don't you think?" the driver asked again, and I finally responded: "It is. Definitely it is." As the song continued, I stared at the two rainbows. It just so happened to be the same Hawaiian version of the classic song that we'd used at Mom's funeral, to accompany the slide show we'd compiled. I'd last heard it as images of my mother had flashed on a screen at her funeral. The smooth voice of musician Israel Kamakawiwoʻole reverberated with haunting beauty, flowing like velvet above the sweet, simple plunking of a ukulele.

Roughly calculating the probability of this particular song—and the same rendition of it we had chosen for Mom's funeral—playing on the radio of a car I traveled in, under a rainbow (or two), I was stumped for an answer. Accepting the serendipity of it, silently I wondered, *Mom, is that you?*

In lieu of an answer, I saw for a moment, in my mind's eye, the double rainbow that had hung over my sister's and my beds in the room we'd shared as children. My mother had once sat beneath this wallpaper rainbow, perched atop one of our beds with one of her lovely legs tucked beneath her; strumming on a guitar and sweetly singing the handful of songs she had learned for our benefit. "Somewhere Over The Rainbow" had been our favorite. She'd also sung of a sweet-flowered lemon tree who grew impossibly piquant fruit; and about a magic dragon who lived by the sea, and frolicked in the mist with a boy named Jackie Paper. We sang along, gathered around my mother on the white chenille bedspread; our bedroom just as magical a place for me as any that lived on in song.

Rolling along in the car from Hartford, Connecticut to Lenox, Massachusetts, I thought about the many miles I'd traveled to find myself right here under a couple of rainbows, propelled by my deep feelings of loss. Over the past year, I'd noticed more than a few uncanny coincidences that had prompted me to look up and ask, "*Is that you, Momma?! Or Oh, Dad, tell me that's you; it simply must be....*" But as coincidences go, this was a doozy. With the first involuntary smile in a while, I imagined my mother having arranged such a grand collaboration. "*Yes, excuse me Lord, but I'm going to need one of those rainbows of yours; oh well, let's make it two. And oh, God, if you wouldn't mind, I'd like a song to go with it—and I just happen to have a copy of it right here!*" This was my mother: someone who did things her way and made you glad that she had.

I might have known that any 'sign' from my mother would be more of a shout than a mumble. This multi-hued banner was more her style than say, a soft breeze or even a bird landing on my shoulder. Was it a double-arrow, of sorts? If I followed one or both rainbows to their ends, would they point me in the right direction to go on without my parents at my side?

Stretching across the heavens, they looked to be pointing ahead in a *forward* direction. Right then and there I decided to take it as a sign: the rainbows, the song, and the small shift I felt within me.

"Yeah, that's crazy!" I answered the driver. "I think maybe it's a sign. I'm not sure of what."

"Indeed," the driver said. (*Indeed*—a word my father often used; an affirmative response to any number of subjects. Another coincidence, perhaps.)

Driver, follow that rainbow and step on it! I wanted to say. He could keep the pot of gold—I only wanted guidance: a map for my future without my parents. And with this thought, to quench my fierce thirst, I took a swig of water from a bottle I did not recall buying, gazing at the spectacular duo of rainbows still shimmering in the distance. Bigger than any billboard, they were just the kind of epic, larger-than-life sign my mother would be likely to send me from her perch in heaven. A sign she knew I could not possibly miss.

THIRTY-SIX

It was exciting enough to dream that I would meet Dani Shapiro and learn about writing from a true master, but I'd taken it farther than that, secretly imagining that she and I would become fast friends, doing all the things that gal pals did, long distance. This was a bit of a stretch, regardless of any interest she might or might not have had in me as a friend, as I did not, typically, seek to make new girlfriends. I could meet them easily enough, but had no interest in collecting them, after that. Women could be tough and I had learned to avoid conflict or disappointment by not making a habit of adding to my micro-circle of friends. Perfectly happy to have a large number of acquaintances, I protected myself from the obligation to connect with most of them; outside of social media. Occasionally I'd bump into someone and we'd promise to meet for lunch but I rarely followed up. It seemed too much was at stake; there was disappointment lurking behind every female friendship.

But I imagined Dani Shapiro to be exactly the opposite of the girls and women I'd found difficult in my past. Dani would be different. Taking me under her wing, she'd guide me like a girl-guru and then (oh, the ideas were coming to me fast now!) I'd design a necklace for us, like the two-part 'mitzpah pendants' we had worn as kids, split in half and shared with a special friend. For Dani, I'd design a cool, grown-up version, set with diamonds, that I'd present to her on the first anniversary of our friendship. Already grateful to her for having written words that had spoken so clearly to me, I imagined that we'd have years of friendship ahead in which I would express my indebtedness to her. She'd inspired and launched my writing career, after all.

Like many of her other fans, I felt as if *knew* Dani. I'd read practically every word she'd written. Although my success paled in comparison to her many titles (Teacher, Public Speaker, Best-selling Author, and even recent Guest on *Oprah*), otherwise I thought she and I were practically matching bookends. And if Dani Shapiro had survived her struggles and risen above great pain in the wake of her parents' deaths, then maybe I could too.

The only place we differed significantly was where Dani, as a teen, had struggled with her blond beauty and fretted over not looking typically Jewish; an affliction I would have fully embraced. Having lived through my own adolescence lamenting unwanted dark body hair and the overactive oil glands of my swarthy ancestors, I considered her pale and hairless limbs a gift, not a curse. While she'd wished for a more 'authentic' Jewish appearance, I'd been busy hiding my hairy adolescent knees underneath the long 'maxi-dresses' that were thankfully then in fashion, worn by all of us female tweens to *Bar and Bat Mitzvah* parties. My mother strictly enforced a "no shaving above the knee" regulation, apparently a belief of the day that I now find amusing. Not shaving (or waxing) beyond my knees made for an awkward transition from the knee up; a fact that I pointed out ardently to my mom, to no avail. Hairs poking out above my knee-socks seemed to defeat the purpose of shaving, but my mother was adamant. I imagined Dani Shapiro had been given a pretty pink electric razor at age 11 by her loving parents.

But what stood out above all for me was the fact that Shapiro had bravely *shared her story with the world*. This suggested to me that the telling of one's story somehow *released it to the universe* and in return, brought back healing—and answers—to the writer. This was exactly what I needed. Though my story differed from Dani's in some ways, at least I knew that I *had* a story—I hailed from a family of storytellers after all. But here was a gal who had *done* something with hers; and because she had, I thought maybe I could, too.

I took the double rainbows that had greeted my arrival in the Berkshires as an auspicious sign, fading from my sight but not from my mind as the car moved smoothly over winding roads surrounded by forest, finally pulling into the entrance to Kripalu just as the computer-voice of the limo's GPS system confirmed, *"You have arrived at your destination."* I supposed I had.

Kripalu's main building was a former monastery and looked every bit the part, albeit nestled in a beautiful place. When I pulled my wallet from my bag, the driver informed me that I had *pre-paid* (funny the things we do not remember doing and the things we somehow can't forget) so I offered a tip, which he seemed genuinely grateful to receive. Pulling my suitcase from the trunk, he offered to take it to the lobby for me but I had a free hand so I took it from him instead.

"Enjoy your weekend," he said.

"Oh, I think I will," I said. "And thanks for pointing out those rainbows!" I added. "I might have missed them if you hadn't."

As I wheeled my suitcase into Kripalu, it seemed like I could hear my mom's voice, urging me to write. *You're a writer, Naomi, like your Dad. You should write, honey,* she'd said. So here I was at a 'writer's weekend' with Dani Shapiro no less! I could hardly wait to get started.

The lobby smelled like incense, and I inhaled deeply, shifting my balance on mid-height heels and smoothing my year-round gabardine wool pants. For the number of guests I saw, the level of noise in the lobby was low, but the quiet was explained when I spotted someone with a name tag that read *I'm practicing silence today.* Hushed but happy humans treaded lightly through the foyer, which was decorated with a life-size mural of Kripalu's namesake swami. Everyone I saw appeared to be heading to destinations of illumination within the facilities that I could not wait to find. Though I was slightly weary from travel, I was eager to join the ranks of the enlightened.

I'd dressed for travel in what I considered to be 'work clothes,' attire acceptable in *any* situation. Yet suddenly I wished I'd dressed differently. Or at least had worn different shoes. These folks looked like the type who regularly sorted and recycled their refuse and wouldn't have dreamed of sacrificing comfort for the three inches of height gained by a platform heel. I tried to shake a mental image of the bags of un-sorted rubbish I'd knowingly pushed down the trash chute of our high-rise apartment building back in Dallas, just that morning. Maybe I'd start recycling when I got back. Shimmying up to the "Welcome Desk" for check-in, I tried my best to look as 'environmentally responsible' as possible; moving casually and assuming the demeanor of someone who wouldn't *dream* of mixing together glass bottles, newsprint and non-biodegradable plastic utensils. I pulled out a black credit card and found myself wishing it was a debit card from a bank known for its antagonism towards fossil fuels. I felt out of my element. And overdressed.

The staff members behind the welcome desk were sensibly dressed in woven fabrics of calming earth-tones, the women noticeably *sans* make-up, sporting the healthy glow of the outdoors in lieu of cosmetics. I myself had applied a fresh coat of lipstick before exiting the limo. Digging my Hermes wallet out from beneath my Prada make-up bag, I unearthed a gilded compact before shoving it to the bottom of my bag. It dawned on me that the new powder-blusher in its bejeweled compact, which I'd bought especially for the trip, had been an unnecessary purchase. Suddenly the shade named *"Orgasm"* seemed gauche, even though I'd removed its $70 price tag. Better to appear as these girls did, I thought: to have achieved my rosy glow the old-fashioned way. And as I was traveling alone and staying in a former nun's room, I'd better not attribute a facial glow to anything that could be misconstrued as "orgasm." I barely knew these people for gosh sakes. I made a mental note to wear less make-up over the coming weekend.

After check-in I followed the young man's directions to find my room, heading to a bank of elevators he said I'd find just past the yoga studios. I rolled my suitcase past heavy, highly polished wooden doors, etched in gold with Sanskrit lettering. I assumed they opened into Zen-like yoga dens. Outside the grand doors were neat rows of uber-practical shoes. My high heels pinched me as I rolled past the line-up of simple slip-ons, flip-flops, and biblical-style sandals. Mentally calculating the probability of an overnight order from Zappos, a pair of similar sandals safely arriving at this remote location in the mountains, I decided against ordering. I'd 'make do' as my mother used to say.

Continuing on past the earth-shoes, I picked up my step, rolling my over-priced Vuitton suitcase towards my room at a pretty good clip. The repeating 'LV' logo practically screamed for attention, making me wish I'd had the good sense to have bought something more appropriate, like an understated North Face mountain-climbing backpack.

I was all but careening now, rolling my ill-fated suitcase down what was turning out to be the Lord's longest hallway to my room, seemingly located as far away from the entry as one could be while still remaining on property. If I'd lost a heel during the run for my room, I'd honest-to-god not have looked back. Someone else could pick it up, and I'd check the lost-and-found later, I thought, before it occurred to me that there probably wasn't a lost-and-found, anyway. Surely these eco-responsible folks owned a more sensible number of possessions than I did and did not constantly lose and misplace their belongings, having been cured of their attention deficits by the constant practice of yoga and meditation. I lost things as a general rule; my relationship with any pair of sunglasses, for example, never lasted long.

Finally I reached my room (and possibly my maximum heart-rate), breathing a sigh of relief. Unlocking the door and shoving my ostentatious bag inside, with one look I could see why Kripalu had been ideal for its original inhabitants, the monks. This was a room only a reverend-mother could love; and it goes without saying that there was no mini-bar. I surveyed the small and sparsely 'decorated' room as the door slammed shut behind me, like the clang of a jail cell. I was overdressed but home at last, in a former monastery in the mountains with no television. God help me.

Well, at least I hadn't opted for the shared bathroom down the hall; I had paid extra to assure I would have a room with its own facilities. Remembering this, my mood lifted slightly, only to sink again when I ducked into the universe's smallest bathroom to unpack my toiletries and discovered that I'd forgotten my hairspray.

A glance in the pitifully small mirror, hanging over the insanely small sink, showed evidence of my hair's ability to droop under pressure. I seriously doubted that Kripalu's gift shop carried hairspray. Remembering that sometimes a quick blast from a blow-dryer did the trick, I looked for the one I'd assumed *every* hotel room provided, but apparently there was no such thing here at Kripalu. *Of course not Naomi,* I told myself. *This was a nun's residence, for God's sake.* Hooks for hanging habits, yes. Blow dryers, no. I'd been there for only thirty minutes, and suddenly I wanted wine or a burger. I was a fish out of water, and craving a steak, at that. Thank God I'd at least requested a view of the mountains. Propelled by this thought, I headed towards the window, crossing the room in exactly 2.5 steps to open the shades.

Outside my window, the rain had started up again. There was no sign of the rainbow I'd seen earlier. I leaned over the radiator placed under the window; it was turned to 'off' to adjust for summer in the Berkshires. These were warm days in May, but still, leaning over the old radiator, looking out the window of a room once resided in by nuns, I shivered.

In the past, settling into a new place, I would have recognized the small ache of homesickness starting up. No matter how much I had traveled, for business and pleasure, I still always felt a pang for the place I called home. But my parents were gone and so much had changed with their passing. No one was 'home' anymore; the old familiar niggle of homesickness had grown into an anguish for a place now forever gone. As I stood at the window, watching the light rain intensify and turned heavy again, I was suddenly frightened by the truth that hit me like a fever: I had no home to return to.

THIRTY-SEVEN

By late afternoon on Saturday, my antsy feelings at Kripalu had reached peak levels. Where was the sense of calm I'd expected after two days of yoga? Fretful, lonesome and badly in need of a glass of wine, I headed to the front desk to inquire about a shuttle, or a ride of some kind, to the nearby town of Lenox. I was told that Kripalu's car only made airport runs. I considered feigning an illness requiring medication from a drug store, but decided that in such a natural and healthy atmosphere I'd probably be offered a holistic cure. So instead I decided to head out on foot. My recollection was that there had been towns on either side of Kripalu, so I figured I'd head in one direction or the other and eventually see civilization. I had seen a sweet-looking little town (with shops and restaurants!) on the drive to Kripalu and remembered it being just down the road, though I would discover that I was off in my calculations by a long shot.

Kicking a can down the road, I contemplated a growing feeling of failure I couldn't quite put my finger on. At the writing workshop and yoga retreat, I'd looked so forward to, I felt I hadn't mastered much of anything. Admittedly, I'd slept through a yoga class or two, but it wasn't that. My three days of journal-writing and sprout-eating at Kripalu would end on Sunday, and now, on Saturday afternoon, I felt like I had failed. Had my efforts to learn or gain something at Kripalu been futile? There was a nagging feeling of having exposed myself in a way I hadn't done before; and wasn't sure I should have. *Sans* make-up and jewelry all weekend, I had been stripped bare of everything I believed to be *distinctive* about me. Consequently, I had been utterly and totally *myself*, and it turned out that I was not very good at playing such an unfamiliar role. I had not impressed anyone; without my usual props and reinforcements, I felt I had not even succeeded at being myself.

I had met my literary idol, Dani Shapiro, but I doubted she knew who I was or would remember me after the weekend ended. Before the trip, I'd harbored visions of chatting with her over coffee about our eerily similar backgrounds and shared childhood frustrations. I'd even dared to imagine that she and I would become friends! Chattering on, we'd be phone and pen-pals who'd proofread each other's manuscripts, she cheering on my inevitable success as a writer.

The truth was that I'd actually introduced myself to Dani only once all weekend. Otherwise I'd blended into the sea of women (and a smattering of men) sitting cross-legged on yoga mats in front of her during her seminars. What would I have said, anyway, that would have been of any interest to such an accomplished writer as she? Sure, I'd had success as a jewelry designer, appearing on national television in sell-out shows and designing for stars like Cher and Jane Seymour. But no one in the yoga-world cared much for accessories; this I'd noted right away, removing my jewelry and tucking it under some shirts in my suitcase. In the gift shop and on the wrists and necks of others at Kripalu, I'd seen semi-precious beads and woven bracelets, but not a diamond among them. I doubted anyone would ask for my business card, with the intention of purchasing handmade diamond jewelry down the line.

I was anonymous that weekend and even *looked* the part. Underdressed and uncertain, like an unpolished rough diamond, I felt less smooth and sophisticated, more *ordinary*—missing my usual 'shine.' Without a Starbucks in my hand and diamonds in my ears, I was just one of the crowd; another aspiring writer hoping to soak up some of Dani Shapiro's wisdom.

"I can look much more impressive!" I wanted to shout.

Having lost the two human beings who'd undoubtedly loved me

most, I wanted someone else to love me, too. True, my parents had adored me through every awkward stage, from braces on my teeth and thick-lensed glasses to chubby pre-teen and even awkward early adulthood. They had loved my soul. But they were gone, and without them I was as plain as I looked. Who would love me now? I had become invisible. I'd even failed at Yoga 101.

While I had sat on a mat in my new yoga togs, trying to clear my cluttered mind of unnecessary thoughts, for two days I'd thought of little else than the ones I had lost. In unfamiliar surroundings, in a faraway place, every dormant insecurity of mine had surfaced. Sitting cross-legged on the hardwood floor, every negative thought or perception emerged as if on cue and circled me like ants at a picnic. Twisted into new yoga poses, I was in no position to argue with my fears, nor was I able to brush them away. Instead, forced to just sit with them, I felt myself crawling with self-doubt.

By Saturday afternoon, I could have sworn I smelled a glass of wine with my name on it in the nearest town. Walking purposefully up the winding road to Lenox, my thighs and calves reminded me that I hadn't moved my body much in the past year. I felt the burn and strain of weary limbs but carried on. Finally I saw a twinkling town ahead, looking even in the distance like the sort of place Norman Rockwell might have frequented; which, it turns out, he had. I breathed a sigh of relief and opened heavy oak doors to a candle-lit restaurant, where background music swelled in my ears like a homecoming movie score.

Ahhhh, culture. In the air-conditioned atmosphere of the restaurant, my skin prickled with delight at the familiar tinkling of toasting glasses and the clinking of silverware on fine china. A classical tune resonated like a concerto off the white linen tablecloths. Enough of the yoga and sprouts, I thought. I would belly up to the sparkling bar with its gleaming glasses and appetizing nibbles, savoring the taste of sophistication.

Sliding onto an elegantly upholstered barstool and sinking into its rich jewel-toned velvet seat, it dawned on me that I had not been greeted at the door. I'd assumed it was acceptable for me to seat myself but wondered why none of the usual suspects had offered me assistance. As a typically fit-to-be-seen woman who dines out with some regularity, I was at least used to being smiled at when I entered a restaurant. A bartender, maitre-d and several waiters were standing by, but none had so much as looked my way. I hadn't expected a red carpet, but I hoped I didn't look like some sort of nobody who had wandered in off the dirt road and didn't belong in this upscale establishment.

After a moment or two, I looked below the barstool to my dusty, road-worn gym shoes and only then did it dawn on me that I wasn't exactly dressed for a Saturday night evening out. Ah, well, I thought, in a town as small as this, surely such things didn't matter. I'd spoken (to myself) a moment too soon, as several chic patrons entered the restaurant for an early dinner or drink and I wondered if I might have underestimated the establishment. I could clearly identify the scent of Chanel No. 5 coming from one of the women who'd entered, and I wished I'd thought to spritz myself. She was smartly dressed in a St. John knit; not my style but considered chic in certain circles.

Tucking a stringy piece of hair behind my earring-less ear, I licked my dry, gloss-less lips and remembered that I was not wearing a stitch of my usual make-up. Suddenly, I wondered—did I look a bit disheveled? I couldn't know for sure, not having even a purse-sized mirror on me—nor a purse, for that matter. I'd tucked a credit card and my room key into a small pocket in my yoga pants and had hit the road empty handed. Though I'd felt out of place at Kripalu, suddenly I wished for the safety of the former monastery; but I was not going to return before I'd at least had a glass of wine.

At last, a bartender slid a cocktail napkin onto the bar in front of me, and I ordered a glass of Chardonnay in a voice that surprised me by cracking with the emotion I thought I'd squelched.

"Our house wine okay, ma'am?" he asked, and I nodded, afraid to speak further.

With no one to talk to and not yet hungry enough to ask for a menu, I drummed my fingers on the bar top while he turned to pour my drink. As if even the universe itself was conspiring against me, one previously well-manicured fingernail broke off and rolled over on the polished bar, lying there like a dead soldier. The bartender turned my way with a half-full wine glass, and I tucked the nail tip under my napkin just in time for my wine to be set atop it like a proper tombstone. I smiled, as much a 'thank you' as I could muster, and put my credit card on the bar, lest he think I couldn't pay for my libation. Hoping he'd take my card and run it immediately, so I could finish my wine and head out, I folded the finger with the broken nail into my fist and pounded my thigh, for no particular reason. Damn it. Damn it all.

My credit card on the bar was facing me and I glanced at the gold embossed letters spelling my name. Once familiar, suddenly my own name looked odd to me: N-A-O-M-I P-E-V-S-N-E-R. Who was I, anyway? Without my parents, I felt less of *me* than I had been. While rationally I knew this to be untrue, at that moment I missed them so desperately I thought I might choke from sadness. *Girl at the bar choking on grief. Heimlich maneuver somebody!* I was alone in a way I'd never known before; truly, deeply and utterly detached, 2,000 miles from home and homesick for a home now forever gone. Right there in the lovely low lighting of the restaurant, I leaned over my glass of wine and began to cry. Big, fat tears fell onto the napkin on the bar—the one I'd buried my broken nail under—and spread into small wet circles around the restaurant's logo.

Somehow, that weekend I had become further displaced and even more lost than I had been before. I'd traveled a very long way from home to find myself—nowhere. I was neither here nor there; neither lost nor found. My beloved parents were dead and more than half my life was officially behind me. My heart was broken and worse, my hair looked terrible. I would have run home just then, but my legs ached as much as my heart did and I wasn't sure what direction to head in.

I could not have known then that this was the very first step towards my finally seeing the light. I settled my tab and headed back the way I'd come, as the sun began to set behind the mountains. My head hanging low, I did the only thing I knew to do, which was to put one foot in front of another and repeat this as many times as it took to arrive back at Kripalu. I'd forgotten just how many steps it had taken and had begun to panic about the possibility of walking in the dark in unfamiliar territory. By the time I finally made it back, the sun was setting and Kripalu looked like a mirage I was very glad to see.

The mountains were now fading in the dark. My legs hurt and my soul ached. No 'welcome back' awaited me; no one noticed I was back, or even that I had been gone at all. As I trudged the long halls to my room, no one and nothing greeted me there either. I unlocked the door to my tiny room with its small bed, simple wooden chair, and no telephone or television. Kicking off my shoes, I headed to the pint-sized bathroom and leaned over the sink to splash my tearstained face. Drying it with the one white face towel I'd been allotted, I saw my image in the small mirror hanging over the sink and recognized it as a face once loved by two remarkable parents. Seeing myself without so much as a stick of make-up, I frowned at my reflection. Compared to the woman in the restaurant dressed in St. John, I looked dreadful.

I hung my towel, sighed and walked the couple of steps to my small bed, where I sat for a while in my nothingness. The journal I'd scribbled in all weekend sat on the bedside table, leaving only enough room for the lamp, which looked as old as electricity itself. I turned the switch on the metal lamp and decided maybe I'd write a bit, for lack of anything else to do. Though I would have sworn that not a word could possibly come out of my inner emptiness, when I set the broken nub of my pencil to the paper I wrote from my heart, with the truest words that I had. *You know the answers, Honeygirl,* my Dad had said. *They're right there,* he said in my dream, pointing to my heart.

That night, in the dim yellow light of a metal lamp with a crooked shade, I began to write in a way I'd not been able to before. *You're a writer, Nomeluh,* my father had said. I wrote what I knew, because it was all I had; the words coming from an unfamiliar, untapped place in my soul, which had somehow always been there. Writing about being lost—about my breaking heart—I realized that it was at precisely such moments when the purest and truest words flowed.

I remembered how I'd begged my father, in my dreams, to tell me what I needed to know. He always said that I already *knew*, which had frustrated me because I swore I didn't. But that night, in the loneliest place on earth, the truth began to echo in whispers of my own voice, which must have been what my father meant. I'd been looking for answers in all the wrong places. For what Dani Shapiro had suggested appeared to be true: that it is precisely when one feels most detached—hopelessly, desperately lost and alone—that the heart of a writer opens up to reveal the soul's truest contents. In *our own words* we discover that our true North *lies in our connection to ourselves*.

I slept without dreaming that night, beneath a rising moon that cast a glow over the Berkshire mountains. My journal lay open, a pencil beside it. Though I had believed that I had failed at yoga, at making new friends and at feeling comfortable in my own skin, I had not really failed at all. They'd been baby steps I'd taken, but steps nonetheless towards remembering what I knew best. Though I felt out of place in that strange place called Kripalu, in time I would discover that I had been exactly where I belonged.

PART FIVE

GOOD FORTUNE

THIRTY-EIGHT

On Sunday afternoons, I'd often stop by my parents' house where they would be going about their usual routines. A typical Sunday found my father lounging in his easy chair while my mother 'piddled around the house' (her phrase) either tidying things, polishing her nails, folding laundry or re-organizing a drawer or a pantry shelf. I realize now that these visits were as fundamental to my feelings of well-being and optimism as most anything else I did to prepare for the week ahead. It was a bit like filling up my gas tank for the week, with enough fuel to keep me going until the following Sunday.

I'd have spoken to both of my parents multiple times during the week, but we'd always spend some time catching up on various other things, before I'd head to their couch for a nap. I'd stake my claim to the brocade couch in the front room, softly lit in the afternoon by sun filtered through two picture windows facing the street. These Sunday afternoon siestas were not just indulgences, but felt like necessary respites for me, during which time itself seemed to stand still. Even as my parents chatted with each other in hushed tones, I'd enter a state of half-sleep, drowsing for an hour in complete serenity. *"Oh, I'm so glad she's resting,"* I'd hear my mother say, in low tones. *"She's been working so hard this week,"* my father might add.

What I have longed for, in these years without them, were their unforgettable voices and the way they rose and fell in soft cadence while I slept. Theirs were the conversations of two people who didn't need to speak at all; as one could easily finish the other's sentence.

Their voices, and the way they two-stepped together, had been calming me since I was a child. The conversations I'd heard floating down the hall, after the three of us children were tucked into bed, were the nightly background music to my life, from the time when nothing had yet threatened the peaceful calm of life at home with the people I loved. It didn't matter that I couldn't hear exactly what they were saying to each other; what I heard in the harmony of their overlapping voices was love. Their conversations were like love songs; their affection for each other evident in the tone of their voices.

My mother's responses to whatever my father said sounded more like validations than just 'yes' and 'no.' "*Oh don't you* know *that's true!*" from my mother, meant that what my father had said was spot on. If, in answer to a question my mother had posed, my dad said "*Well, you know best, darling,*" my mother would know once again, for the millionth time, that he supported her every thought, every whim, and every opinion.

As I lay on their couch as an adult daughter, the sound of their voices in duet reminded me of who I was and where I had come from. Wrapped in their voices on those Sunday afternoons, (satiated by whatever 'lovely' leftover my mother had artfully plated and practically force-fed me), nourished me in a way that nothing else ever has. That couch, on those Sunday afternoons, was always there for me; unless my brother had beat me to it, in which case I'd head to the other couch.

It was the small pleasure of these Sunday afternoon naps that I pined for after my parents were gone. Beyond the quiet comfort of their always-immaculate home or their soft sofa, what satisfied me in these quiet moments was the belief that as long as I was on their couch, all was well with the world.

I hadn't anticipated the difficulty of all the Sundays that would come after their deaths, but it hit me full force on one particular Sunday when I found myself driving by what had been our old house on Hillbriar Drive. Pulling up in front, I allowed myself a moment or two of what I considered an indulgence: imagining our bygone time in that house. I didn't want to stay too long, in case the current owners came out to wonder about the woman sitting and weeping in her car. But for just a moment, I could 'see' my father moving the sprinkler from the front to the side yard, walking carefully on his prosthesis and sidestepping across the Bermuda grass he'd nursed from squares of soon-to-be turf to the plush green lawn of which he was so proud.

I looked towards the windows to what had been our dining room, with the kitchen just beyond it, imagining my mother flitting about, wearing the yellow rubber gloves she always donned to protect her perfect hands and manicure as she washed the plate she'd used for Dad's lunch. In my imagination, the phone on the kitchen wall rings and it's her sister or cousin Henry from Florida and they chat. I can almost see her twisting her pretty fingers into the coiled cord of the yellow phone as she speaks. She doesn't sit down but keeps moving, from sink to butcher-block counter and back. I marvel at her ability to never sit down or 'take a load off.'

"Oh, someone's at my door, Henry!" I imagine her saying into the phone. "It must be one of the kids...." She'll put the phone in its cradle, remove her rubber gloves and lay them by the sink, before rushing to greet one of us at the door.

I noticed a car pass me and slow down; perhaps the driver is wondering if I am the current resident, pulling up to check the black metal mailbox (the one my father bought at Ace Hardware and installed himself) before going round to the garage to park. I snapped out of my fantasy, waving briefly at the person driving by before pulling away from the curb and reluctantly rolling to the corner of Hillbriar and Woodbriar, ten feet away. I wondered how many times I had turned at this corner, knowing I'd be back home later. But it was different now.

Now I would head home to the brand-new multi-level, ultra-modern townhouse we'd rented, having sold both our Plano and Dallas homes to free ourselves up to consider buying the place of my dreams in the Berkshires of Massachusetts, to which I'd begun traveling on a regular basis—sometimes with Richard in tow. Entering the apartment, no one greeted me at the door—not even my little dog, who didn't hear me enter in this cavernous glass house with its high ceilings and built-in noise reduction. I kicked off my shoes and padded back to the bedroom to find little Gigi, her happy licks lifting my mood slightly. She and I headed out to the turf dog park in front of the building, where I wondered if this little pup missed the scents and sounds of our former hilly grounds with real grass. Obviously pleased to be outside, she ran in happy circles and chased the ball I tossed rather feebly. She had me and that was all that mattered; oh, to be a dog, I sighed. Gigi did her business and we headed back up to the apartment, where the twin couches under the sparkling walls of windows beckoned. I stretched out on one of them and Gigi hopped up next to me, arranging herself on a pillow by my head and promptly dozing off.

I closed my eyes too, feeling more weary than tired or sleepy. It seemed I'd lost everything but weight lately; I hadn't been exercising like I used to, and this in itself might have added to my lack of energy. Besides, I had nothing much to do. I fell into a half-sleep, allowing myself to drift, but hoping not to dream—preferring not to think at all.

After a while, I heard only the breath of my little dog. Then, in the silence, I began to hear the memories of my parents' voices, hovering nearby. Hers, lilting and lovely, animated as always; and his, soft, deep and authoritative in a news-anchor way, but sweet-tempered and patient, pausing periodically for my mother to speak and agreeing with whatever-it-was that she said. In this way, their voices wrapped together and then separated again, drifting and weaving, riding above and below each other, with unintelligible words that clearly spoke of love. I remembered this like a song I'd heard a hundred times.

My parents' calming voices had found me here, in a place I'd barely lived in long enough to call home. On a Sunday afternoon, as I lay half asleep with my little dog beside me, the voices I was longing to hear blanketed me with their familiar inflections and magical murmurings, convincing me that at least for that hour, all was right with the world.

THIRTY-NINE

A post-it note with a phone number had been sitting on my desk for weeks. I'd shuffle it around, sticking it on one surface or another, reluctant to make the call. It was the phone number of a psychiatrist who had been recommended to me as 'someone to see about grief.' Somehow in my mind mourning seemed more acceptable than the stigma of clinical depression, so a psychiatric specialist seemed like overkill—but nevertheless, I'd kept the number.

I'd had my first experience with the perils and pitfalls of pharmaceutical cures for depression in the early 1980s, when I was in my twenties, and I still remembered the various side effects of the limited number of anti-depressant medications available in those days. Extreme fatigue, weight gain, problems with memory, and more; and over the years I was never convinced that the meds helped much anyway. So it wasn't likely I'd wake up one day and smack myself in the forehead—like the commercial for V-8 vegetable juice—saying: *I coulda had a Deseryl!* I was *mourning*, I thought—and so far, bereavement seemed to be in a class of its own, much worse than any bout of depression I'd had over the years.

It was an affliction I'd apparently inherited from my father's side of the family. I had my first experience of the almost-impossible-to-describe dark, sad feelings of deep hopelessness as a college freshman, 200 miles from home at the University of Texas. My parents assured me that I would settle in, but I never did. I would call home constantly, in spite of my parents' limited budget long-distance calls in those days before the Internet or cell phones. They were part of a generation not accustomed to 'talking about feelings,' and the possibility of a mental illness like depression was not on anyone's radar then. Constant worry, extreme anxiety and a wide-ranging fear of the unknown became constant companions, which I dealt with as best I could. In hindsight, so much of my life would have been different if I'd known there was help for what ailed me.

It was only after baby Marissa was born that the debilitating symptoms of depression became too hard for me to hide or deal with on my own. Even then, 'postpartum depression' seemed more acceptable than other mental illnesses; a better excuse for what I saw as weakness. Those few with whom I'd share the embarrassing subject reported feelings of exhaustion or melancholy after child-birth, so I assumed my funk would 'pass' like theirs had. I might have recognized—but didn't—that I was feeling the same dark, chok-ing desperation I'd experienced years before as a college student. Over the years I'd been told that I might have 'treatment resistant' depression, a diagnosis I accepted because I never noticed much improvement when I was on medication, especially as I dealt with difficult side effects like fatigue and weight gain.

Two dismal years after my mother had gone, I still hadn't con-sidered that my old friend Depression might have moved in as a companion to my grief, in a whopping double-whammy. I knew there was no way around grief but through it, but I had forgot-ten that there were shortcuts to moving through clinical depression. There was talk-therapy (from which I'd benefitted in the past), as well as a slew of newer medications that I had not yet tried; meds that corrected neuro-transmitted brain connections with far fewer side effects.

The extreme heat of a typical Texas summer returned right on schedule, but so much else about my former life in Dallas did not come back. *Everything changes, Nomeluh,* my father had always said. And he'd been right. As a child, I'd splashed the summer days away, staying cool in the JCC pool but now I faced those long hot Texas summers with dread.

One hot, sticky afternoon, I cranked up the air conditioner and stared at the Post-it note on which I'd scrawled the number for Dr. Glass, a psychiatrist. Fingering the note, I considered tossing it in the trash but something made me hold on to it. I gazed at the nearby phone, thinking morosely about the many times I had picked it up to call my mother or my father. It seemed inconceivable that the same phone no longer connected to either of them.

Still indecisive, my eye was caught by a framed photo of my grandfather, sitting on a shelf beside his old scale. Grandpa had been wearing a tuxedo for a cousin's wedding and the photographer had captured him well, cropping out the bedroom slippers he'd worn underneath the dress pants. He'd been dressed for comfort—at least from the ankles down.

"Don't worry, Grandpa. It's just a phase," I sighed.

Looking at the balancing bowls on his familiar scale, one sitting higher than the other, out of habit, I roughly calculated how many of the tiny brass weights it would take to bring both bowls into balance; remembering how my grandfather had skillfully added just the right combination to bring the lower bowl up to equal the weight of a diamond. Suddenly a thought came to me that stopped me in my tracks.

I was carrying too much weight. *The grief had become too heavy.*

"I need to balance," I whispered out loud. Where, I wondered, were those small brass weights of his? Suddenly, they seemed important. As I rifled through some drawers to find them, I remembered fingering those little weights and asking my grandfather how many he thought it would take to balance the diamond he was weighing.

"We can't guess, Sweetheart," he'd said. *"We have to try different sizes and see. But you will* know *when it balances."* And he'd been right.

I found the box containing the tiny brass weights and opened it up reverently. They little sat in a cluster, their service no longer needed; no telling how many years it had been since they'd seen the light. I picked up a few of the weights and made myself into a scale, my hands becoming the bowls. It was time to find my balance.

I looked down at the number on the yellow sticky-note and picked up the phone to call Dr. Glass.

FORTY

A year into therapy, I had begun to look forward to my visits with Dr. Glass, who seemed pleased, maybe even proud, of my progress. For me, a born 'people-pleaser,' this provided its own incentive. The Seroquel he prescribed was working its miracle, helping me cope with so many small things that would have overwhelmed me in the past. *Everything is easier,* I told myself with wonder. The Seroquel was different than the anti-depressants I'd taken previously; it worked. Remembering my first appointment and how skeptical I'd been about the possibility of a psychiatrist or medication helping me, I knew I'd come a long way.

Dr. Glass had been different than I'd expected. Tall and lanky, he wore small round spectacles and a camelhair jacket. He spoke soothingly and asked pertinent questions. Surprisingly, it did not feel odd to reveal such personal details to someone I'd just met. I spilled my misery through constant tears, one soaked tissue after another, as he listened. I sensed an unexpected empathy from him, noticing how he leaned forward when I spoke. He was attentive in a way that wasn't condescending, and it seemed like he understood my pain.

Now, a year later, so much had changed. Progress and turning points had been subtle, and remembering where I'd been showed me how far I'd come. As I stood to leave his office, I wanted to voice my appreciation for how he had patiently guided me from hopelessness to happiness, but I wasn't sure quite what to say.

"I can't thank you enough, Dr. Glass," I said. "Truly, I just…." My voice trailed off, as I knew that if I said more I would need one of those tissues I had thought I was done with.

He nodded his head in a humble sort of gesture and looked directly into my eyes. "*You* did the work, Naomi," he said. I knew what he meant, and I supposed it was true. He put a hand on one of my shoulders, adding, "They're *in* you, you know."

I took a sharp breath in, as if to inhale his words and take them straight into my heart. Perhaps his status as a Doctor of Medicine added perceived value to the words he'd offered. I fancied it practically *science* if Dr. Glass said it, though obviously, he had not presented this comment as a medical fact. Even so, his words had as much certainty to me as if, in the space for "diagnosis" on an insurance form, he'd written: *beloved, deceased parents are inside of patient.*

I raised my hand to my chest, in a gesture meant to indicate that I would take his tender comment to heart. I turned to leave, managing to blink back all but one renegade tear, which clung momentarily to the thick bottom lashes I'd inherited from my father, before traveling down the straight plane of the nose that had been my mother's. Smiling, I allowed Dr. Glass's statement to float in the air behind me as I left his office, hovering around me like a sweet scent or a familiar fragrance.

It seemed such a lovely premise, that my parents could somehow "live in me." This was *something*; something I could consider. Whereas before they'd been nowhere, now they were somewhere—in an ideal place, *my heart.* Like the red balloon that followed the lost child in a story my mother had read me long ago, the doctor's suggestion lingered, bobbing and floating somewhere just above me, happy to follow me on my journey forward.

A few days later, I took a 'girl's trip' to the beach at Rockport with my sister-in-law Debbie, my daughter and twin nieces, and a few of their friends. Although I thought of my parents as always, now I was smiling instead of crying as I sat by the bay with a lively group of teenagers, all of us laughing while a flock of seagulls dove for the crumbs we tossed their way. Sitting by the water in late summer, surrounded by family, all of us a-glow with summer tans and full of the spirit of vacation, it felt as close to perfect as I could imagine. I savored the moment, leaning back in my chair as I admired the glow of the sinking sun delicately backlighting the girls' summer-streaked hair, creating halos that crowned their heads.

"A toast to Texas summers!" Debbie said, clinking her wine glass to mine and inspiring the younger ladies to follow suit.

"To cousins!" Paige said.

"To sisters!" Haley followed.

"To Chardonnay!" Marissa chimed in, eliciting laughs from all.

Glasses clinked and the dinnertime chatter rose and fell until the food came. On a table covered with white paper we cracked mounds of crabs with wooden mallets and cleaned off cobs of sweet corn. Chunks of potatoes, boiled soft, were dipped into blobs of ketchup or sweet mustard that had been squeezed onto the paper table-top. The conversation only lulled when mouths were full. Set to a soundtrack of teenage giggles, piles of shrimp tails and shells rose in the middle of the long table while the rise and fall of young voices reviewed the day's highlights and discussed plans for the rest of the evening.

This was the stuff of memories worth making, I thought to myself. This right here, right now. I closed my eyes behind my sunglasses and took a deep, slow breath, as if to inhale the moment.

With bellies full and tabs paid, we pushed our chairs away from the shell-strewn tables with great effort, rubbing our overstuffed middles, happily licking our lips. As we did, an expression came to me from absolutely nowhere—an expression I uttered in my own voice, but somehow wrapped in someone else's, too. It was a phrase long tucked away in memory, just then deciding to float up and out in my voice to sail off on the bay breeze.

"Let's go, kidlets," I said.

This was something my father had said to us as children; words that had lain dormant for decades, as I didn't recall him ever saying it to his grandkids, but only to the three of us—my brother, my sister and me.

It was a little thing, but Dad had called us *kidlets* when referring to the three of us, and once upon a time, that's *who we were*. For just a moment, as the moon rose over the bay in the fading glow of the summer sunset, I wondered where I had drawn that long-ago expression from.

Then I smiled. Ahhhh…of course, I knew.

As I followed the gaggle of girls through the restaurant and out to our cars, I looked up above to where I imagined my parents might be, taking a deep breath of the cooling seaside air. But then I realized that I didn't need to look any further than where I stood. Because that's where they were, too. I carried them both in my heart, tucked safely in a place where their shining spirits could still float up on a breeze, at just the moment when the setting sun gives way to the silvery rising moon.

"They're in you, you know…." It was indeed just as the good Doctor had said that it would be.

FORTY-ONE

Having received an offer too good to refuse, Richard and I sold our charming Avondale house rather unexpectedly. On moving day, I stood like a traffic cop directing movers carrying furniture and boxes out the front door. My mind wandered to the day we'd moved in, the year after my mother had died. I had known instantly that my mom would have loved this house and its endless charms, and with her on my mind, when a favorite photo of her floated out of a drawer that day, I'd taken it as a sign. I was positive I'd stuck it into a moving box, so when one of the movers brought it to me later, saying it must have fallen out of a box, I considered it my mother's way of saying, "I'm here, darling. I loved this house, too!"

I had mourned my mother there, in that lovely house on Avondale. Although just brick and mortar, the house had wrapped me in invisible arms during that difficult time and I'd come a long way there. Reminding myself that the sale put us one step closer to a future place in the Berkshires, I kept my chin up and in fact, I was *in* the Berkshires on the day of the real estate closing that Richard attended; I'd signed all necessary paperwork ahead of time. Goose bumps rose up on the back of my neck when Richard told me later about what had happened just after the closing, when he had handed over the keys, pocketed the check, and stepped onto the elevator in the building of the title company.

Riding down to the lobby with an attractive woman, pleasantries were exchanged and, as the elevator descended, Richard was surprised when the woman asked, "Aren't you Naomi Pevsner's husband?"

She had seen Richard's picture in my Facebook posts, so she recognized him immediately; but, not a fan of the social network himself, Richard did not know her.

"Yes I am," Richard said. "I'm Richard Fogel, and I'm sorry, but do we know each other?"

"I'm Kay Hester," she said, a faint trace of a Midwestern accent in her voice. "You don't know me, but I know you. I was a neighbor of Naomi's, a long time ago" she began, as the elevator opened at ground level and both of them stepped out. "We were neighbors in Illinois and played together every day as kids. Our parents were dear friends, too."

"Well I'll be darned!" Richard said. "I can't wait to tell Naomi. She would have been here but she's in the Berkshires of Massachusetts right now."

"Oh please do give her a hug for me!" Kay said. "I will never forget the day the Pevsners left for Texas. We were so sad; all of our parents were hugging and crying and then we watched them drive off." Kay frowned. "But just recently we found each other again on Facebook, and we're planning to get together soon!"

As Richard recounted their meeting in the elevator, I was amazed by all of the coincidences and serendipitous occurrences that had spoken to me of my parents and had felt like 'signs' from them. It seemed symbolic, somehow, for my childhood friend Kay Hester to have had ridden along with my husband just after our house closing, on an elevator many hundreds of miles from River Forest, Illinois, where 50 years earlier my parents had turned over their keys to new owners on that long-ago moving day.

I knew now, as I had not known then, that my parents had taken a huge leap of faith as they'd driven away from Chicago, the only city they'd ever known as home, with the three of us kids in tow. We'd driven away, Illinois in our rearview window, growing smaller and smaller and finally dropping off and out of sight. My parents had told us that *moving on* led to the opening of new doors that led to brand-new adventures. And indeed, had I not have lived in Dallas, I would never have met my former husband Cass, given birth to my darling daughter, succeeded in business, married my dear Richard or ten thousand other things that I could only have accomplished by looking *forward,* not backward on that summer day. We'd been right not to look back.

On the day Richard and I were leaving our familiar home behind, my long-ago life found itself standing shoulder-to-shoulder with the life I was living now. I wished I could tell my mom or dad, but I decided that they probably already knew. While I wasn't on the elevator that day myself, I considered the moment that Richard met Kay as a wink from my parents, proof positive of the power of possibility that hangs in the air around every corner. Perhaps the 'magic' that my mother always swore to be true, was real, after all.

FORTY-TWO

My trips to the Berkshires had become more frequent as my memoir began to take shape. I looked forward to my trips out of Dallas, to this new place I had fallen in love with. Though I didn't enjoy leaving Richard alone; I loved him all the more for supporting my travels and the book project. When he could join me he would, but many times I'd go alone; at first renting a car at the airport, and eventually shipping my own car from Dallas to Lenox. When I came home to Dallas, Richard and I would share a car and it was certainly convenient to leave mine at the Hartford airport when I'd commute, which is where I'd just retrieved it. Heading back to Lenox, I pulled into the tollbooth between the airport and the Berkshires, smiling at the memory of my parents and the 'tollbooth police.'

In the 1960's, when we drove along Route 80 from Illinois toTexas, the three of us kids would immediately snap to attention in the back seat, whenever our car pulled in to a tollbooth. Any ongoing unruliness was immediately quelled by the knowledge that *the uniformed attendants in each booth were stationed there specifically to remove misbehaving children from their cars*, a warning our parents concocted and we did not question. The three of us would sit stick-straight and motionless during the slow approach to the tollbooth, with our hands neatly folded in our laps, looking as innocent as possible. Rolling up to the tollbooth window, our hearts beat faster at the first sight of the guard in the booth, standing in a small cubicle, just large enough to allow a child or two to be squeezed into alongside the uniformed toll-taker. To authenticate the farce, my father would roll down his window, and as he extended his arm to deliver the coins or a dollar bill, and he'd say to the tollbooth attendant, *"They've been very good, sir."* After this, he'd roll up his window and drive on through, the three of us in the back seat breathing triple-sighs of relief and daring to relax; at least until the next tollbooth.

None of us were ever irritated or offended when we eventually learned that the whole thing had been a ruse; on the contrary, once we became aware of the wool that had been pulled over our six little eyes, we laughed as hard as anyone, imagining our parents pulling away from a toll booth, no doubt poking each other across the front seat—out of our view—and stifling laughs.

Even into adulthood, I joked with my parents about feeling uneasy whenever I had to drive through a tollbooth. Although they were no longer manned by attendants, I claimed I still became clammy and felt anxious, the deeply imbedded fear of being hoisted out of a car for pinching a sister or annoying a brother still present. What I loved about the tollbooth story was what it said about the little secrets my parents had shared. It was easy to imagine them giggling about it later, after the three of us children were tucked in our beds. They were a happy, loving couple who had good fun together. In those days life was good, and things to laugh about were easy to find.

Fifty years later, I was approaching a tollbooth on the Massachusetts Turnpike, glad to be in my own familiar vehicle. As I reached for money to pay the toll, a smiling toll-taker greeted me cheerily.

"Texas, huh?" the uniformed man said, referring to my Texas plates.

"Yessir," I said.

"You drive this Mercedes all this way from Texas, young lady?" the tollbooth attendant asked. I appreciated his use of 'young' with 'lady' but wished I were driving a truck rather than my shiny Mercedes, which seemed ostentatious out of its big-city element.

"No sir," I answered. "I didn't actually drive here; that would have been a tall order to have attempted that long a drive on my own."

"Well, you look like a pretty capable gal to me," he said and I smiled at the compliment.

Decades had gone by since we'd first driven from Chicago to Texas, piled into the family car with bingo, blankets and pillows. Driving through Connecticut on my way to the Berkshire Hills of Massachusetts, I'd become familiar with the comments about my Texas plates. Nonetheless, I tried to blend in and—luxury vehicle aside—I thought I was beginning to do just that. I wasn't the girl on the billboard, here in the Berkshires, and I was glad of it. Although I was far from home, I was beginning to bloom where I was planted.

FORTY-THREE

The screen on the caller I.D. says "The Tradition" and if my mother had been alive, a phone message from the director of the senior living facility she'd resided in might have frightened me. *We're calling because your mother has had an accident.*

But my mom was gone now, so I knew that it wouldn't have been a call about her having taken a fall. A small joke began forming in my mind, based on the repeatedly-run commercial about a woman who fell and could not get up. If my mother had been able to add to the commercial's tag line—"Help, I've fallen and I can't get up!"—she would have said something like: *"Well, I'll say I've fallen and can't get up, alright!...Six feet under is how far I've fallen, to be exact!"* She would have delivered these lines with perfect comedic timing, laughing broadly at her own joke.

Checking my messages, I saw it had been Linda Faulkner who'd called—the marketing director for the retirement community where my mother had resided, who'd also known my mom from their days together at Neiman-Marcus, when she'd been the PR Director and my mom the downtown Couture Manager. Linda had told me once that when she'd initially interviewed for the position at the Tradition, she'd bumped into my mother as she'd left one of the interviews and promptly decided to take the job. "If Sandra Pevsner lives here, it simply *must* be fabulous!" she thought, and shortly thereafter she joined the Tradition 'family,' where she and my mother enjoyed a re-kindled friendship for the two wonderful years my mother lived there.

In 'grand exit' style, my mom had died, but not before enjoying a gourmet dinner served in multiple courses in the beautifully appointed dining room of the Tradition, where she'd been loved by all who knew her. And anyone who didn't know her needn't have worried, for she'd have introduced herself in short order. The belle of any ball, my mother was as adorable in senior-hood as she had been at every stage of her beautiful life. And oh, the stories she loved to tell of her days at the Tradition, where she had clearly been a crowd favorite. One story I'd laughed long and hard about was the one about the day she had met "a very nice new neighbor *on the floor of his bathroom.*"

Puttering around my kitchen while talking to her on the phone, I'd been listening but at that point I thought my mind might have wandered off. "Sorry Mom, I thought you said that the guy you met *was lying on his bathroom floor.*"

Yes, she confirmed, she had indeed said just exactly that. Apparently—as she merrily continued her story—it had just-so-happened that a neighbor frantically knocking on my mother's door had desperately needed help. The woman's husband had fallen in the bathroom and the woman could not lift him by herself. Forget about the fact that my mom was five feet tall and weighed in at around 110; any port in a storm I suppose, so this neighbor had come to my mom for crisis assistance.

Donning her invisible cape (already wearing her imaginary tiara), in true 'Sandra style,' my mother had raced across the hall to see what sort of load the two of them would have to lift. Entering the apartment and scurrying to the bathroom, my mom had observed this gentleman lying flat on his back on the bathroom floor. Even before estimating his heft or the probability of two smallish women successfully lifting him, my mom had reached out with her perfectly manicured fingers to shake his hand, offering a hearty and heartfelt 'How-do-you-do,' typically reserved for individuals standing on two feet.

"*Well hello Mr. So-and-So,*" she'd said, leaning over him and smiling widely. "*I'm Sandra Pevsner, your across-the-hall neighbor!*"

To which, according to my mom, the man on the floor looked up and without missing a beat, replied, "*Pleased to meet you, Sandra.*"

At this point, my mom claims that the fellow on the floor, still holding her hand, added, *"Please excuse my not getting up."* But I only heard this part the *second* time she told the story, pointing to the possibility that she had added this detail under the allowable exception for poetic or literary license; which she wholly believed in and practiced often. In fact, I don't actually remember the end of that particular story and am not even sure that my mother provided it; for the part she'd told was just too perfect as it was. They no doubt called some maintenance man, who dragged the poor guy to a couch where he watched the Cowboys lose to Philadelphia; end of story right there. My mother knew we wouldn't be interested in that part of the story, so she took the liberty of editing it before presentation. This was my mother's genius; her endings were always better than what might actually have occurred.

Thoughts of my mom's entertaining stories aside, there was that message from Linda Faulkner to consider, so I supposed I'd best call her back sooner rather than later. My usual two-to-four-day phone call follow-up had been improving a bit lately, as I'd felt more 'myself' in recent months and hoped this trend would continue. Besides, the procrastinator who'd set up camp in me after she died knew this was about my *Mother*, for God's sake. If she had been here, she would have all but dialed the number for me.

Linda answered her phone and we chatted, gushing about my mom and how fabulous she was, occasionally becoming sniffly and emotional about the memories we shared of her. Getting to the point eventually, Linda explained that she had called about a photograph of my mother still being used in promotions, front and center on the Senior Living Community's website. Mom had been their 'model resident,' her image just the type they wanted to use to attract other upscale retirees to sign up and move in. Linda explained that they were planning to use the image again, in a beautiful, tastefully deluxe brochure promoting a new property. Remembering my mother telling me about the day of that photo shoot, I knew she'd been especially thrilled about the fact that, coincidentally, her coral lipstick had perfectly matched not only the jacket she'd been wearing, but also the flowers sitting in a vase on the table in the photo shoot. *Well, of course, they had,* I'd thought to myself. *This was my mother after all!*

Needless to say, I did not have to think more than a moment before assuring Linda that yes, of course, they were more than welcome to use any and all images of my beautiful mother for anything at all, whatsoever; a sentiment I knew my mother would have agreed with. As Linda went described the elegant new brochure they were putting together, I could feel the part of my mother that lives in my heart making its way to the front, chiming in with a resounding, "YES! You simply must use my image!" I knew my mom would not only have approved of the use of her picture, but would have insisted on it, and would have gone on to claim that she was part of the success of the new brochure in attracting new residents. By the time all was said and done, my mother would have told anyone who'd cared (and even those who did not) that she herself had had a hand in filling the new facility to capacity, and you'd not only have believed what she was telling you, but—if you were a senior—you would have kicked yourself for not having jumped on board yourself before it had sold out.

This habit of hers for enhancing or augmenting a story was an obvious offshoot of her knack for optimism in every imaginable situation. She never sounded cocky or full of herself; it was just part of her unshakable confidence in herself and her point of view, and whatever the root of her positivity, you wished you had some too. A line from a Rob Reiner movie that she and I both loved might have crossed your mind while listening to her: *"I'll have what she's having!"*

Ahhh, to be more like her...to possess the skill for putting an artful spin on any situation, no matter how negative or dire it might seem. My mother could find the most elusive silver lining, and from it she could make a double-sided all-weather parachute to carry her to a safe landing. Somehow she could reframe any difficulty that came her way, often with a built-in *"Thank God it wasn't worse"* mentality. So just when you might be thanking your lucky stars that you didn't have to deal with whatever-it-was she was facing, by the time she'd finished with you, you'd walk away wishing to be as *lucky* as she was. You might even feel as if you'd seen the result of some sort of slight of hand or a magic trick as she convinced you that a 'very bad' thing could have been *ten times worse*. The sleight of hand you'd not seen was that she'd been telling herself this too.

I believe her ability to see the silver lining had been just the thing that saved her, time and time again, from real-life difficulties she'd faced. Tough times and true tragedies were no match for her power to put a positive spin on each and every one of them. Since she died, I've often said that if my mother had survived the last surgery, by the time we'd all heard her tell of it, each of us might have wanted to run out and get one of the colostomy bags she'd have been sporting. No doubt she'd have touted its benefits and 'sold us' on the conveniences of having all of one's 'unspeakables' routed through to one neat little bag. My mother could be so convincing that perhaps, heading to our own bathrooms with our morning papers, we might have thought of her with a touch of envy, knowing that she could sidestep the whole morning bathroom-toilet routine we were stuck with.

This, in a glamorous nutshell, was my mother. And this was exactly why I knew she would have been thrilled for her picture to be used in any advertisement, now and until the end of time. She would have expected no less.

After I hung up from Linda, I smiled for the rest of the afternoon. I was pleased that my beautiful mother's image still 'had what it takes,' and I knew that my mom's delight would have equaled mine. In life, my mother had been the Pied Piper of anything she believed in, so it stood to reason that this quality of hers could not have been quelled by something as 'inconvenient' as death.

Actually, before I'd gotten that call from Linda, I'd driven by a life-size version of my mother, draped across several feet of a chain-link fence surrounding the new building site. Luckily I had not swerved off the road, though it had startled me, but in the very best of ways. A maniacal u-turn later, I pulled over and exited my car to find myself standing in front of a humongous image of my mother. Right there on well-traveled Lovers' Lane, where a new Tradition facility would rise from its foundation, I stepped out of my car, not crying but smiling, and said, "Well, hullo Momma!" to no one in particular.

The new facility was being erected just across the street from where the Yves Saint Laurent Boutique had once stood: the beautiful store that my mother had opened and managed for the iconic French designer in the 1970's. There had been other times I'd felt that certain 'signs' had been little winks from her, and on the day I'd seen that enlarged image of her, I had been missing her terribly, so I'd taken it as one. Besides, my mother never did things in a small way, so this mammoth image of her would have been just the sort of super-sized 'wink' I would have expected from her. Why use a smaller image when a larger-than-life one will do?

My mother had been one of those people whose light shined so brightly in life that it left a lasting impression even afterwards. Like the pop of a flashbulb and the replica of light remaining in the dark behind our eyes, she left an indelible image that never faded. She captured us at first glance, in that fleeting moment when we are already sold.

FORTY-FOUR

In Mitch Albom's magical book, *The First Phone Call From Heaven*, a phone jangles from a caller who has long since been deceased. To Albom's credit, in the context of the story, we readers are completely convinced that a call can indeed come from heaven; while the characters in Albom's lovely story are somewhat harder to convince. While the characters in the story hesitate, questioning their own sanity, we grip the sides of the book and squeeze, wanting to shout: *My God, it's really happening! Answer your damn phone and you'll know!*

I finished Albom's book in two sittings, devouring it while imagining myself as one of the lucky characters in the story waiting for my own mother to call, my father at her side in heaven, as usual allowing her to speak for them both. Albom's book was on my mind as I stood in my kitchen on a late summer day in Lenox, Massachusetts, staring out the window over my tiny but flourishing garden to the green hillside rising up beyond the trees. Taking in the perfection of the small patch of God's green earth beyond my window, I felt suddenly humbled at the good fortune that had allowed me to claim this little piece of heaven on Earth. But my happiness was suddenly tempered by the sobering realization that *my mother no longer existed in the world outside my window*—nor outside any other window, anywhere, for that matter. I was momentarily overtaken by the duality of tremendous loss alongside marvelous beauty. Feeling both these sensations at once was overwhelming and unsettling, all the more so because today was the date of my mother's *Yarzeit*. What were my chances, I wondered, of finding a proper *Yartzeit* candle in the small New England town of Lenox? They were easily available at any grocery store in Dallas; perhaps, I thought to myself, I had brought one with me from Texas?

I dried the tears I'd allowed to blur the beauty of my bursting garden and turned to rummage through my kitchen cabinets and drawers, searching for a candle. Peering into a deep drawer next to the stove, a tangled collection of household items revealed everything but a candle. Moving some batteries aside, I lifted a box of matches from the drawer and remembered that I had had a *Yartzeit* candle but had used it for my father's *Yartzeit,* a couple weeks earlier.

Damn. Why hadn't I bought two? I wondered, thinking of my Grandma, Bama, who had been famous for buying everything in bulk. We'd teased Bama lovingly about her habit of stockpiling multiples of everything from frozen bagels to Baggies, a habit I suddenly began to appreciate. She would never have been caught without a *Yartzeit* candle on hand—in fact, she probably had them individually labeled and catalogued by name of deceased relative and month-of-passing. Meanwhile, here I was, without even a single candle for my mother.

Like my mother and me, my grandmother had been a 'foodie.' When she spoke of a *crusty* roll and the *crunch* of its toasted crust, one could practically *see* the steam coming from its broken shell—all soft and warm inside, just awaiting a pat of butter spread by her expert fingers. Even the way she said *chicken* could make my mouth water; something about the way she rolled the 'c' and the 'k' together made you long to pull apart the crackling skin of a roasted breast to get to the bones, where the sweetest meat lies.

Ahhhh…maybe I'd roast a chicken this afternoon, I thought, reaching for my keys and deciding to head out to the store to buy both a roasting chicken and a *Yartzeit* candle—if I could find one for sale in town. *Well, Mom, I'm going to be an hour or two late in lighting your candle,* I thought to myself as I grabbed a straw sun-hat I'd never wear in Dallas. Suddenly a ringing phone turned my head towards the one on my own kitchen wall. Had I been a character in Mitch Albom's book—standing in the kitchen where the first phone call from heaven had come in—I would have thought it was my mother, telling me she had a perfectly good *Yartzeit* candle I could use.

It hadn't actually been the phone, but the ringing of the oven timer I'd set to alert me that the squash I'd been baking was ready. It was my first full-size, home-grown squash from my first-ever garden. I didn't typically bake squash in the morning, but my excitement had prompted an early-morning experimental baking of a whole squash, with no preparations except a few pokes from a fork. To me, that little bulbous beauty was quite an accomplishment, my first collaboration with Mother Nature in the Berkshires. She and I had not worked together much back in Dallas, where I'd had no luck growing vegetables—or much of anything else—under the blazing sun of a fiery Texas summer.

Truth be told, since my days of swimming as a child, I had avoided spending time outdoors during the hot, humid summer days. In Dallas, the open spaces between my car and the entrance to a building were nothing but rain or wind or natural inconveniences sure to ruin my hairdo. But so much had changed. Here in the Berkshires, I cared little about my hair, smashed under my favorite gardening hat for a trip to town. I'd spring out of bed in the morning, not to adorn myself with a new outfit for a luncheon, but to brew coffee as the sun came up so that I could go out to see the perfectly formed baby butternut squashes clinging to a vine in my garden. Earlier this morning, I had plucked the fattest of them and carried them inside as gingerly as if it were a basketful of baby rabbits. After a quick rinse, I'd carefully pierced the whole squashes with a fork, all the while apologizing under my breath for the few quick stabs necessary for steam to escape. I knew that the details of my first homegrown squash baking would have delighted my mother, and on her *Yartzeit* it was a pleasure to imagine the pride she would have had for my newly burnished horticultural prowess. She, who'd believed I could do *anything*.

I had all but forgotten about the little roasting round when I heard the bell ring. I knew it couldn't have been a phone ringing because we didn't have a landline, only a decorative antique wall phone. Putting my keys down, I turned the ringing timer off and grabbed a potholder to carefully pull the steaming squash from the oven. It was perfectly done; I marveled at its gleaming glossiness and inhaled its aroma as if I'd never smelled anything quite like it. Setting it atop the stove to cool while I ran to the store, it occurred to me to check another drawer by the back door, just in case it might hold a candle.

When I yanked the drawer open a bit harder than necessary, the entire thing came out and fell to the floor, scattering its contents across several rows of alternating black and white tiles. *Oh, darn.* A dog's ball bounced, a couple of woven potholders flopped and several coins rolled in different directions. As I squatted and scooped up the scattered items to return them to the drawer, a funny-looking thing-a-ma-jig caught my eye. I saw its electrical prongs first and, then, recognizing it, I was suddenly whisked away into the memory of the first time I'd seen it.

My mother had held it in her hands then, standing in my Dallas kitchen simply ecstatic about the new discovery she'd pulled from her purse, waving it wildly and all but chomping at the bit to demonstrate it. For as long as I could remember, my mother had been bringing me new items, which she would present with such enthusiasm, you might have thought she was the inventor of what-ever-it-was. That day, she'd been simply percolating with excitement as she produced this thing, with prongs on its underside. For me, the sheer joy she exuded as she shared her incredible new find was half the fun.

She unwrapped the object carefully from its protective pouch, handling it as if it were the Holy Grail. Even if I'd known what it was, I would not have wanted to deprive her of the pleasure of tell-ing me. Holding it in her hands, she presented what appeared to be a small, black, plastic box with some gold Hebrew lettering across its curved top and a white stripe down its middle. As usual, she wanted me to guess, before she revealed its purpose. I couldn't imagine what it was, but wouldn't have dreamed of "giving up." I noticed that there was a tiny light bulb at the top of the white stripe, but she was mov-ing the damn thing around so fast I couldn't tell for sure. I honestly didn't have a clue as to its purpose or name, but I'd been down this road a time or two and knew I was expected to make a few random stabs at naming it.

"*Is it a Pill box?... a night light?... Ummm...a Christmas ornament?!*" I offered my initial guesses as if they might be winners, though her smug look and slow head shake told me I wasn't even close. They had been throwaway guesses—who would want a Christmas ornament with Hebrew lettering in the middle of summer?—but I had to start somewhere.

"Give up?" my mother asked with a widening smile, less a question than an order to do so; to which I responded with the only answer she was looking for and the one I could always be counted on to give her. "Okay, so what is it?" I asked. This of course was music to her ears; her face lit up like a Chanukah Bush.

First, she would offer me a hint. When we played these guessing games, I never thought of turning from the object in question with a yawn, saying, *Okay, I'm a little bored; just tell me what it is already.* To deprive her of the delight of these moments would have been cruel.

The two metal prongs coming from the bottom of the black component offered a big clue, suggesting that the thing could be plugged into a wall socket. She pointed these out with one glossy red fingernail. *Ah-HA!* I said, as if this had been a revealing trove of intel—which it wasn't. Based on the Hebrew lettering, I kept my guesses kosher. *Passover Nightlight?! Electric Tefillin?* While my mother rolled her eyes at my ridiculous guesses, my mind momentarily wandered, the entrepreneur in me considering the marketability of a plug-in heated prayer shawl and making a mental note to revisit the idea.

Eyes twinkling wildly now, my mother moved the electrical thing a little closer to my face. I didn't flinch. Was it a Jewish water-squirting device? Maybe a miniature fan to blow tiny breezes my way? Before I could speculate further my mother spun around on one pretty heel and asked, "*Where's your nearest outlet?*" It was both a question and a directive. "Probably behind the..." I began, trailing off as I saw she wasn't waiting for my answer anyway—she was already ducking into the laundry room. I followed her to where she stood in front of an electrical outlet above the washing machine.

In five seconds, she'd cleared a space on the washer's top—so I knew a demo was coming. And oh my, how my mother loved a demo! Especially if it was a product that only *she* could demonstrate to some previously un-enlightened soul.

"So, you'll note the *candle* you see here?" my mother asked, pointing to the front of the plug-in object.

"Yes, Mother, I see it," I said. I never called her 'Mother' but she was too busy to notice or to acknowledge my sarcasm, as she pointed one perfect fingernail at what was—upon closer inspection—a tiny candle painted on the front of the 3-inch-high, black plastic thing-a-ma-jig. It was not more than an inch in height, with an orange flame on top, and Hebrew lettering just below. I could still read a bit of Hebrew from my years of the forced training 'offered' to every Jewish kid—so I might actually have been able to read the words printed in gold if she had quit moving the darn thing around.

"*Well, watch this...*" my mother said, spinning around to plunge the prongs of the electric device into the bottom socket of the outlet. As she shoved it home, I fully expected the Israeli National Anthem to play, or at least for the garage door to go up and down; but as far as I could tell, nothing was happening. My mother stepped aside to allow the world's greatest thing to shine; and sure enough...it actually *did*.

Plugged into the outlet, the tiny flame appeared to be 'flicker-ing' in miniature, an impossibly tiny candle-wick that fluttered back and forth. No bigger than a seed, I could see that the 'flame' would continue to 'burn' until someone pulled its plug. It was interesting, I thought; I didn't want to burst her bubble, but between you and me, it still wasn't screaming "world's greatest thing."

Thankfully, my mother ended the guessing game with just one word. "*Yartzeit*," she said, in a tone indicating that no other words were needed.

"Whose *Yartzeit*?" I asked. My innocent question provoked a dramatic response: she was now looking at me as though I were an electrical toy, short a battery.

"Why, ANYONE'S!" she answered, as if I had missed the glaringly obvious.

"Whose *Yartzeit...*" I heard her mumble, the repeating of my query further illustrating the ridiculousness of what I'd asked.

At this point, I wasn't just placating her with my cluelessness; I truly did not know what she was getting at and was beginning to question my own intelligence. Though I was in my fifties, I still felt for a moment like a dimwitted ten-year-old.

"Well, I was at the Synagogue Gift Shop today," she began, her voice rising and then trailing off, to indicate that this was a clue. Ah-ha! She was throwing me a bone. And then—allowing me to keep the bone but apparently not to run with it—she sprinted ahead for the big reveal. Well played, Mom.

"THIS," she proclaimed, pausing for effect as she swept her lovely hand back towards the plastic piece in the plug, looking just like Vanna White standing in front of a billboard for a trip to the Bahamas—"This is *the NEW Yartzeit Candle*," she said with great satisfaction.

Her revelation hung in the air like the cloud over Mount Sinai on the day Moses received the Ten Commandments. Had been proclaimed by God, I wondered? And what had become of the old-school, white waxy versions, with wicks that were guaranteed to burn for 24 hours? I had no time to ask, as she continued with her demonstration.

She gestured the striking of a match on a matchbox and said, "NO longer does one need to actually light a *Yartzeit* candle."

"So dangerous!" she pointed out, shaking her invisible match as if to extinguish it just before it set one of her manicured nails ablaze. "Now..." she said, "THIS is all you do!" By 'This' she clearly meant plugging in the black thing and by 'you,' I had to assume she meant every living Jew. I couldn't help but wonder how many of us, besides me, had been early beneficiaries of this really big news and also, what would become of all those poor, dusty old-style *Yartzeit* candles, now practically extinct according to the Temple Shalom Gift Shop and my mother.

The obvious question left unanswered was who exactly had determined that the age-old Jewish tradition of lighting a real memorial candle could now be replaced by a plug-in.

So: "Says who?" was the question I asked; assuming I was allowed at least one.

Her green eyes widened, as if I'd said something incredulous.

"Says *who?*" she repeated, underscoring the ludicrousness of my question. "Says…well…says EVERYBODY!"

"Everybody?" I asked, with a bit of doubt in my voice. "Like, ya mean, God?" I added, poker-faced.

"Well…I…" she paused here.

And then, a smile: "Oh, stop," she said, brushing me off with the realization that I was just egging her on.

"You're teasing me!" she said, continuing on undeterred.

"Why, I am telling you, Naomi, THIS is the newest thing! One simply plugs it in, wherever one likes…"—she spun a half circle to deftly pluck the electric thing-a-ma-jig from its socket, then held it up—"…and 24 hours later… Why, you just pull the plug…and… (turning back to face her audience of one) "VOILA! *YARZTEIT OVER!*" she said.

Setting the thing face down on the top of the dryer she smiled and said, "You simply put it away until next year! You're done!" she exclaimed, brushing her hands against each other, as if washing them of a task.

"No mess, no fire, no danger, no waste!" she declared, grinning with this big finish. The longtime 'hassle' of allowing a memorial candle to burn on a kitchen countertop was now 'simplified.' Thank God above.

There were about a dozen obvious comments I could have made then, including my observation that she seemed just a bit too happy for someone demonstrating a product associated with death; but she seemed so darn excited, I opted to do what I always did: I told her it was truly a clever find.

Mission accomplished, my mother had already twirled around to return to the kitchen, as if just wrapping up an episode of *Wheel of Fortune*. I considered the 'thing' lying there—and with my father's *Yartzeit* approaching, I figured I'd plug the 'virtual candle' in on the upcoming date and no doubt giggle to myself when I did, remembering my mom's undying enthusiasm and unstoppable adorableness.

Following her out of the kitchen that day, I had no way of knowing that all too soon, it would be her *Yartzeit* I'd be facing. And surely it had not been a coincidence that on the day of my first squash harvest, I'd found the electric 'candle' just when I'd needed it.

Getting up off my Berkshire floor, I picked up the electric Yartzeit candle and went in search of the perfect outlet for my mother. I headed straight to the living room, with its lovely view of the meadow stretching out towards the trees. It was a place of honor worthy of Mom; she'd love it. But I'd forgotten that all of the outlets were located low to the ground. As I squatted with plug in hand, I imagined a wee version of my mom's voice coming from just below the baseboard molding, saying, "Hey, way too low! I can't see a thing down here!"

Knowing this wouldn't do, I stood with hand on hip, scanning the charming old house for a better spot. It suddenly dawned on me that not only were the outlets positioned down near the floor, they were also set into the wall horizontally, which meant that the plug could not be inserted vertically, with its tiny candle upright. Hmmmmm…I considered my options and headed to the bathroom, but the plugs were the same—and not only would the electric *Yartzeit* candle be sideways, but it would also be placed directly opposite the commode. I knew this would not have gone over well with my mom.

Hell-bent on vertical positioning, I wandered through the house to confirm that while all of the outlets might have been electrical code compliant, none of them were vertically installed. So I headed back to the kitchen, wondering what my mom herself would have said of such a predicament.

"What now, Momma?" I asked, as I aimed the prongs towards the horizontal outlet with my head at a 45-degree angle.

If she'd been around, she would have shown up with some Rabbi-approved adaptor or kosher converter, which she'd have pulled from her purse, having found it just that week at the synagogue gift shop—on sale, to boot!

I knew that we would have giggled together about the sideways plug, and just thinking about it made me laugh out loud in my kitchen, on the anniversary of her death. This small thing—the ability to laugh about a memory, rather than cry—was proof of my slow but steady journey towards healing.

Though no telephone rang from heaven, I could hear her distinctly through the receiver in my head, and see her clearly in my memories of the way she spoke, moved and gestured. As I plunged the prongs into the outlet, the tiny candle lit, flickering in miniature, and illuminating the Hebrew words that translate to: *I Remember.* Standing as reverently as I could in my bare feet, I beheld the thing-a-ma-bob; and assuming that the traditional blessing would still be applicable to the electric adaptation of the old-style candle, I began the Hebrew prayer that I knew by heart.

In our sun-washed cottage in Lenox. Massachusetts, on that May 18th, I sang the mourner's prayer in a voice that did not crack with emotion, with the memory of my mother strong in my mind. As I sang, I bent at the waist and leaned left, my head cocked to the side as far as it would go in order to be parallel with the direction of the plug-in candle, a detail I knew would have tickled my mom immensely. *A perfectly good Yartzeit gone sideways!* she'd have quipped.

She, of all people, would have found the humor in her *Yartzeit* leaning left. And that morning, standing in my Berkshire kitchen, redolent with the scent of roasted squash, so did I.

FORTY-FIVE

Inside the glittering and glamorous Northpark location of the famed Neiman Marcus store, the 'Mermaid Bar' beckons. A favorite among weary women-who-shop and ladies-who-lunch, well-dressed patrons sink into leather banquettes to enjoy finger sandwiches and orange souffles as light as air, beneath ceramic mermaids hand-painted in pastels and hung above bistro tables on peachy-pink walls. I sat at a corner table in the tony cafe on a rainy Saturday, awaiting my girlfriends Shari and Patti to join me for lunch.

My trips back 'home' to Dallas had become shorter and farther apart over the last few years, so I tried to connect with my closest girlfriends when I was back from the Berkshires. I spotted a pretty mother and her young daughter sitting at a table across the café, sharing lunch as my mother and I had once done. A fancy lunch with my mom, in this very same place, had been a delight and a real treat, and I sighed at the memory, waiting for two of my besties at a table set with my favorite MacKenzie-Childs china. Whimsical and cheerily checkered in black and white, the plates on the table reminded me of my mom, as they'd been her favorite china too. I fingered the edges of a bread plate, tracing the colorful hand-painted butterflies fluttering there and thinking that perhaps they were like the ones over the rainbow.

My mom had been on my mind since I'd walked through the gleaming glass doors of the famed Neiman Marcus store; the very place she had started her career in fashion, as a "Greeter" in the high-end Couture department at this same store. The three of us kids, finally in school all day, became 'latch-key kids' for a couple of hours after school, while she worked at her new job. She'd been a natural, looking every bit the part of a glamorous hostess, welcoming afflu-ent shoppers into the pricey Couture department. Often they'd ask to work with her, admiring her knowledge, style, beauty and taste, resulting in Mom's promotion to from hostess to sales. She became the top salesperson in no time, and then quickly rose to become department manager. Sitting in the sparkling cafe waiting for my gal pals, I realized that I still knew the phone number of this very store by heart. My siblings and I had called the number countless times over the years for various reasons, most of them less-than-urgent and surely annoyances to our hard-working mother. "Joe is being rude to me!" Or, "Can Sara and I bake a cake? I'll be responsible for handling the hot pans and turning off the oven."

Eventually, she was lured away from her beloved Neimans by the only one who could have done so: the French designer Yves Saint Laurent. When he opened his famed *Rive Gauche* boutique in the U.S., its first jewel-box location was Dallas. My mother had always sworn she had French blood coursing through her veins and it took little to convince her to climb happily aboard a flight to Paris, courtesy of YSL, to accept the position she'd been offered. Opening the YSL Rive Gauche Boutique in Dallas to great success, my mom claimed that the $500 blouses and $1500 jackets practically walked themselves out the door, but we knew it was largely her doing. The world's finest ready-to-wear seemed to suit Dallas' most discerning women just fine and even in the 1970's it sold at pricing our own mother could ill afford. But she lived and breathed the iconic French designer, whose larger-than-life black and white headshot graced one entire wall of the boutique. Yves Saint Laurent became my mother as much as my mother became YSL. Theirs was a love affair that lasted well beyond the great designer's lifetime and certainly as long as my mother's. Even the personalized license plates on her car read YSL, and she had 'gone down in the annals of history' by winning a land-mark tax case supporting her claim that the expensive YSL clothing she purchased to wear at work was a required uniform and should, therefore, be a tax-deductible expense. Indeed, the shy but brilliant 'genius of fashion' Yves Saint Laurent would have been at the top of my Mom's list of fantasy guests with whom to dine. And lunch at the Mermaid Bar would have suited just fine.

As I sat and waited for Shari and Patti, I couldn't help but tear up when I thought of my mother. I missed her desperately, but seated in the pretty surroundings of the Mermaid Bar at Neiman's, somehow I felt a bit closer to her memory. I was sitting in a place where she had actually BEEN in life, so it was a bit like 'hallowed ground.' It was a place where her energy had once floated in life, which begged the possibility that perhaps it lingered still. *Isn't it true that energy never dies?* I thought to myself. *If so, maybe a bit of her remains here.*

There were times like these when I felt her close to me in a way I couldn't explain. When it happened, I'd almost expect her to sashay up behind me. I'd imagine that at any moment I'd sense her fragrance under my nose, and then I'd hear her sing-song voice and I wouldn't have to miss her anymore. Of course, this never happened. But when I found myself missing her so much that I could almost smell her, a coincidence would often present itself in her place. I had tried to explain this to my brother, the non-believer, and he scoffed at such things. But I wanted to believe.

While I waited, I sipped a spiced tea and prepared to forgo such fantasies, but as if on cue, two good-looking young men strolled in. They were screamingly handsome, but what caught my eye was that both of them were wearing fitted black shirts emblazoned with the signature 'YSL'. My mother would have approved, I thought.

When Shari and Patti arrived, after hugs and greetings, we sat and arranged ourselves around the table. As luck would have it, the two men were seated close enough for us to chat while we waited for our lunches. They were reps for the famed designer's Couture collection, and except for the matching Hermes belts they wore, both young men were beautifully dressed head to toe in YSL. I told them about my mother, and we talked about mother love—both of them said they simply could not imagine life without their moms. I had decades on both of them but admitted that I was still trying to imagine it, myself. They were so handsome and stylish, I asked if we could take a picture together so I'd remember the day. They were very accommodating, posing happily with me. I wouldn't be able to show it to my mother, but it seemed like a picture worth having.

I wanted to remember the moment, one in which I'd lunched with friends in a place I'd once sat with my mother, like the little girl I saw across the restaurant, eating fancy finger sandwiches with her own mom. I'd enjoyed lunch with my dearest old friends, in the company of two of Yves Saint Laurent's picture-perfect modern-day men and we'd clinked our topaz teas across the table in a toast to friendship. Enjoying a typical Dallas afternoon, we had caught up over scoops of chicken salad and tiny orange-molded terrines, and I had to admit that I'd missed this side of Dallas. I'd missed my friends. They were as much a link to my past as anything; I'd known both Patti and Shari since my early days in Dallas, and we'd managed to remain close over the years. I hadn't even minded when they teased me about the highly 'un-designer' bag I carried, perfect for the Berkshires, but perhaps not sufficiently Dallas-chic, its burlap front emblazoned with the words "Re-use, Re-Cycle"—to which Patti exclaimed, "Girl, you need to recycle that bag... straight to the trash!" But I was part 'Berkshire girl' now, able to laugh at such materialism.

I leaned into the soft back of the booth and listened to my girlfriends chattering about their college-age kids. Across the restaurant, I watched the little girl and her mother rise and collect their things, going out the door and melting into the crowd of well-dressed Neiman's shoppers. I wondered where they were going next. Perhaps to do a bit more shopping before heading home to join the rest of their family; as my mother and I had once done. I imagined them going to our old house on Brookshire and setting their iconic Neiman-Marcus shopping bags on our old kitchen counter. I smiled at the memory of the white linoleum of the countertops in our kitchen; funny, the things we remember.

Just then, I noticed a familiar scent in the air, but I couldn't place it exactly. I breathed in deeply and decided it was a scent I recognized; one that had perhaps drifted in from one of the cosmetics counters just outside the Mermaid Bar. Patti and Shari were checking their cell phones so I didn't ask either of them if they recognized the scent; I just leaned into it and closed my eyes for a moment. Fragrant lilies blended with notes of something slightly mysterious and finished off with a scent that was unmistakably French. It was a fragrance I would know anywhere; my mother's perfume. For just a moment, I was wrapped in the scent of her; surrounded by old friends, in a place where she had once been. And I was smiling.

FORTY-SIX

After lunch with the girls, I stopped by the dress department at Neiman's, thinking I'd need a dress for a young cousin's upcoming *Bat Mitzvah*. Perusing the racks of stylish clothes with unapologetic price tags, I considered the possibility that dresses might not be required, or even expected, at a Reform synagogue in this day and age. It had been a while since I'd attended a *Shabbat* service, even at our Conservative synagogue, so times might have changed since the days of required skirts at services. I decided black pants and a jacket would be appropriate enough.

I was excited about seeing many of the relatives who'd be coming into town for the *Mitzvah* especially since rumor had it that an extra-special guest would be in attendance, one I'd had the honor of meeting for the first time some forty years before, at my own *Bat Mitzvah*. Our family *Torah*—the V.I.P. attendee—would be shipped in a specially crafted wooden crate, lovingly wrapped with great care and respect for both its contents and its age—having been carried here from Russia by our ancestors well over a century ago.

Our family *Torah* was the stuff of legends. Its hand-scribed scrolls of the Five Books Of Moses were rolled around tall wooden arms and cloaked in a velvet cover with the names of my great-grand-parents *Zalman and Naomi Pevsner* embroidered in gold, below a gold tasseled border that shimmied when the Torah was carried. The cover had been added in recent years, as had the ornate silver crowns atop the wooden handles; the *Torah* itself had come to America in the early 1900's with my family from Russia, though parts of the story remain as veiled as the scrolls under cover. We know that my great-grandfather came through Ellis Island with my grandfather and his brothers and sisters, then small children, but the story of how they were able to get the *Torah* here has different versions. Travel, for Jews of that era, was not easily afforded or allowed but somehow my ancestors had managed it and the rest—as they say—was history.

A few days later, at cousin Diane's *Bat Mitzvah*, I was sitting with my husband in the sanctuary while the same Rabbi who'd officiated at my mother's funeral stood at the podium next to my young cousin, a petite blue-eyed version of her great-grandmother Dinah, the woman for whom she'd been named. My great-aunt Dinah had been the loving wife of my Uncle Sam Pevsner; himself one of the brothers seated around my grandfather, in an old photo of the six of them as children. I'd seen this photo for the first time only the night before, at a family gathering to which we'd all been encouraged to bring pictures to share. Later I came to know that the photo had been taken on the steps of their farmhouse in Connecticut, just down the road from the Hartford airport I'd flown into on my way to Kripalu; unknowingly landing in the same place my ancestors had, in a previous century. Just like them, I'd been stepping into a new life.

My early ancestors had been treading on new ground, just as life without my parents seemed like alien territory to me—and we'd all wandered into the same place, albeit several lifetimes apart. The tobacco fields on either side of the car I'd hired had been standing in welcome poses to greet me under a rainbow, as I'd entered strange new lands once farmed by those who'd come before me. I hadn't farmed tobacco, as they had, nor had I ever heard of 'the Berkshires' before—but like my ancestors, I found something in the rolling fields and mountains of the same green corner of the world: I found a new peace of mind and enough quiet to hear my own heart.

The highlight of the lovely Sabbath service was seeing little Diane carrying the massive *Torah*—almost as big as she was—around the sanctuary to the tune of a centuries-old, celebratory prayer. Returning to the pulpit, she stood on a step that raised her above the opened scrolls so she could follow the words with a silver *Yad,* a tiny hand with a pointed finger to glide along the parchment line by line. Diane chanted flawlessly in Hebrew with a sweet-sounding voice, reaching high notes I remembered from my own *Bat Mitzvah*. Age-old melodies filled the sanctuary as background music for the words she read, penned long ago in another century, on another continent.

Afterwards, she carried the towering *Torah* to where my cousin Henry sat, in a special seat on the *Bimah*, and she passed the *Torah* off to him, no small feat for a young lady of her size. Henry held the ancient scrolls upright, steady and straight, while his two young grandsons stood beside him, ready to do the honors of replacing the *Torah's* cover. The congregation stood—an ovation for the holy scrolls—as the boys in their hand-knit *yarmulkes* slowly pulled the velvet cover from the top to the bottom of the *Torah*— carefully covering its scrolls until the next time they'd be unfurled, on another *Shabbat*.

As they did, I squinted my eyes, not from the light reflecting off the stained glass windows, nor to keep from tearing up at the sight of it all. I was squinting to see the image of my great-uncles—sweet Uncle Leo and his brothers, my grandfather and my precious father, too—*all standing* beside the holy scrolls tucked into a velvet coat bearing the names of those who'd brought us here long ago, from other shores. I could almost see my ancestors there, their eyes fixed on the *Torah* Henry held, its biblical stories rolled together from one side to the other between heavy wooden arms reaching to the heavens, adorned with silver crowns.

I imagined I saw my cousin Robert there, too, whose *Bar Mitzvah* in Chicago had been the first I'd ever attended. I remembered how he'd read from the same *Torah*, and how years later I'd cried to learn he had passed away too soon, only in his 30's. My beautiful cousin Marsha, his sister, had passed away decades before him, a child herself at only 14 when she died of cancer; the first half of a double family tragedy. But Marsha had read from this *Torah* too. It had touched so many of us—and as it passed by in a procession led by Diane, we had all touched it back.

The family *Torah* had traveled to Texas for my own Bat Mitzvah in 1971 and returned for my daughter to read from it in 1999; and now here it was, back once again; all of us gathered around it. Had the relatives who'd carried these scrolls from old-world Russia known how much it would mean to those of us here and now? Perhaps they had. Perhaps they'd done it for just this reason, and we, here tonight, were the fulfillment of their dreams.

Other legacies seated in the sanctuary carried not just the DNA of our ancestors but their names, as well. Little Leo Bernard—named for my grandfather and uncle, sat in my lap exhibiting patience beyond his three years. My beautiful daughter Marissa had been named for my cousin Marsha, who we'd imagined had been met by all our relatives at the gates of heaven. And I'd given Marissa my paternal grandmother Lucy's Hebrew middle name—*Leah*—in memory of the sweet and gentle spirit of the mother who'd adored her son Barry, my father. So many legacies stood with us that night, all of us together beneath the 'eternal light' at the front of the sanctuary, that never darkened or dimmed. This *Torah...this* is our legacy, I thought.

I'd long regarded the *'legacy of the five generations of diamond purveyors'* as something sacred, but elevating my profession to this level of importance had made it hard for me to give up the parts of it that no longer served me. Running a jewelry business (that had begun to 'run me') disallowed wanderings, day trips, forays into writing or painting or any of the other things I wished to do. I'd struggled with this reality for years, but especially after the deaths of my parents I had felt trapped in a 'job' I considered 'my legacy.' It was my birthright, after all; far too important to be 'cast off' for other dreams or different journeys.

But on the evening that Diane chanted her *Haftorah*, I glimpsed the larger legacy left to us; wrapped around our gathered family like the scrolls encircling the great wooden arms of our *Torah*. An inheritance that shimmered around the edges as brilliantly as diamonds set in gold, as meaningfully as the words of the Old Testament, written long ago on parchment that never faded. More than dazzling diamonds or chests of gold, this *Torah* was our family jewel, and we were its legacy. I'd had inklings of this truth but knew it for sure only that night. The value of this inheritance was no less precious for being less tangible than other riches.

That evening I felt the significance of all those whose shoulders we stand upon, and how we honor them by how we live and by what we do. I'd seen how we immortalize these souls by allowing the magic in the memories to come to light in the midst of religious ceremonies we have cared enough about to preserve. We are the guardians of these age-old traditions, which held blessings in their cores that far outweighed the burden of safe-keeping them.

I felt the presence of loved ones in spirit, surrounding us just like the rows of high windows running the length of the walls of the sanctuary. I felt my father and the other patriarchs of my family as surely as if I'd actually seen them standing on the pulpit alongside my cousin Henry, holding the *Torah*. I stood with the congregation before an open Ark, facing the pulpit where my ancestors stood as tall as my memories of them.

After the late afternoon service, there was a *Bat-Mitzvah*-style celebration lasting into the night, worthy of Diane's stellar performance and years of study. We ate and danced and as the festivities began to wind down for the night, we bid our farewells. Leaving the synagogue, my husband and I walked with Marissa into the moonlight towards the car and I breathed in the evening air, still thinking of the images of the men I'd imagined on the pulpit. My dear departed relatives—my darling father and my grandfather, too—had all *been there*. I felt warmed, still, by the sight of them.

We'd been together, heedless of space and time, called to assemble in the shadow of a legacy: a *Torah* that had journeyed across centuries and continents to be lifted up in prayer and carried in a procession led by one of the smallest of us, to the tune of an ancient prayer. Diane's steps with the *Torah* had been in the direction of the next leg of its journey, from one generation to the next. *L'dor va dor*, as we say in Hebrew. And those who'd walked with the family *Torah* from the beginning were there in spirit—leading us around the sanctuary and never missing a step. Ours was a legacy stretching farther, even, than the long lengths of parchment, rolling out across generations to stop for a time, in a place where we'd gather together, before going forward.

Arriving at the car with Richard and Marissa, I smiled at the stars winking in the heavens. My beloved relatives, even if only in memory, had been with us that evening. Under an ink-blue Sabbath sky, I was suddenly certain that that was enough.

FORTY-SEVEN

It was Christmastime and I was home in Dallas. There would be no snow; a cold rain would have to suffice. It has been said that if you're looking for a Jew on Christmas Day, you need look no further than your neighborhood Chinese restaurant; and indeed this was exactly where Richard and I were heading, in the rain. Perhaps the noblest among us Jews had spent the earlier part of the day volunteering at local hospitals or serving the homeless in a food line, as my father had done for many years. But come evening, while our Christian friends bask in the glow of a well-lit Christmas tree, assembling toys with impossible numbers of loose parts, we would be waiting in the bar area for a table—because no Chinese restaurant worth their soy takes reservations on Christmas Day.

There is an old joke I cannot remember most of—which is true of 99% of the jokes I've ever heard—about Jews who own *three*, rather than the customary *two* sets of 'Kosher' dishes: one reserved for milk, another for meat and the third for *Chinese*. Kosher be darned, nothing says 'here-comes-New-Year's-Eve' to a Jewish person like an order of barbecue spareribs and tightly rolled pancakes of steaming moo-shu-pork.

And so it was, on the chilly and misty evening-after-Christmas, that Richard pulled up to our neighborhood *Royal China* to drop me, dry-shod, in close proximity to the restaurant entrance, before driving on by himself to search for a parking space in the nearly-full parking lot. I exited the car with a sigh, thinking about another holiday having come and gone without my parents.

I knew that my mother and father would surely have been here with us if they'd been alive. My father would have been driving right behind Richard, and, after dropping my mother off, would have circled the parking lot trailing my husband. Both consummate gentlemen, each would have wanted to defer the first available space to the other; both mouthing the words *"You take it! No...you take it,"* gesturing wildly for the other to pull in. Ultimately, my father, with his prosthetic leg, would have taken the absolute farthest-away spot, thereby 'out-gentleman-ing' my chivalrous husband, until Richard—walking in the opposite direction of the restaurant—would join my Dad in the hinterland of remote parking so that the two of them could walk slowly back to civilization together.

But we were not meeting my parents. Instead, we were gathering with Richard's family that evening: sons Kirby and Kurt with their respective wives Barri and Ruth, their assorted children and even Richard's former wife, Melanie. *Royal China*, our meeting place, was the exact same Chinese restaurant at which I'd dined with my own family as a child, once believing that the "Happy Family" combo had actually been *named for us*. In those days it had been called *Sing's Chinese*, and it was where my father's infamous 'fortune-cookie joke' had elicited laughs from us kids for years. It had been our tradition to open our fortune cookies and go round the table, each reading our fortune out loud. When my Dad's turn came, he would open the cellophane wrapper carefully and, breaking the cookie into two parts, pretend to read an actual fortune that was always the same.

"Oh, my!" he'd say. "Mine says, *'HELP, I'M BEING HELD CAPTIVE IN A CHINESE FORTUNE COOKIE FACTORY!'*"

We'd laugh and roll our eyes, rising from the table contented and satiated; the fortune cookie gag our cue to head out of the restaurant and pile into the family car. As if that memory had suddenly come to life, two little girls, looking not unlike me and my sister, burst from the restaurant and ran towards me, dissipating those thoughts of long-ago days. With squeals and hugs, Richard's two darling granddaughters bounced like little jumping beans, the perfect antidotes to my holiday gloom.

Ella and Brooklyn surrounded me and—each one talking faster than the other—began lifting my spirits considerably. Each was wearing a new outfit that they *had* to tell me about, and both wore fancy new necklaces. I also noticed that both had pint-sized pocketbooks hanging from their shoulders, no doubt stuffed with *Hanukkah gelt* (the cash and/or coins practically required by Jewish law to be included in a gifted wallet, purse or handbag, lest ill-fortune or hard times befall the recipient of said goods). The girls were simply a delight—and as both of them could speak with the clarity and intellect of tiny adults, the three of us had *lots* to talk about.

We headed into the restaurant and waited for "Grandpa Richard" to make it back from car-parking, as next-to-arrive Melanie, Richard's former wife, came through the door. In the early days of my marriage to Richard, I'd sworn that Melanie hated me with a passion; but in recent years she had softened somewhat and (don't tell her this) I had even started to suspect that she actually *liked* me a little. I liked her a lot (let's not tell her this either) and after what had been a rocky first few years, I'd become determined to win her over—and believed that I finally had.

Excitedly greeted by the little girls, Melanie and I exchanged hellos, and even leaned in to *hug* each other, both of us smiling genuinely as we did. I complimented her sincerely on her hair and the great-looking sweater she had on; Melanie is truly a pretty lady with great taste and an appealing sense of style. What I'd originally perceived as a hard edge, I now appreciated and saw as a personality virtue I could use a bit of myself, at times. We'd come a long way, she and I.

Soon, older son Kirby arrived, with our darling daughter-in-law Barri and their three kids in tow, and it was hugs and squeals all around. They'd come to Dallas from their home in San Antonio, where twins Max and Ben—fresh from their rockstar performances at a double-billed *Bar Mitzvah* we'd all attended a few months before—escorted their sister Samantha, two years younger than her brothers and at 10 years old already a willowy, wonderful teenager-in-training.

Samantha and I had bonded early on over our mutual love of art and her aspiration to be an *artiste.* I had been brought to tears by a school paper she'd written about her visit to my *real-life* art studio, complete with a flattering and touching reference to me as her "lovely grandmother"—the first time one of Richard's grandchildren had referred to me as anything other than Naomi. In her beautiful penmanship and prose worthy of a trip to Disneyland, she'd gone on to describe the day we'd spent painting and creating in my studio.

"*And then... at the top of the stairs,*" she'd written, " *there I saw it...*" (I admired her use of pause for emphasis) "*...my lovely grandmother's ART STUDIO appeared and was the most beautiful thing I had ever seen....*" I'd hung on every word as she described my studio in dramatic detail. This little artist-in-training and burgeoning writer reminded me of myself at her age. I respected and appreciated her love of art and whenever I knew I'd be seeing her, I would always tuck some supplies into my bag: a pad, special watercolor pencils or colored pens. From an early age Sam knew to check my purse or tote for "professional artist's materials" meant for her use.

In the crowded restaurant, after a short wait, a pretty Asian woman called our name: "*FOGEL, party of ten!*" she said; and, recognizing my married name, it dawned on me that this was *all* of our names: Naomi *Fogel,* Richard *Fogel,* Melanie *Fogel,* and on down to the little ones whose names would be carefully written in block-letters on lunch bags and backpacks by their mother; all of us *Fogel.* Though my parents were gone and I felt this to my core, here we were: *the FOGEL party of 10.* With this thought, I smiled as we walked single-file to a long, cloth-covered table near the back of the restaurant, with stops at various tables of friends to say hello. Over the din of rising voices in the crowded restaurant, I *felt* it, even if I couldn't identify it just then: *Something small had shifted in me.*

Joining the human train of Fogels, I fell in line behind little Samantha and in front of my husband and perhaps in that very moment, although I did not yet fully realize it, I left part of me behind in the waiting area. Minutes before, I'd been a woman in her 50's, mourning a family whose most beloved members were gone; and in the new normal of life without them—my remaining family members no longer pulled by the magnet of our elders and orbiting elsewhere—I had truly felt like a *party of one.* But on that Christmas

Day, as the dusk settled in and the rain slowed and then ended, I'd walked out of a shell of sadness and left it—as a cicada slips from its shell—to walk on together with another family. One that, I now began to see, had been mine all along.

Melanie sat at one end of the long dining table and I sat at the opposite head, listening as conversation flowed, platters were passed and egg rolls were dipped into sweet sauce made palatable by a touch of sour. Plates clinked, children's giggles joined adult laughter and holiday toasts were exchanged. A tradition as simple as meeting at a Chinese restaurant on a holiday had continued, albeit with different voices rising and other players in attendance this year. I felt a part of something that night. A family. Mine. I hadn't yet officially 'graduated' from grief; but I was doing a *bit better*. And I'd only realized it just then.

Pocketing handfuls of fortune cookies and exchanging goodbye hugs, all of us exited the warm, festive atmosphere of the restaurant and stepped out into the chilly evening air. Richard squeezed my hand, saying he'd go for the car and be right back to pick me up, but I didn't let go of his hand as he turned to walk away, instead following him along the walkway towards the parking area. "No, I'll go with you, honey," I said.

Buckling seatbelts over full stomachs, we cranked up the car's heat and drove through the shopping center to turn onto the familiar road home. I was surrounded by storefronts I knew from my childhood, bearing different names now. Once I'd held my mother's hand and walked these very sidewalks as a child. On my left had been *Sandy's Shoes*—perhaps the only children's shoe store in town, in that day, to carry the orthopedic shoes my siblings and I were prescribed for our impossibly flat feet. I smiled at the mental image of me, seated next to my beautiful mother, while Mr. Sandy gently urged my small foot into a shoe with the silver shoe-horn he kept in his pocket. I'd daydream as he laced it; there was something hypnotic in his technique.

Next to *Sandy's* had been *T. G. & Y,* a now-defunct dime store where we'd fill our baskets with school supplies each September; taking them home and laying them out like spoils from a hunt, carefully writing our names on each folder, pencil-pouch and pad. My brother had decided that the initials T. G. & Y. stood for 'The Greatest Yet," early evidence of a future in marketing and advertising—if he hadn't gone into law.

As we drove by, I saw *Dougherty's Drug Store* (which had been *John Cobb's Pharmacy* before the Doughertys took it over) where once I'd been forced to return to the 'scene of the crime' by my father, who insisted I return a green animal-shaped eraser that I had "failed to pay for"—the exact words my father had used as I'd stood before the store's manager that day, my head hanging in shame. I had simply not been able to resist the clever pencil accessory as it had smiled up at me: a tiny hippopotamus, adorably fashioned to fit over the existing eraser of a pencil and perch there until needed, as one wrote one's schoolwork. I shuddered at the memory of that embarrassing incident but smiled at the lesson my father had wanted to teach his 8-year-old daughter. And indeed, he *had*.

Passing what had once been the movie theater where I'd watched *Mary Poppins* enough times to have nearly memorized every scene, we were slowed by other cars waiting at the light to exit the parking lot, and stopped momentarily in front of what was—and still is— *Tom Thumb Grocery*, where a colorful open-binned display of *Brach's Candy* always called to us kids. We were allowed to choose ONE piece, which thrilled us; somehow it was enough—I don't know that we ever asked for more. My pick was always the Neapolitan, with its perfect stripes of chocolate brown, cherry-pink and white coconut waiting beneath the cellophane wrapper I'd unwrap oh-so-slowly before eating one tiny section at a time. All these decades later, I could still see that scene playing out behind that *very window*, where our car was now reflected. Thank God for my memories, I thought.

The light changed and we rolled ahead. We drove in silence for a moment or two until Richard turned up the radio to an oldie I recognized as a tune my mother had played to us as children, singing softly and strumming her guitar. While Peter Paul and Mary played (*Lemon tree very pretty and the lemon flower is sweet...*"), thoughts of sweet songs and the once-loved cellophane-wrapped candy reminded me of the fortune cookie I had taken from the Chinese restaurant. I pulled it from my pocket, opened it slowly and snapped it in half. Its white slip bearing good fortune was unreadable in the dimly lit car but I could see Richard's smiling face in the light of the street lamps shining through our windows, and it told me he was as pleased as I was about the dinner with our family.

Crunching one half of the cookie, I offered Richard the other half and held the fortune up to the light but still couldn't read its small lettering. "You wanna hear my fortune, honey?" I asked him.

"Sure, babe," he said. "How can you see it in the dark, though?"

"Let me see," I said, pausing and squinting to enhance my performance.

"Oh!" I said, not actually reading but reciting from memory instead. "It says…." I paused again here for effect: "HELP! I'M BEING HELD CAPTIVE IN A CHINESE COOKIE FACTORY!"

And with this, both of us smiled with the knowledge that—in a lovely way—my parents had been right there with us that evening, too. They were tucked safely into my heart, always, and lived on in all the memories I had of them, which would always come back to me just when I needed them: in a coincidence, on the front page of my morning paper, or on the wind through the leaves of the lemon tree whose praises my mother once sang.

FORTY-EIGHT

Long before the advent of drive-through fast food, there was but a single set of golden arches rising high above the very first McDonalds in Des Plaines, Illinois, just a six-mile drive from our home in suburban Morton Grove. I have vivid recollections of my brother, my sister and me perched like three birds on a limb on a bench outside the McDonalds, our noses pressed to the glass windows, through which we could watch our father standing inside. Like ticket holders at a circus, we waited with great anticipation, as if trained bears or flying acrobats were about to emerge, rather than just burgers and fries. From our ringside seats, we would watch our father at the red-and-white tiled counter, delivering our orders to a paper-hatted attendant. We could see him count out the bills that then disappeared into the drawer of the cash register, and the few coins that were scooped out in exchange, as we waited and watched for the white paper bags to be filled with our food.

On those evenings that I remember so well, nothing else mattered. As children, we knew nothing of 'what lay ahead,' nor did we ponder any of the realities or difficulties that our future lives might bring. We thought only of the familiar food that always satisfied our palates and never disappointed. As kids, there was only that moment... and then the one that followed. In those days, living in the moment was all we knew.

When the time came for us to scramble down from our bench, three small smudges of descending order and height remained on the glass. Returning with the bags of burgers and salty fries, Dad stood by while Mom arranged the three of us around one of the picnic tables outside of the iconic restaurant. Neatly unfolding a napkin for each of us, she'd spread one out in front of all five places and carefully squeeze circular globs of ketchup onto a corner of each makeshift placemat. Once settled, my father would slide into a bench beside one of us kids, and if I close my eyes, I can still see his fingers un-creasing and unfolding the tops of the bags to open them wide and allow the heavenly smells to escape, wafting right under our little noses.

"*Well, what have we here?*" he'd say. The question, needing no answer, added to the anticipation already at a high level around our table. "*My cheeseburger!*" "*My fries!*" "*My plain hamburger with no pickles!*" the three of us would cry, all at once.

Reaching into the bags, he'd pull out just exactly what each of us had ordered, distributing our sandwiches (yellow paper wrapper for cheese, white for plain) and our individual bags of fries before finally plucking a cold soda for each of us from a cardboard tray. Once settled in, an uncommon quiet would ensue: our mouths were full and our simple needs were met.

In this sweet memory, the five of us sat, dipping fries into ketchup and munching burgers while night edged its way into our little corner of the heartland. If there were clouds in the Midwestern skies on those balmy evenings, they all scattered before drifting into my memories; for the only shadows I remember were those cast by the golden arches we sat beneath. These dinnertime recollections still shimmer around the edges for me when I think of them, grounding me in a way that nothing else does. They are the simplest of memories, but today, I would not trade them for treasure chests of gold.

I know now that there is a flip-side to happiness. To truly know a thing, one must first have known the exact opposite. It was not unlike my grandfather's diamond scale and the way he once taught me to balance brilliant diamonds in one basket with equal amounts of tarnished brass weights in the other. As if to recognize joy, one must have known sadness; or to appreciate plenty, one must have experienced scarcity. I believe I *knew* what I'd had, all along, but I did not fully appreciate its weight until the time came (as it must) to calculate it.

I was beginning to understand that the unbearable sadness I felt after losing my parents was perhaps the correct and proper balance to all the joy I'd *had* with them. For how does one calculate the weight or the worth of days such as the one where I sat around a table outside a McDonalds and knew for sure that I was loved beyond measure? To have been a part of my family of five, munching burgers on a warm evening, under arches as golden as the memories we were making—how could I quantify how far this evening alone—even before those yet to come—had tipped the scales in my favor?

A half-century of love would surely require a basket of sadness to equal its weight. So the grief, which I believed had lingered for years too long, was the true balance to all the love I'd once had. If I'd realized this earlier on, I would have known that my sadness would be weighty; understanding it now makes all the difference. Now I know that grief takes its own time; it is beyond our power to start or stop.

My parents' great love had created our family, the heart and soul of the real legacy left to me, which was not—as it turns out—jewelry or the jewelry business. The legacy, in the end, is *love*. And this love remains, appreciating at immeasurable increments without any bank or safe. I know that such things are impossible to measure, yet still there are times when I try to weigh it all in my mind. And as best as I can figure, each time I calculate it the answer is always the same: love is more precious than all the jewels in the world.

The memories that my parents cared enough to create for my siblings and me are the real jewels, every bit as precious as diamonds and gold. Each remembrance is valuable beyond measure, but I don't keep them in a safe. Instead they surround me every day as I move towards new adventures; new memories in the making that need no weights or scales to measure. My precious memories tip the scales and are my greatest treasures, reminding me that I was once—and still am—the richest girl in the world.

ACKNOWLEDGMENTS

Having a tale to tell is one thing; actually turning it into a book is another, and and none of it takes place in a vacuum. I owe an immense debt of gratitude to the many individuals who made it happen, including you, my reader (especially if you've made it this far!). As we all carry our own stories and memories, I thank each and every one of you for allowing me to share mine here.

To Dr. Jennifer Browdy—whose passion lies in developing and leading others to success—my complete thanks for the gift of time you've shared and for going to the ends of the rainbow for my story. Your dedication to mentoring and for 'growing' and leading others is a gift to all of us. Your gentle guidance and unending support is the glue that binds this book.

To Jana Laiz, the other half of my Green Fire Press dream team, my sincerest thanks for such exceptional editing and no-nonsense direction just when it was needed most. I am humbled to be in the company of great writers like yourself.

To the women of the Berkshire Festival of Women Writers, gifted writers all, my gratitude for listening intently to my very first scrawlings and for cheering me on; and for graciously sharing your remarkable personal stories. Your triumphs over adversity touched and inspired me.

This book evolved with the constant support of my peers. My love and thanks to Shari Krage, Todd Maley, Andy Siegel, Janelle and Larry Friedman (kudos to Larry for excellent legal advice!);

to Billy Gutow for being my first reader and cousin Marcie Glaser for spotting every hidden typo. To John Owen, Scott and Shelby Dabney and the Clayton Dabney Foundation for support and my first book-related speaking engagement! To Paul Green for all the fireside barbecues and for everything he does, including sharing his friends Kristen and Emily. Sipping sangria with the three of you, on a summer afternoon in the glory of the Berkshires, is heaven on earth. To Carl Bowling, Kay Hester, and Becky Aft. And to the extraordinary Doctors Cynthia Curry and Robert Shiekh, my admiration and sincerest gratitude for your dedication to the work that you do. The two of you saved me.

To my oldest, dearest friend, the late great Karen Greenberg, who didn't live to read the book; I think of you every day and hear your unmistakable voice (and that laugh!) in my head. Yours was the friendship of a lifetime and I shall carry it always. And to many more darling friends I cannot squeeze into limited space; you know who you are and how much you mean to me.

To my brother Joe—there are no words in any language to properly express my love and admiration for everything you do. I am—and have always been—your best audience. Undoubtedly, I won the big-brother lottery.

To Debbie, my sissy-in-law and my friend; your grace and charm won over my brother—and me.

To my sister Sara—in our matching dresses we were constant companions and each other's first best friend. The little girl with the big voice, you are every bit the superstar you were when you rocked the stage. Beautiful Berkshire winters, snowed in with you, munching popcorn and watching a marathon of movies, these are my very favorite days. You cheered me on, never tired of hearing first drafts and tossed me just the right synonyms when I needed them. I love you little sister.

To cousins Hank and Linda for all the love and homemade meals. Finding you in the Berkshires (in my own backyard!) was kismet.

For my daughter Marissa, the light of my life, who inspires every word I write, I love you with all my heart. You are the best parts of me and your dad. And to David, my thanks for all that you do for Rissi and thus for me! I am so happy and proud to be your mom-in-law.

To my husband Richard, whose love and support stretched all the way to the foothills of Massachusetts. You are the safe place to rest my head and wherever you are is home for me. I love you.

To my late grandfather, 'Mr B.' who taught me about diamonds and about so much else of life; and whose words inspired the title of this book. And to the inimitable Annabelle Sholdar, our 'Bama' whose memory floats between these pages and whose words inspire me still.

And finally, to my beloved parents, who live in my heart and were the inspiration for this book. Like diamonds, the memory of them shines, lighting my path from where they are: somewhere over the most brilliant rainbow.

Naomi Pevsner
Spring 2020

Naomi Pevsner is a fifth-generation diamond dealer whose ancestors were purveyors of diamonds to the Czars of Russia. An award-winning jewelry designer and entrepreneur, Naomi's designs are red-carpet regulars, coveted and collected by Hollywood royalty including Cher, Christie Brinkley, Jane Seymour, the late Eartha Kitt and more. With her husband and family, she divides her time between Dallas, Texas and Lenox, Massachusetts, always with her little dog Pearl in tow.

ABOUT GREEN FIRE PRESS

Green Fire Press is an independent publishing company dedicated to supporting authors in producing and distributing high-quality books in fiction or non-fiction, poetry or prose.

Find out more at **Greenfirepress.com**.

Other Green Fire Press titles you may also enjoy:

A Short Course In Happiness After Loss, by Maria Sirois, PsyD.

A lyrical gem of a book, combining positive psychology with the wisdom necessary to thrive when facing life's harshest moments, rising through pain into a steady, resilient and open heart.

Nature, Culture, and the Sacred: A Woman Listens For Leadership, by Nina Simons

Bioneers co-founder Nina Simons offers inspiration for anyone who aspires to grow into their own unique form of leadership with resilience and joy. Winner of the 2018 Nautilus Gold Award.

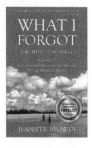

What I Forgot...and Why I Remembered: A Journey to Environmental Awareness and Activism Through Purposeful Memoir, by Jennifer Browdy, PhD.

"Inspires us to see how we can reclaim our lives for the sake of life on Earth" —Joanna Macy.

Finalist for the 2018 International Book Award.

*The Elemental Journey of Purposeful Memoir:
A Writer's Companion*, by Jennifer Browdy, PhD.

Month-by-month guidance for memoir writers.

Winner of the 2017 Nautilus Silver Award.

*Writing Fire: Celebrating the Power of
Women's Words*, edited by Jennifer Browdy,
Jana Laiz and Sahra Bateson Brubeck.

More than 75 passionate women
writers share their voices and visions
in this powerful anthology.

*Wisdom Lessons: Spirited Guidance from an
Ojibwe Great-Grandmother*, by Mary Lyons

The culmination of a lifetime steeped
in Indigenous spiritual traditions,
Grandmother Mary offers invaluable
lessons for anyone interested in living
in alignment with their higher self.

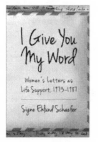

*I Give You My Word: Women's Letters as Life
Support, 1973–1987*, by Signe Eklund Schaefer

A forgotten box of letters in a dark attic
corner, messages from women friends written
decades ago. An intimate record of a time of
great transition in how women experienced
their daily lives and imagined their future.

Made in the USA
Columbia, SC
17 December 2021

51943879R00174